JESSE T. MOORE, JR.

PRIMITIVE TRAITS
IN RELIGIOUS REVIVALS

PRIMITIVE TRAITS
IN RELIGIOUS REVIVALS

A STUDY IN
MENTAL AND SOCIAL EVOLUTION

BY

FREDERICK MORGAN DAVENPORT

SUBMITTED IN PARTIAL FULFILMENT OF THE REQUIREMENTS
FOR THE DEGREE OF DOCTOR OF PHILOSOPHY IN
THE FACULTY OF POLITICAL SCIENCE
IN COLUMBIA UNIVERSITY

NEGRO UNIVERSITIES PRESS
NEW YORK

CONTENTS

CONTENTS

CHAPTER VIII

PAGE

CHAPTER IX

CHAPTER X

CHAPTER XI

CHAPTER XII

CHAPTER XIII

CHAPTER XIV

CHAPTER XV

PRIMITIVE TRAITS
IN RELIGIOUS REVIVALS

PRIMITIVE TRAITS IN RELIGIOUS REVIVALS

CHAPTER I

THE REVIVAL ESSENTIALLY A FORM OF IMPULSIVE SOCIAL ACTION

RELIGIOUS movements of magnitude have often assumed a mode which sociologists call sympathetic likemindedness. It is a term which perhaps deserves or requires a further word of description. Likeminded people are those whose mental and nervous organizations respond in like ways to the same stimuli. They might conceivably respond *unconsciously* to the same stimuli, as animals do. We should then call them instinctively likeminded. But it is at least doubtful whether there are people so low in the scale of mental development that they are not to some extent conscious of feeling, thinking and acting together. When we rise a step higher, however, we come upon a phenomenon which has played a great part in social, political and religious movements among all races of men. It has played a *conscious* part, though rational consciousness has by no means always been the controlling factor. This phenomenon has been called sympathetic likemindedness,[1] and

[1] Giddings, "Inductive Sociology," p. 136 f.

the predominant mental characteristics of a population under its influence are suggestibility, imitativeness, imagination and emotion. These are exceedingly primitive and probably universal mental traits. Just as every human being tends to respond to a sensation by some reflex movement, so every human being tends to respond to an idea implanted in his consciousness. He is suggestible. He is imitative. He is also more or less a creature of imagination and emotion. In proportion as these tendencies in a population are held in check, we have a population under control. We have deliberation and public opinion and social evolution rather than revolution.

But whatever else may be said of sympathetically likeminded people, — and much that is good may be said of them, — they are not likely to have their primitive and instinctive nervous tendencies and mental traits under the governance of the higher inhibitory centres. With them, suggestion and imitation, imagination and emotion, pass swiftly, impulsively and often resistlessly into the united action of the lynching mob, the super-emotional revival or the political revolution.

Normally, subjective and sympathetic likemindedness manifests itself in forms of objective and impulsive social action. And in our time these peculiar social movements have been studied and have been found to conform to law.[1] There is the law of origin, that impulsive social action origi-

[1] Giddings, "Elements of Sociology," p. 136.

nates among people who have least inhibitory control. This does not mean that the thinking out
of the plan of action has its origin with this class
of the community, but it does mean that the first
movement towards carrying out the plan is likely to
be made by the people who are least self-controlled.
John Brown and Harper's Ferry preceded Grant
and Vicksburg. An ill-balanced young lawyer led
the Paris mob to the storming of the Bastile. Over
and over again in the pages that follow we shall see
the nervously unstable, the suggestible, the inex-
perienced, affected by the highly emotional revival
earlier than the dignified and intelligent people
of judgment and standing. This law is strikingly
illustrated in that remarkable sympathetic social
movement of the middle ages, the Crusades. We
are in the habit of thinking of the Crusades as a
series of organized and orderly military expeditions
led by princes of Christian blood to wrest the Holy
Land from the infidel — and so in fact they were
before the Crusades were done. But first there
were three great unorganized movements. By the
middle of the eleventh century Jerusalem was in
the hands of the Seljukian Turks, who cruelly
harassed Christian pilgrims and heaped insult
upon their sacred shrines. Peter the Hermit, on
his return from a pilgrimage to Jerusalem, at the
instance of Pope Urban II, travelled widely and
depicted the calamity vividly to the imagination
of Christendom. In 1095 a great council of the
Church resolved upon the deliverance of the Holy

Sepulchre. No movement of armed forces was organized until two years later under Godfrey of Bouillon. But in 1096 Walter the Penniless, the ringleader of a mob of twenty thousand men, the dregs of humanity, passed through Germany, Hungary and into Bulgaria, devastating the country through which they passed with robbery and murder. Finally, on the verge of starvation, they stormed Belgrave, were crushed, and only the shattered remnants of a disorderly host found its way to Constantinople. Then Peter the Hermit led forty thousand men, women and children. In attempting to cross the Bosphorus they were routed and decimated. Later in the same year a horde of fifteen thousand lawless vagabonds under Gottschalk, a German priest, entered upon their sacred mission by massacring all Jews who unhappily crossed their path. But the most astounding outburst was that which preceded the fifth organized Crusade. In 1212 a great host of children, boys and girls, three armies of them,—one from France and two from Germany, —started on the pious pilgrimage. Some of these little ones returned to their homes, but it is probable that most of them perished of starvation or disease or were sold into slavery. . . . The initial step in sympathetic social action is taken by those who have least inhibitory control over the nervous and mental processes.

And the second law is the law of spread. Impulsive social action tends, through imitation, to extend and intensify in geometrical progression.[1] One individual influences a second, the two influence four, and like a stone thrown into a lake of still water, the single centre of impulse moves on in ever widening circles of suggestion and imitation, emotional action and reaction. This law is illustrated in the remarkable growth of early Christianity. On the day of Pentecost there were apparently about six hundred Christians confined to Palestine. At the accession of Constantine early in the fourth century, it is estimated that there were about ten millions of Christians, or one-tenth of the empire's population. Gibbon places the figure at five millions, and others as high as twenty millions. Ten millions is probably approximately correct. If there had been a great number less than this, Constantine would hardly have chosen the Christians as the support of his empire. If there had been twenty or twenty-five millions, the persecution of Diocletian would no doubt have been impossible. A feeble six hundred on the day of Pentecost, a powerful ten millions in the days of Constantine! Now one reason for the great spread of early Christianity growing out of the social conditions of the time, is often left out of account. There were great families of slaves, sometimes two or three hundred in a family. Christianity entered the house through a slave and ran by suggestion and imitation through the whole slave body. There were also large numbers of clubs

[1] Giddings, "Elements of Sociology," p. 139.

and fraternities of all kinds in the early empire to whom the doctrine of the brotherhood of man was exceedingly congenial. And the cardinal precepts of the new religion swept through these organizations like a flame.[1]

The great wave of religious interest which passed over the United States in 1857 furnishes another clear exemplification of this law. During the summer there had occurred many business disturbances which slowly approached a climax of financial disaster. And finally on a single day, between 9 A.M. and 4 P.M., scores of banks and thousands of families were ruined. Wall Street collapsed, and the tremendous force of the almost unparalleled financial calamity was felt throughout the country. A few days later a solitary man, one Jeremiah C. Lanphier, a lay missionary in the employ of the Dutch Reformed Church in Fulton Street, New York City, became impressed with the idea that an hour of prayer, from twelve to one o'clock, would be beneficial to business men. He instituted it, and advertised it somewhat, but sat out the first half of the first meeting alone.[2] At the end of the hour there were six present. Lanphier kept a diary and a record of the increase. At the second meeting there were twenty, at the third forty and at the fourth one hundred, and

[1] I am indebted to the Church History lectures of my former preceptor, Professor A. C. McGiffert, for this illustration.

[2] Cf. Prime, "The Power of Prayer," an account of the revival of 1857.

then the numbers increased so rapidly that it was impossible to accommodate the people in one room. Overflow meetings were held in many churches in New York and Brooklyn, and great crowds went away unable to get into any of them. Men were organized by occupations, firemen for example, with an attendance of two thousand. Business men thronged the churches, all the means of access were blocked before the hour of prayer commenced and hundreds stood in the street during the hour. Soon the revival spread to Jersey City, Hoboken, Paterson and, a few days later, to Philadelphia, and ran rapidly through that city; then through New England to Boston, and up the Hudson to Albany, Troy, Schenectady, Rochester, Buffalo; and to Baltimore, Richmond, Charleston, Savannah, Mobile, New Orleans, Vicksburg, Memphis, St. Louis, Cincinnati, Pittsburgh, Chicago and other cities throughout the nation. The movement was resistless and cumulative, characterized by strong emotion but not by wild excitement.

And the third law of impulsive social action is the law of restraint. Sympathetic popular movements tend to spend themselves with abandon, and are held in check only if there are a considerable number of individuals scattered through the population who are trained in the habit of control, who are accustomed to subordinate feeling to rational considerations and who act as bulwarks against the advance of the overwhelming tide of imitation

and emotion.[1] We shall see in the pages that
follow that in the more primitive religious revivals
there is little or no restraint until the wave has
spent its fury, while in others, calmer leadership
within and critical judgment from without combine to hold in leash the natural excesses of the
movement.

We must notice, also, that there appear to be
certain physical and mental conditions which predispose to emotionalism. For example, sudden
changes of climate from summer to winter, combined with monotony of topography, seem to be a
factor in fixing the type of mind of the inhabitant
of the Russian steppe.[2] Physical surrounding has
probably had its influence in establishing among
the people of the great western plains in America
a more radical and impulsive religious and political
habit than that which characterizes the New Englander. There are other predisposing conditions
of which we may speak with more confidence.
Instinctive fear, when a population is under the
spell of it, arouses great volumes of imagination
and emotion, and powerfully induces sympathetic
movements. We shall find, for example, that certain distinctive features of the Edwards revival in
the first half of the eighteenth century in New
England, and of the Kentucky revival of 1800, are
explained by the environment of fear — fear of
starvation, of wild beasts and savages — in which

[1] Cf. Giddings, "Democracy and Empire," p. 56.
[2] Giddings, "Inductive Sociology," p. 140 f.

the colonists had lived, in New England for a century, in Kentucky for a shorter period.

Difficulty of communication and a great amount of ignorance in a population predispose to emotional movements. The three millions of white people in the southern mountains from Virginia to northern Alabama are known chiefly for their moonshine stills, their feuds, their murders, their excitable religious temperament and their illiteracy. And the last is to a great degree the cause of the others. They live in one of the great land-locked areas of the globe, comparable with the Basque country of the Pyrenees. They were early shut off from the remainder of the southern people, socially by an aversion to the institution of slavery, and economically by the fact that their mountain holdings furnished no such resources of wealth as the rich plantations of their neighbors in the low lands in the old slave days. And educational opportunities throughout their whole history have been very meagre and are exceedingly meagre to-day. It is not at all likely that they are lacking in capacity, for their Scotch-Irish and English ancestors have been a great element of national strength. But they have been shut in by poverty and the mountains, their horizon has been limited by ignorance, and they have been at the mercy of primitive passion and primitive superstition.

And finally we must bear in mind constantly as we proceed that the effect of a sympathetic religious movement is greatly increased by the massing of men and women in a psychological "crowd," a camp-meeting for instance. This is a purely social condition and has such important consequences that we shall return to the subject farther on. It will be sufficient here to remark that the natural result of the assembling of men in crowds, especially when skilful speakers engage their attention and play upon the chords of imagination and emotion, seems to be the weakening of the power of inhibition in each individual, and the giving of free rein to feeling and imitation. And when under these circumstances a powerful emotion, especially that of fear, is aroused in the consciousness of the assembly, all the phenomena of suggestion — even the highly reflex phenomena of hypnotic suggestion so called — are likely to develop. This will be most in evidence among primitive, superstitious and unlettered people, of course, for civilization shows itself in nothing more clearly than in the growing capacity for individual self-control, but they will also appear in the relatively higher stages of culture and experience if the combination of conditions, physical, mental and social, is strong enough to develop them. In fact there is no population, there are comparatively few individuals in any population, who cannot be swept from the moorings of reason and balanced judgment if brought under the mysterious and potent influence of the psychological "crowd."

CHAPTER II

THE MIND OF PRIMITIVE MAN

THE term "primitive" as applied to man is often used in two senses. It sometimes occurs as a synonym for aboriginal humans, and sometimes for contemporary savages. The mental capacity and characteristics of savages we know a good deal about from direct research among existing tribes. The mental capacity and characteristics of aboriginal peoples we know very little about except from a priori reasoning. It certainly would be unsafe to make too wide inferences of original human traits from what we know of savage traits and count upon these inferences as absolutely accurate, for existing savages have unnumbered thousands of years of inheritance stretching back of them, and there has probably been some mental development in their history, although this development has been in the main arrested.

There are not wanting marked indications that the mind of the animal no less than its physical organization is the result of a process of evolution. Certainly it is true that in all animal life up to man, the development of intelligence and the development of the nervous system proceed together. There has been a slow and steady evolution of the regulating centres — first the uniform spinal cord is supreme, then the medulla and the cord, then the basal ganglia, then the cerebrum.[1] And the appearance of these progressively higher centres has always marked successive stages in the advance of intelligence. When we come to man, we find "a ganglionic apparatus far surpassing in delicacy and complexity that of any other animal, and in correlation therewith we find man manifesting an unequalled range and variety of psychical function." [2]

Now the mind of man is an inheritance from the animal mind, by extraordinary variation it may be, but an inheritance nevertheless. The question at once arises whether, as one school of anthropologists hold, the brain of man is an extraordinary variation and the mind of primitive man has potential capacity approximating that of modern civilized man, or whether, as another school of anthropologists hold, the original variation was small and mental complexity and capacity themselves have been an evolution. The first school, resting upon inductive research in the field, points to the fact, for instance, that while the heavy brain is more frequent among the Europeans than among the negroes, the actual statistical average of weights and sizes would not be very different for the negro and the European white. The bulk of the brains of each race would probably fall within about the same limits. And it is reasonable to suppose,

[1] Cf. Spencer, "Principles of Sociology" (1–2), p. 520.
[2] Rice, "Christian Faith in an Age of Science," p. 270.

therefore, they say, that so far as actual capacity goes, there has been no great advance. It would indeed be a formidable task, with our present knowledge, to attempt to decide between these opposing views, but happily it is not necessary to our purpose. For however the two schools of anthropologists may differ with respect to original potential capacity, the first as readily as the second would admit that there has been a considerable development of latent mental capacity along with change of environment and increase of experience.

Although the mind is a unity, it is not a rigid entity, but a group of conscious states or tendencies, which, within normal limits, shift even from day to day. It is also a matter of common observation that one personality displays a certain group of mental tendencies and another personality a higher or lower group. We say the two persons are not of the same type of mind. So, at successive stages of racial development, higher and higher groups of mental qualities have blossomed, so to speak, into higher and higher types of mind. And the primitive type which we see at least imperfectly represented in the savage and which a priori reasoning would urge as having been probably represented in the early human, is a physically active, highly emotional type, with feeble reasoning powers, — child of conjecture and imagination, — a type which ranges, to use a psychological phrase, from ideo-motor to ideo-emotional. It is this type, representing the infancy of humanity, so far as we can study it among contemporary primitive people, to whose mental and nervous characteristics I wish to give some further attention. Whether or not contemporary primitives are practically aboriginal primitives, it is at least certain that we have among populations yet dwelling with us an exceedingly rudimentary and undeveloped type of mind.

With the more obvious mental traits and those not so important for our present purpose, we need not linger. For instance, the primitive man has a keen sense in directions in which that sense has been particularly trained. He is a remarkable hunter, and finds tracks of his game under circumstances that would present great difficulty to the eye of the man of much higher culture. He is strong in perception, but weak in logical interpretation of his perceptions, lacking in logical connection in his conclusions.[1] This is no doubt largely the result of a crude experience. He has no abundant and more or less accurate tradition with which to compare and by which to test his new perceptions. And here arises a very interesting advance in the mental evolution of primitive man. ›He fills in the gaps, he makes connection between the perceptions, by the use of his imagination. And so the imagination among primitive people finally reaches a very considerable state of development, because of its tremendous

---

[1] Cf. Boas, "The Mind of Primitive Man," address of the retiring president before the American Folk Lore Society, Baltimore, December 27, 1900.

utility. In its early period it is very crude, as it is to-day among the negroes of the United States, whose religious thinking, both lay and clerical, is very frequently one long stretch of most astounding images. Thus they fill in the gaps in the thought. I once heard a colored brother in a religious meeting in Tennessee, in the midst of mighty enthusiasm and the most lively assurance that he carried his whole audience with him, declare that the first thing he wished to do when he reached Heaven was to bathe his soul in the sea of glass! And one hears frequently such experiences as the following recited in religious meetings, that at the time of conversion, when the recipient of the experience was in a cataleptic trance — as so many negroes are at that time — a little white man chopped open the breast with an axe, took the heart out, poured out the black blood, washed it pure in the purple stream, put it back and closed up the opening. This reminds one of the belief among the primitive Mohammedans that Mahomet's heart was actually taken out, washed and replaced by the Almighty.[1]

And this vividness of imagination among primitive peoples has important consequences. Whatever the savage vividly conceives he believes with all his soul. And this helps to account for his credulity, for the dreadful hold that superstition has upon him. His imagination peoples his environment with a world of spirits, good and evil,

[1] Cf. Spencer, "Principles of Sociology" (1-1), p. 343.

dwelling in trees and animals and in the whistling wind, in the darkness, in the tempest, in the shadow, in the echo, in all things animate and inanimate, more powerful than himself, powerful to aid, powerful to harm. A large part of his conscious life is devoted to propitiating the friendly, and warding off the hostile, spirit. Hence the rapid growth of charm and magic, medicine-men, exorcists and conjurers. These superstitions have made their way so deeply into the mind of the race that they are by no means rooted out even in highly developed communities. And among primitive people everywhere they show much of their pristine strength. The negro people in the South to-day, for example, are enveloped in a cloud of superstition. The belief in signs, charms, spells, dreams, except among the few intelligent members of the race, is very general.

" Many neighborhoods have an old man or woman who possesses unearthly powers and who is constantly appealed to for assistance in connection with love-affairs and the quarrels of the colored people and in cases of protracted or mysterious sickness. The belief in the power of the evil eye is nearly universal, as is the notion that persons, domestic animals, wells and particular places can be tricked — that is, have a curse or malign spell put upon them — by anybody who knows the charm or method of procedure which will produce such a result. In matters of love, courtship and marriage, the negroes are usually

extremely jealous and suspicious, and magical arts
are commonly invoked to secure affection and to
alienate those who are already attached to each
other.   They usually include the use of a scrap of
clothing which has been worn by the person that
is to be tricked, or a shred of his hair, a piece of a
finger nail or toe nail or even some dust from his
shoes." [1]   Of course it is easy to recognize in these
peculiar forms a principle of magic that is widely
disseminated among primitive people, namely that
for the purpose of control of the individual, it is
only necessary to have a part of him or his belong-
ings, even the most minute.   These are only everyday examples, among a people whom we know, of
a vast mass of superstition which overlays the life
of primitive man.   The records of ethnological
study are full of it.

And it is a natural inference from what has
been said of the primitive man's view of the world,
peopled by demon spirits, that perhaps his strongest emotion should be fear.   Of this I think
ethnological research leaves little doubt.   Herbert
Spencer was so convinced of it that in his sociological system fear of the living among primitive
people becomes the root of all political control, and
fear of the dead the root of all religious control. [2]
And Professor William James places fear with lust
and anger as one of the "three most exciting
emotions of which human nature is susceptible,"

[1] *Atlantic Monthly*, February, 1882, " Studies in the South."
[2] Spencer, " Principles of Sociology " (1-1), p. 437.

and says of it that it is a "genuine instinct and one of the earliest shown by the human child."[1] And we have here an explanation of the perfectly enormous amount of latent fear that exists in every population on the face of the earth, an inheritance from the primitive days, showing itself in theatre panics and army routs, ever ready to burst into activity in spite of the fact that, in general, progress is measured by the elimination of actual outward fear.

And finally we may mention together a group of primitive characteristics, the chief of which is nervous instability, with its inevitable accompaniments of remarkable imitativeness and suggestibility and great lack of inhibitive control. I think perhaps the characteristic of nervous instability applied to primitive man may arouse some opposition in the mind of the reader. There is a popular impression that the South Sea Islander, for example, knows nothing of nerves, and that the North American Indians are an exceedingly phlegmatic race. But there is a good deal of evidence accumulating which indicates that while these primitive people may not suffer from derangements of the nervous system as the more highly civilized suffer, it is nevertheless true that their nervous and mental organization is in a very plastic, unstable condition. We find some excellent confirmations of this among the northern Siberian peoples. Castren observed long ago that

[1] James, " Psychology — Briefer Course," p. 408.

if the Samoyeds were sitting around inside their skin tents in the evening, and some one crept up and struck the tent with his hand, half of them were likely to fall into cataleptic fits. The shock was probably associated with some dreadful mythical tale, and the superstitious fear thus aroused threw them off their delicate nervous balance. The investigations of Bogoros and others just published in the reports of the Jesup Northern Pacific expedition reveal this condition of nervous instability as very widespread among such Siberian tribes as the Wukaghir, Lamut and Chukchee. They are so extraordinarily susceptible that if the observer makes a motion, they will instantly follow it with a like motion, and whole groups may be thrust into hypnotic trance with little difficulty.

I call this peculiar condition normal nervous instability, for there seems to be no evidence of any large amount of nervous disease or insanity among primitive men. In fact, in spite of this extraordinary susceptibility, there is probably less insanity than among civilized peoples. The causes which make for nervous derangement in a later stage of progress and environment do not yet exist.

I think this view will be even more fully substantiated in the mind of the reader, when we come to the chapter upon religious phenomena among the North American Indians, where it will be seen that in the development of the Shaker religion among the tribes of Puget Sound, and later in that

extraordinary Indian revival brought to the attention of the country in the spread of the famous
ghost-dance religion, the highest degree of nervous
instability and suggestibility is exhibited. The record
of this revival as compiled by the Bureau of Ethnology at Washington is one mass of trances, hypnotic rigidities, dreams, visions, rapid imitations,
involuntary tremblings, violent spasmodic actions,
wild excitement and dancing kept up until at least
one hundred out of three or four hundred persons
engaged were lying wholly unconscious, and were
left lying in this state until they recovered, as they
were supposed to be beholding visions of the spirit
world. Such a revelation is calculated to change
our views somewhat of the essentially phlegmatic
character of the red race in America.

I add one further bit of testimony from Swetten-
ham, the distinguished student of the Malay race.
He affirms that any simple device will serve to
attract the attention of these artless, unsophisti-
cated children of nature. " Then by merely looking them hard in the face, they will fall helpless
into the hands of the operator, instantly lose all
self-control, and go passively through any performance whether verbally imposed or merely suggested
by a sign." [1]   In all these cases nervous instability
appears as a fundamental primitive trait, with im-
pulsiveness and a high degree of imitativeness and
suggestibility as its natural consequence.

[1] In " Malay Sketches," 1895, quoted in Keane — " Man, Past
and Present," p. 236.

And so it follows that primitive man is led to action by impulse rather than by motives carefully reflected upon. His opinions are chiefly beliefs, that is, they are products of imagination and emotion. And because there is so much emotion in his opinions, it carries him quickly into action. His will power, in any high sense, is relatively weak. He lacks inhibitive control. Not entirely, however. The Eskimo will sit motionless at a seal hole for five, eight, twelve, fifteen hours, if necessary, with his spear all the time uplifted to strike. In earlier days, the Indian could endure torture at the stake without a tremor or a cry. But in general it may be said, I think, that civilized peoples exhibit a far wider range of powers of inhibition than the primitive man. And, as much as in anything else, therein consists civilization.

It is with some hesitation that I offer the suggestion that a correlation which others have contended for between nervous instability and a large subliminal field of consciousness [1] may find further confirmation in an investigation of the mind of primitive man. I know that many psychologists believe the subliminal to be vague and a term to conjure with. And so, no doubt, it has often been. But the fact remains that there is a wide margin of what may be called, for want of a better term, subconsciousness, stretching away beyond the horizon of the full consciousness of every personality. And from that shadowy land come at call many

[1] Cf. William James, "Varieties of Religious Experience," p. 251.

elements which make up shifting mental states and momentary conscious experiences — long-forgotten memories, impressions, convictions. And there come, too, without our willing, many factors which we cannot account for, the superstitions, fancies, impulses, dreams, that seem to belong to another personality — though they may be our very own, by brain-cell inheritance from a dim and distant animal and human past, incubated unconsciously by our own mental mechanism.

However this may be, all I wish to call attention to here is that among primitive people the appearance of the sensory and motor automatisms — active convulsion as well as hallucination and vision, all that group of reflex phenomena which everywhere follow upon overpowering imagination and emotion, as well as the so-called demoniac states — the appearance of all these seems usually to be marked by a considerable fading of the field of normal rational consciousness, and very frequently by the emergence into view of that mysterious and active double personality which has so puzzled psychologists. There is an interesting collection of these phenomena from the Shantung province of China in a little book called " Demon Possession," by the Rev. John L. Nevius, for forty years a missionary to the Chinese. This gentleman took unusual pains in the gathering of information from many sources, and was himself for a long period an observer. His interpretation is distinctly theological, but that does no harm to

the book as a storehouse of material. The observations made disclose a high degree of nervous
instability among the thoroughly healthy, ignorant
and primitive populations of the interior of China.
Under the influence of autosuggestion without excitement, or in a time of unusual perturbation in
the community, there are developed in every village many cases of possession wherein the supposed demoniac passes into an abnormal state,
sometimes of depression and melancholy, sometimes of ferocity or malignity and sometimes
of mental exaltation and ecstasy. "The subject
is often thrown into paroxysms more or less violent and falls senseless upon the ground. And
the most striking characteristic of these cases
everywhere is that the subject evidences another
personality, and the normal personality for the
time being is partially or wholly dormant." [1]

These are only Castren's Samoyed cases over
again, and the traditional belief of the Chinese in
evil spirits and the superstition and fear thus
created, play their powerful part in causing these
dreadful automatisms.

The kinds of reflex phenomena so common
among these primitives of China are worthy of note
in view of their likeness to those we shall observe
later in connection with several of the famous religious revivals of our own country and Great
Britain. The subject has visions and dreams; he
laughs, rolls on the ground, leaps about, exhibits

[1] Nevius, "Demon Possession," p. 143 f.

contortions of the body or twistings of the neck, changes color; the body shakes violently, becomes rigid; the subject falls in a fit.[1] And the interesting fact is that the possession disappears naturally in an individual who is taken out of his environment of superstition and ignorance and brought by the missionaries under the dominion of intelligence.[2]

It is perhaps safe to say that the mental and nervous characteristics of primitive man are in these broad outlines similar throughout the world.

[1] Cf. Nevius, *op. cit.*, pp. 53, 56, 57.   [2] *Ibid.*, p. 18 f.

CHAPTER III

MENTAL TRAITS OF A PSYCHOLOGICAL " CROWD "

PERHAPS no book of recent years has done more to awaken interest in social psychology than Gustave Le Bon's study of "The Crowd." It is possible to say this and yet hold that there is a great amount of exaggeration in its teaching. But there is a great deal of truth in it also, and I think the general theory may be applied in an enlightening way in the study of the religious revival. Le Bon is a foremost pioneer in this field, and this chapter presents chiefly a summary of the principles enunciated by him and by other social psychologists. Durkeim had preceded him with a study of the coercion or intimidation of the individual by the mass. The stage fright of the actress when she first appears before the footlights, the terror of the man who is about to make his first speech, the dread of the candidate who appears before an examining board, these are illustrations that occur to everybody of the strange psychological influence of mere numbers over against the helpless individual. It was Le Bon's task to develop this everyday bit of psychology into a broad study of the psychological "crowd." It is not the

25

mere physical sense of the word, the mass of men, of which Le Bon is thinking. He means a group of persons, small or large, who are for the time being in some kind of mental agreement, who are a mental unity or practically so. A lynching party is a crowd. A political meeting is a crowd. Le Bon reasons that the individual is one thing in such a company, and another thing out of it. The crowd for the time being swallows him up, and has feelings of its own, thoughts of its own, a character of its own. The large sprinkling of respectable farmers who made the imbecile march in Coxie's army from California to Washington and who sunk every dollar they had in the world in the enterprise, if they could have considered the matter objectively, would have laughed to scorn such a method of accomplishing reform. But the judgment of each was swallowed up in the impulse of many.

The mind of the crowd is strangely like that of primitive man. Most of the people in it may be far from primitive in emotion, in thought, in character; nevertheless the result tends always to be the same. Stimulation immediately begets action. Reason is in abeyance. The cool, rational speaker has little chance beside the skilful, emotional orator. The crowd thinks in images, and speech must take this form to be accessible to it. The images are not connected by any natural bond, and they take each other's place like the slides of a magic lantern.[1] It follows from this, of course,

[1] Cf. Le Bon, "The Crowd," p. 69.

that appeals to the imagination have paramount influence.

The crowd is united and governed by emotion rather than by reason. Emotion is the natural bond, for men differ much less in this respect than in intellect. It is also true that in a crowd of a thousand men the amount of emotion actually generated and existing is far greater than the sum which might conceivably be obtained by adding together the emotion of the individuals taken by themselves. The explanation of this is that the attention of the crowd is always directed either by the circumstances of the occasion or by the speaker to certain common ideas, such as "liberty" or "democracy" in political gatherings, and "salvation" in religious gatherings, or to certain emblems or symbolic images, such as the flag, the native land, the church, the Scriptures; and every individual in the gathering is stirred with emotion, not only because the idea or the shibboleth stirs him, as it would if he were by himself, but also because he is conscious that every other individual in the gathering believes in the idea or the shibboleth, and is stirred by it too. And this enormously increases the volume of his own emotion and consequently the total volume of emotion of the crowd.[1] As in the case of the primitive mind, imagination has unlocked the flood-gates of emotion, which on occasion may become wild enthusiasm or demoniac frenzy.

[1] Cf. Giddings, "Elements of Sociology," p. 123.

The very fact that men in a crowd are so close together and can so readily communicate with one another makes them particularly liable to a swift contagion of feeling. The force of this contagion is so great that it often carries off their feet men who are in no sort of mental agreement with the purpose of the gathering. We shall find numerous instances of this in the records of religious revivals.

Wherever reason is subordinated and feeling is supreme, the influence is always in the direction of the sweeping away of inhibitive control. The critical faculty is dormant; but at the same time that it is repressed, other faculties are brought to a high degree of exaltation. Instinct, impulse, imitation, emotion — the primitive characteristics — are awake and extraordinarily alert. People who are easily subject to suggestion become more thoroughly so, and people who are by no means naturally susceptible become suggestible under the control of a crowd. This suggestibility ranges all the way from the normal to the abnormal or hypnotic, under the influence of the skilful orator or preacher. And we shall therefore expect to observe in the great religious audiences of primitive men which we are to study a large number of the reflex phenomena that are everywhere the peculiar evidence of remarkable suggestibility and nervous instability.

The means of influencing their audiences upon which skilful speakers universally depend, are appeals to imagination and emotion, direct and indirect suggestion, affirmation and repetition. Repetition is one of the surest means of getting an idea firmly into the mind of a crowd as well as of the child or of the savage. As Mr. Dooley phrases it in his philosophy — " I belave annything at all, if ye only tell it to me aften enough."

The crowd, like the individual, but to a greater degree, easily falls under the sway of the instinctive emotions, particularly latent or actual fear. Under the stimulus of a panic the latent fear of inheritance is brought to the surface to intensify the influence of actual and present horror. It was so in the Iroquois theatre. I do not offer it as the sole explanation of the phenomenon, but it is more than a coincidence, I believe, that the great revival of 1857 in the United States followed directly upon the terrible business disasters of that year, when men's minds were crazy with financial fear. It is more than a coincidence that the most frightful period of the appalling mental epidemics of the middle ages should have been the last quarter of the fourteenth century, when men's minds were under the thrall of terror from the Black Death, the most terrible plague in human history.[1]

Under this analysis the crowd presents itself as the great driving force, so to speak, of impulsive social action. "From the moment that reason finally loses its control over masses of communicating men, they fall under the power of imitation

[1] Cf. White, "The History of the Warfare of Science with Theology," Vol. I, p. 187.

and hypnotic suggestion; and emotional fury sweeps through them with increasing volume and accelerating velocity, as a conflagration sweeps through accumulations of combustible material." [1]

There are at least two factors to be mentioned in conclusion, which tend to modify the effects described in this chapter. The differing temperament of populations is one. The Anglo-Saxon crowd is one thing, the Latin or Celtic crowd quite another. The extent, intensity and character of the sympathetic outbreak will vary considerably with populations of different races and different degrees of development within the same race. It is also necessary to make an important modification in the whole theory of Le Bon. His "foule" or crowd includes not only those who have come together in one place for a common purpose, but also a group or multitude of persons easily communicating in any way whatsoever. [2] His conclusions in their radical form are by no means true under the latter circumstances, and under the former circumstances they are in need of substantial abatement. If a crowd never comes together in close physical contact, or if, coming together, it periodically breaks up, there is time for rational inhibition to intervene and do its perfect work. If Le Bon's theory were completely true, popular government would be a snare. According to his view you never get in a popular assembly the wisdom of the mass, but only illusion,

[1] Giddings, " Democracy and Empire," p. 56.
[2] Cf. Giddings, " Principles of Sociology," p. 151.

delusion, hallucination and other evils which follow upon impulse and suggestion. But Abraham Lincoln had saner vision when he said that you can fool all of the people some of the time and some of the people all of the time, but you can't fool all the people all the time. The instinct of the multitude is sound, and wise popular government is always possible with the aid of constitutional checks and balances and rational leadership — a leadership that depends not upon hypnotic arts, but upon honest, straightforward thinking. The application of this modification to religious revivals will appear in good time. It is at once manifest, however, that a religious camp-meeting such as formerly took place in the central south — in Kentucky or Tennessee, for example — which continued for days together, morning, noon and night, which never broke up until the food supply gave out, and which was characterized by fervid appeals to feeling and imagination rather than to intelligence, would be a very hotbed of disorder and mental disintegration. And such indeed it often was. While on the other hand, religious gatherings controlled by sound sense and rational though deep feeling, with alternation of meeting and separation, with opportunity for private meditation, might have very different effects. But with this modification, our conclusion must be that the unrestrained tendency of the psychological crowd is to lay bare in the individuals composing it primitive and uncontrolled mental and nervous traits.

CHAPTER IV

THE GHOST-DANCE AMONG THE NORTH AMERICAN INDIANS

THE fourteenth annual report of the Bureau of Ethnology at Washington contains some exceedingly illuminating material with respect to religious revivals among a primitive people.[1] There have been two of these of considerable magnitude among the North American Indians within the last twenty years, the Shaker and the ghost-dance revivals. The latter had far greater extension, but the former is notable for its peculiar method which was copied in the ghost-dance. We shall therefore pause to examine it briefly. The red-skin Shakers of Puget Sound are of course not in any way allied to the white-skin Shakers of Watervliet and other places in the eastern states. They are an entirely distinct religious denomination, but the name of each rose from the same phenomenon — a nervous twitching which characterized the white Shakers in the days of their origin and the red Shakers within our own time. The following facts with respect to the movement I glean from the ethnological report mentioned above. The founder of

[1] "The Ghost-dance Religion and the Sioux Outbreak of 1890," by James Mooney.

the religion is Squ-sacht-un. His chief high priest is Ai-yäl. Both are of the Squaxin tribe. In the early eighties the founder fell into a trance one morning, and remained therein till mid-afternoon. He dreamed himself at the entrance of heaven, from which the angels kept him back and charged him to return to earth and teach his people what they must dó to enter finally the happy hunting-grounds. Accordingly, as soon as he awoke, he embarked upon his divinely appointed mission. Of course he was familiar with Christian customs and Christian doctrines, for white missionaries had been in that field for years, without however producing any such result as the Shaker movement. Christian form and Christian principle were to some extent, therefore, sprinkled through their practices from the beginning, making it a curious mixture of Christianity and savagery. At their first meetings, the ceremonial quite largely followed that of the ancient sacred and secret society of their savage days, in which persons went into hypnotic trance and became rigid. The votaries of the new faith, therefore, like the votaries of the old "tomahnous," dreamed dreams, saw visions, and were overcome by violent shaking. "With their arms at full length, their hair and arms would shake very rapidly. Gazing into Heaven, their heads would also shake, sometimes for a few minutes, sometimes for a few hours, sometimes for half the night." The shaking took possession of entirely normal people, but it finally became so extreme that it seemed likely to cast great numbers of them into insanity, at which crisis the agent interfered. When the shaking was discouraged it very largely ceased, although some declared at first that they could not stop. However, when the excitement died away, they found they could bring themselves under control.

It spread most easily among the ignorant — those who had not yet learned to read, or been under any of the wholesome restraints of proper secular or religious instruction. The movement, as well as the shaking, spread by imitation from camp to camp about Skookum Bay, Mud Bay, Squaxon, and then among the Nisqually and Chehalis Indians, and later among the Yakima and other eastern tribes of the Columbia region. And Dr. Livingston Farrand tells me that when he still later visited the coast of Washington, the movement had spread among the Nez Perces, and even into Idaho. The suggestibility of the Indian race in that part of the country was so marked that almost nobody could withstand it. There were frequently not ten members of the tribe that were not converts. The Indians spoke of it as being as catching as the measles. "Many who at first ridiculed it and fought against it and invoked the aid of the agent to stop it, were drawn into it after a little and became its strong upholders."

The prominent feature of their revival method, which the ghost-dancers have probably copied, is naked hypnotism. Indian medicine-men from one end of the country to the other have always understood how to produce many of the effects of suggestion, although they have not understood the force they were dealing with and have honestly considered it a supernatural endowment. By the use of this art they are able to bring about, under right conditions, involuntary trembling, spasmodic action, rigidity and finally unconsciousness. This hypnotic method is used not only to influence to conversion, but as a means of throwing the devotees into trance communication with their departed friends, and also as a preventive and cure of disease.

It will no doubt be interesting to many to learn that the primitive red wards of the nation are very modern in their religious differentiations. Millerism flourished among the Cherokees of Alabama and Georgia some time before it appeared among the white people in the state of New York and elsewhere. Early in the last century many members of that tribe, expecting the end of the world, left their bees, their orchards, and all that they possessed and made for the mountains of Carolina, among the highest summits of which their original William Miller told them they must be on a certain day to escape destruction. And as late as 1890 something very like spiritualism was in a state of active existence among the Arapaho and Cheyenne, and many members of the tribe professed to have been in heaven where they talked with their dead friends, then came back and brought messages from the other world. And among these Shakers of Puget Sound the faith-cure doctrine has flourished like a green bay tree. This branch of the sect was headed originally by the brother of Ai-yäl, and is still in existence. Their cure for disease consists in the members of the cult "shaking in a circle about a sick person, dressed in ceremonial costume." The religious practitioner waves a cloth in front of the patient "with a gentle, fanning motion, and, blowing at the same time, proceeds to drive the disease out of the body, beginning at the feet and working upward. The assistant stands ready to seize the disease with his cloth when it is driven out of the head."[1] And they are able to boast of many real cures.

The Shakers of Puget Sound present a strange combination of superstition and ignorance of the grossest sort with some really ethical religion which they have learned from the white missionaries; for it must be said to their credit that they make vigorous onslaughts against drinking and gambling, the two great Indian vices.

But of greater interest is the remarkable spread of the famous ghost-dance religion during the later eighties and the early nineties of the last century. It is probably by far the most extensive religious movement among the Indians of America within the historic period.[2] It had its prophet, Wovoka,

---

[1] Fourteenth Annual Report, Bureau of Ethnology, p. 761.
[2] Ibid., p. 927.

the Messiah of the ghost-dance, who lived among the Paiutes in western Nevada. There is some evidence that he was initiated into the newer hypnotic mysteries of the Shakers, but his doctrines, through the medium of imitation and of that peculiar form of psychological crowd, the ghost-dance, spread far and wide throughout the tribes both west and east of the Rockies. The hope of this movement was of a paradise regained, a happy hunting-ground here below, the whole Indian race, living and dead, leading a life of aboriginal delight upon a regenerated earth.

The ghost-dance was the driving force of the movement. Mr. Mooney came upon the instructions which the Messiah had sent to the Cheyenne and Arapaho which were in effect to hold the gatherings every six weeks, and dance four successive nights. On the last night, the dance was to be kept up until the morning of the fifth day, when all were to bathe in the river and then disperse to their homes.

This performance was not a variety of the war dance, as many have supposed, for no weapon of any kind was allowed to be carried during its progress. It was a sacred dance. The name is taken from the ghost-shirt or ghost-dress of white cotton cloth worn by males and females. The origin of the costume has been traced with some plausibility to the trance of an Indian woman who had seen her friends in heaven thus attired. Among the Shoshoni and Paiutes, sometimes a thousand people would take part. The excitement was very pronounced. "When the dancers were worn out mentally and physically, the medicine-men would shout that they could see the faces of departed friends and relatives moving about the circle. No pen can describe the result. All shouted in chorus and then danced and sang until they fell into a confused and exhausted mass on the ground." [1]

This sacred dance really took the form of an Indian camp-meeting. A teacher on the Pine Ridge reservation has given us a very suggestive and detailed description of one which she attended on White Clay Creek, June 20, 1890.[2] I abridge from her account.

Three hundred tents were placed in a circle around a large pine tree. In the centre were gathered the medicine-men, also those who had been so fortunate as to have had visions and in them had seen and talked with friends who had died. A company of fifteen started a chant and were marching abreast, others coming in behind as they marched. The crowd gathered about the tree. The high priest or master of ceremonies spoke for about fifteen minutes. Then they arose and formed a circle. Three or four hundred persons marched around, setting up the most fearful and heart-piercing wails, moaning, shrieking, naming over their departed relatives and friends, raising their eyes to heaven with hands clasped high above their heads, invoking the power of the Great Spirit to allow them to see and talk with their people who had died. After fifteen minutes all sat down and listened to another address of encouragement and assurance of the coming Messiah. When

[1] Fourteenth Annual Report, Bureau of Ethnology, p. 806.
[2] *Ibid.*, p. 916.

they arose again, there was intense excitement. This time they danced more rapidly, their hands moving from side to side, their bodies swaying. In the ring were men, women and children, the strong and the robust, and some who were in poor health who it was thought could be cured by joining in the dance and losing consciousness. Under the power of the emotion, and of the hypnotic method employed by the medicine-men, of which more will be said later, first one and then another would break from the ring, stagger and fall down. Some would appear conscious but with every muscle twitching and quivering; some appeared to be perfectly unconscious; some would run, stepping high and pawing the air in a frightful manner. Those who fell were never disturbed, and no notice was taken of them save to keep the crowd away. They were supposed to be enjoying a season of refreshing in the spirit world. The dance was kept up until fully one hundred persons out of the three or four hundred who took part were lying absolutely unconscious. Then they stopped and seated themselves in a circle, and, as each one recovered from his trance, he was brought to the centre of the ring to relate his experience.

I am reminded of the incident of the visit of the Emperor of Brazil to the exposition at Philadelphia in 1876. They showed him the Corliss engine. Some one told him how many revolutions it could make in a minute. " Goodness ! " he is reported to have exclaimed, " that beats a South American Republic." It may be said of this Indian gathering on White Clay Creek that it beats a Kentucky camp-meeting of the pioneer days. But there are some suggestive similarities between them, as I think my reader will aver when we come to examine in detail the great revival of 1800.

As among the Shakers, the revival method is

thoroughly hypnotic.   The medicine-man stands within the ring, holding in his hand an eagle feather or a handkerchief, white, black or any other color. Sometimes he holds the feather in one hand and the scarf in the other.   The dancers circle round him singing songs in time with the dance step. The first indication that an individual of least self-control is being affected is observable in a slight muscular tremor.   The first subject is usually a woman.   The medicine-man is on the watch, and he comes immediately and stands in front of the subject, "looking intently into her face, and whirling the feather or the handkerchief, or both, rapidly. in front of her eyes, moving slowly round with the dancers at the same time, always facing the woman. All this time he keeps up a series of sharp exclamations, Hu! Hu! Hu!, like the rapid breathing of an exhausted runner.   Soon the woman is overcome, and staggers into the ring, while the circle closes up behind her."[1]   The medicine-man then gives his whole attention to her until he completes his work and she becomes rigid, uttering low moans, with her eyes fixed and staring, and then totally unconscious.   Immediately he begins the same process with some other who has become susceptible.

These phenomena have been common in several of the great revivals in the civilized white populations, and many examples of pretence have been ferreted out in them all — notably by Charles Wes-

[1] Fourteenth Annual Report, Bureau of Ethnology, p. 925.

ley in the cases which resulted from his brother's preaching — and there are undoubtedly instances of pure deception among the Indians. But competent witnesses assure us that with them, as with the more advanced peoples under similar influences, the great proportion were unquestionably genuine and beyond the control of the subject. While we are still speaking of this matter, it is worthy of note that not all the leaders in the ghost-dance have this power of influencing suggestibles in the same measure. And so it comes about that a process of selection of medicine-men takes place. Any man or woman who has been in a trance and derived inspiration from the other world is at liberty to go within the circle and endeavor to bring others into that condition. Superior ability selects the religious leaders as in the old days it selected the military leaders.

It was matter of observation with the representative of the Bureau of Ethnology that young women were the first to be affected with the ghost-dance, then the older women and lastly men, though sometimes a man of a particular temperament was affected first. The subjects were usually strong and healthy as the average of their type. Temperament, more than physical condition, decided who should first lose self-control.

As to the spread of the ghost-dance religion, it was taken up nearly simultaneously by the Bannock, Shoshoni, Gosuite and Ute in the early part of 1889. All these tribes are neighbors of the

Paiutes and closely akin.[1]   It swept through many tribes west of the Rockies, but not through all, then it passed rapidly east of the Rockies into the plains, where considerable numbers of tribes were caught in the contagion.   All together thirty or thirty-five tribes west and east of the Rockies, having an aggregate population of sixty thousand souls, received the new religion.[2]   Some of these were practically unanimous in acceptance of the new doctrine, — the Paiute, Shoshoni, Arapaho, Cheyenne, Caddo and Pawnee, — while others, as the Comanche, were not largely affected by it.   About one-half of the twenty-six thousand Sioux took active part in it, and their dances were among the wildest of all, many of the tribe becoming practically crazy, falling as if dead and foaming at the mouth.

The only controlling influence was exerted by the Indian agent, who usually did not interfere, so that this great emotional movement followed a natural course and did not cease until it had completely spent its fury.   It is now largely extinct, save in certain tribes in Oklahoma where the dance has become a part of the tribal life.

In this unique development of Indian faith we have a revival with accompaniments of primitive simplicity.   Here is the dance, the rhythm, the trance, the vision, the ecstasy, all the reflex phenomena which belong to primitive savage man.

[1] Fourteenth Annual Report, Bureau of Ethnology, p. 805.
[2] *Ibid.*, p. 927.

This is grotesque and debasing. But there is also mingled with it much that is beautiful and uplifting, and of which no man should speak with disrespect. It is impossible not to see something besides the extraordinary suggestibility of this primitive race in the picture of the men and women of the Arapaho flocking to Mr. Mooney, the government representative, on his return from the country where their Messiah lived,[1] "the tears rolling down their cheeks, the whole body violently trembling from stress of emotion — something more than bald superstition in the simple trust of these red children, that after shaking hands with one who had seen the Messiah whom they would never see, they might be enabled in trance visions to catch a glimpse of the coming glory." It is one more picture of natural human need and longing.

A warrior of the Arapaho, who are the most spiritual of the Indian tribes, said to Mr. Mooney when his little boy died, "I shall not shoot any ponies, and my wife will not gash her arms. We used to do this when our friends died because we thought we would never see them again, and it made us feel badly. But now we know that we shall all be united again." As among the Shakers, so also among the ghost-dancers, emphasis is laid upon the reformed life with respect to the two great Indian vices, drinking and gambling. It is evident that this new religion had in it two distinct elements, which may be dissociated, and which

[1] Fourteenth Annual Report, Bureau of Ethnology, p. 778.

have no part or parcel one with the other. There is the barbaric dance and the cataleptic vision, but there is also the hope of immortality, the ethical uplift, the attempt at righteousness. We shall come upon these diverse elements again in religious revivals among peoples long civilized. It should be as easy to dissociate them there.

CHAPTER V

THE RELIGION OF THE AMERICAN NEGRO

No one doubts, I suppose, that in the negro people, whether in Africa or America, we have another child race. The old slave system of the Southland snatched the ancestors of this race from savagery only one or two hundred years ago. A century or two is not a long period in the social evolution of any people, especially one whose early abode was in the African jungle beneath a tropic sun. And so we would expect to find among the masses of the black people, as we do, many clear marks of their inheritance. Dense ignorance and superstition, a vivid imagination, volatile emotion, a weak will power, small sense of morality, are universally regarded as the most prominent traits of the negro in those sections of the country, notably some parts of the black belt, where he appears in his primitive simplicity. In other parts of the South, where the influence of real education has been at work, the mental and moral character of great numbers of the blacks would not so exactly fit this description. Both slavery and emancipation days have brought to them ideal and aspiration. The culture of the

white race has been imitated. They are in possession of much of what may be spoken of as the
Anglo-Saxon consciousness. Many members of
the negro race have shown capacity for high
thought and heroic deed. But in general there
has not yet been time enough for more than a su-
perposition of higher elements upon their inherited
mental, social, and religious nature. Of true
mental development in the race as a race there
has been little. Civilization and savagery dwell
side by side in the same spirit, and the result is
often flagrant contradiction in thinking, in feeling,
in conduct. According to the chance of the moment, the one or the other shows itself with its
appropriate accompaniment of utterance and act.
I once spent part of an August evening on the top
of Lookout Mountain in the northwestern corner of
Georgia, listening with a company of friends to an
old hermit darky's account of his religious conversion. He was a powerful giant of a black man,
sixty-seven years of age, a recluse, but known
favorably by the dwellers all over the mountain.
He spoke to us on the porch of our hostess's resi-
dence, in the darkness, with only a flickering light
shining in his face. He had reached the climax
of the recital, was in a considerable state of
ecstasy, and was very anxiously seeking to impress
us all with his spiritual experience, when suddenly
his dog began barking furiously just behind him
and utterly broke the continuity of his thought
and of his speech. I think no one of us will ever

forget the dash of savagery that came into his face as he turned with flashing eye and foaming lip upon that canine intruder. It was a startling transition, revealing the crater of primitive passion just underneath the crust of religious culture and nurture.

The most prominent activity of the negro race in America is religion. Of course I mean religion of a certain type, which can only be understood when viewed historically and in the light of the mental development which this people has attained. A little time ago, comparatively speaking, their ancestors were practising primitive rites on the African west coast. And the slave ships brought to the West Indian sugar fields, and to the Southern states ultimately, a people who were saturated with superstition. Many accounts have been written of negro Voodooism which have no doubt been much exaggerated. Voodooism was a cult in which the snake was regarded as a sacred animal, as it has been in various parts of the world. It is a phase of the animistic faith of the early children of nature. It seems certain that this rite, among others, existed in Hayti in early slavery times and that mixtures of Voodooism and other rites with Christianity were common in the old plantation days in the South. I have referred before to the practice of charm and magic so well-nigh universal to-day among the mass of the black race in the lower Mississippi Valley. This phenomenon is reflected clearly in the negro's religious experience — he must have some sign of conversion. The sun must stand still at the moment of the great change, or the moon must exhibit a strange transformation of color, or a star must twinkle in a peculiar way.

The childlikeness of their conceptions, even in a more advanced stage, is shown in the growth of such a sect as the "sheep-calling Baptists" in parts of Alabama, with whom the communion is observed two hours before day. They meet out in the woods or sometimes in the church. The people gather inside and then disperse among the trees and the bushes outside. The preacher dons his robe, and in the character of a shepherd goes forth to gather in his sheep. "Coo-oo sheep! Coo-oo-sh'p — Cooshy-coo-oo-sheep!" he calls, and the men of his flock from their place in the forest answer, "Ba! Ba!" and the women from the bushes answer likewise, and they follow him into the church. They employ two kinds of bread in administering the sacrament, — the black bread for the outsider who is "not of this fold" and the white bread for the true sheep.

With the American negro the church is the exclusive social centre, and in the South practically every man and woman of the race is a member of the church. Thoroughly religious animal as he is by nature, with extraordinary emotional endowment added thereto, he would find it very difficult to withstand the almost constant tide of revival

that sweeps over his community.   Every religious
meeting has a tendency to fall at once into the
revival form, and anyway he cannot escape those
great gatherings of the country people at camp-
meeting each year when the crops are " laid
by."

The negro preacher is a figure of singular interest.   The descendant of the medicine-man of
the African clan, " he early appeared on the plantation and found his function as the healer of the
sick, the interpreter of the unknown, the com-
forter of the sorrowing, the supernatural avenger
of wrong and the one who rudely but picturesquely
expressed the longing, disappointment and resent-
ment of a stolen and oppressed people." [1]   He
became the leader in the early quasi-Christian
institutions which preceded the negro churches,
and finally the pastor of the regularly organized
societies.   Since the days of freedom, the colored
preacher, as the most prominent man in the community, has often been not only the spiritual
leader, but the political boss, the idealist on the
Sabbath, the very practical opportunist during the
week, whose claims to morality, either political or
personal, would not bear minute investigation.   Of
course I am speaking not of the city pastors of
the border states, where are to be found cultivated,
intelligent and thoroughly moral men in the younger
generation, nor would the representation be an
accurate one if applied universally anywhere, but

[1] "The Souls of Black Folk," Dubois, p. 196.

there is no doubt about the type. The colored minister has been the social radical, proclaiming the equality of the races according to the Scriptures, always the emotional orator swaying his audiences at will, expounding the doctrines of depravity and damnation and too often illustrating them in his daily practice, appealing to the instinctive emotions of fear and hate as well as love, the mourner, the shouter, the visioner, rioting in word pictures, his preaching an incoherent, irrational rhythmic ecstasy, his thinking following absolutely the psychological law of the blending of mental images. Here is a primitive man with primitive traits in a modern environment.

And the religious method ? Like that of the Indian ghost-dance, emotional and hypnotic to the core. The sound of religious music, the personality of the preacher, are like tinder to the nature of the black man. He is in the highest degree suggestible.

I once attended a simple " experience meetin' " of black people in Tennessee in which these influences were very visibly at work. At the outset the interest was not intense, and I noted several colored people on the fringe of the crowd sound asleep. Testimony flagged a little, and the leader called for that expression of tense emotional excitement known among the negroes as "mournin'." One speaker was floundering in a weltering chaos of images and seemed likely to sink without anybody to rescue him, when the leader arose and with animation on every feature shouted to the audience, "Mourn him up, chillun!" And the audience began — all except those who were asleep — at first soft and low, but rising higher and higher until they fell into a rhythm that carried everything before it, including the disciple who had been floundering for words in which to phrase his religious experience. But he had no trouble longer. Images flashed through his mind with great rapidity and found quick expression on his lips. He spoke in rhythm, and the audience rhythmically responded. He was speedily in full movement, head, arms, feet, eyes, face, and soon he was lost in ecstasy. And the contagion swept everything before it. Even the sound sleepers on the fringe of the crowd were caught and carried into the movement as if by a tide of the sea. At the very climax of the meeting, a woman rose to her feet, moved forward to the open space in front of the pulpit, evidently under the compulsion of the lyric wave. Having reached the front, in one wild burst of pent-up emotion, she fell rigid to the floor and lay there motionless during the rest of the service. She was not disturbed. Like the devotees of the ghost-dance, she, too, was believed to be enjoying visions of the unseen world.

But the most perfect example of this extraordinary suggestibility of the colored race that has ever come within the range of my investigation is one that I am now about to relate. I would not print it if I did not believe it to be absolutely genuine. It is such a perfect illustration because it dissociates the hypnotic element so completely from any true spiritual element, and shows the power of suggestion in its nakedness. In a little town between Cleveland, Tennessee, and Chattanooga, it was the purpose to give a donation to the colored minister. One of the brethren in the church volunteered to make a collection of the offerings from the various homes of the members, and an old colored woman, somewhat well to do, loaned her cart and a pair of steers to this brother to facilitate the gathering of the donation goods. After he had been throughout the neighborhood and secured a reasonable load of groceries, provisions and clothing, he drove off to Chattanooga and sold everything, including the cart and the steers, pocketed the proceeds and departed for Atlanta on a visit to his relatives. Consternation and then indignation reigned supreme in the home community when it became known that he was gone. After some time the culprit drifted back, in deep contrition, but having spent all. Indignation once more arose to a white heat, and it was determined to give him a church trial without waiting for any legal formality. The day was set, the meeting was crowded; the preacher presided, and after a statement of the charges, announced that the accused would be given a chance to be heard. He went forward and took the place of the preacher on the platform. " I ain't got nuffin to say fo' myse'f," he began in a penitent voice, " I'se a po' mis'able sinner. But, bredren, so is we all mis'able sinners. An' de good book says we must fergib. How many times, bredren ? Till seven times? No, till seventy times seven. An' I ain't sinned no seventy times seven, and I'm jes' go' to sugges' dat we turn dis into a fergibness meetin', an' eberybody in dis great comp'ny dat is willin' to fergib me, come up now, while we sing one of our deah ole hymns, and shake ma hand." And he started one of the powerful revival tunes, and they began to come, first those who hadn't given anything to the donation and were not much interested in the matter anyway, then those who hadn't lost much, and then the others. Finally they had all passed before him except one, and she stuck to her seat. And he said, " Dar's one po' mis'able sinner still lef', dat won't fergib, she won't fergib." (She was the old lady who lost the steers.) " Now I sugges' that we hab a season ob prayer, an' gib dis po' ole sinner one mo' chance." And after they had prayed and sung a hymn, the old lady came up, too !

At many of the "big quarterlies" and the " protracted meetin's" which are held in the South, there are scenes of frenzy, of human passion, of collapse, of catalepsy, of foaming at the mouth, of convulsion, of total loss of inhibition, compared with the scorching heat of which the Indian ghost-dance seems at times only a pale moon. To be "mad with supernatural joy "[1] is with the negro the great test of supernatural presence. The influence of the demon worship of his ancestors in the African forest is still interwoven with the mental prepossessions and the nervous organization of the race.

There are a few of the primitive phenomena which particularly distinguish the religion of the negro so interesting as to warrant our observing them a little more closely. The group of motor manifestations, the rhythm, the shout, the "falling out," are exceedingly characteristic. High feeling,. discharging itself in muscular action, and discharging itself rhythmically, is everywhere a spontaneous manifestation of children and of child races.[2] If this feeling discharges itself through the muscles of the vocal organs, we have the shout. If through the feet, we have the dance. The sacred dance is, of course, not so common among the negroes as among the Indians. But it is quite common. I have had several instances of it brought to my attention. There is a small sect near Granada, Mississippi, who sing and preach and dance in turn. A correspondent writes me that there is a church near Appomattox in which great preparations are made for the revival every September. Certain of the membership are specially trained for the " flower dance," which takes place in the church and is not

[1] "The Souls of Black Folk," Dubois.
[2] Cf. Spencer, " Principles of Sociology " (2–1), p. 17 f.

very unlike the red-Indian variety in its form and
in its effect.   In the country districts of Alabama
we hear of the "roper dance," which consists of
an excited embrace of the sexes followed by a
march around a central figure who claps his hands
and shouts vociferously.   My informant avers that
this procedure takes place at the close of the meeting, and in many cases results in gross immorality.
The Primitive Orthodox Zion Baptist Church at
Yamassee, Florida, holds a "Rocking Daniel"
dance at the close of the communion service.
The membership forms a circle in front of the
pulpit, in the centre of which the leader stands.
They move around the leader in single file, singing
"Rock Daniel, rock Daniel, rock Daniel till I die."
Then they fall into regular step and gesticulate and
shout till exhaustion intervenes.[1]

No one who has listened to a typical negro
preacher or a typical negro congregation has failed
to observe the rhythmic cadence into which they
unconsciously drop.   Rhythm is the line of least
resistance for high emotion.   A change in tone
level is a rest to the muscles which are producing
the vociferous effects.   The same phenomenon
has appeared among the Hard Shell Baptists, the
Friends and the early Methodists, and has always
the same significance.

When the emotion is very violent, muscle con-
traction becomes abnormal and we have the phenomenon of "falling out."   This circumstance is

[1] "The Negro Church, a Social Study," p. 67.

held by probably the major part of religious
colored people as the clearest evidence of divine
grace and conversion. It used always to be a necessary attestation of the "call to preach." Booker
T. Washington in his autobiography describes the
process as it took place in his early home in West
Virginia. "Usually the call came when the individual was sitting in church. Without warning
he would fall upon the floor as if struck by a
bullet, and would lie there for hours, speechless
and motionless. If he were inclined to resist the
summons, he would fall a second or third time.
In the end he always yielded to the ' call.' " This
of course fostered a tendency to the oversupply of
ministers. Mr. Washington speaks of one church
with which he was acquainted which had a total
membership of about two hundred, eighteen of
whom were regular preachers. One of the surest
evidences of the growth of intelligence, civilization and good sense among the blacks is the considerable decline in the number of those who are
thus "called to preach." Under the influence of
education and enlightenment, the grade of ministers
is steadily changing for the better. But the great
majority of the older and the untrained men still
depend upon mere noise and hypnotic excitement
for the conversion of their hearers. Anything else
with them is degeneration. "It's all booklarnin', "
they say, "dey ain't no Holy Ghos' in it at all."

In the earlier days fasting among the negroes
was a common custom precedent to conversion.

Dr. Charles T. Walker of New York City, a distinguished preacher of the colored race, known as
the "black Spurgeon," a man of intelligence and
cultivation, assures me of this, and once described
to me his own experience. The incident is also
related in his biography. On Wednesday of a
certain week in the month of June while he was
hoeing cotton he decided to become a "seeker."
He followed the usual custom. When he reached
the end of the row, without saying a word to anybody, he jumped over the fence and went into the
woods. Without eating or drinking, without see-
ing any one, he remained in the woods until the
following Saturday afternoon, when he was "happily converted." The custom of fasting, as many
know, has a primitive origin and is very widespread.
It was not an invention. It was often a grim necessity. But the hunger of the savage brought him
vivid dreams and visions, seemed to give preternatural acuteness to his spirit. And then fasting
grew to be an institution. The Indian boy regularly fasts about the age of puberty. He goes off
into the forest, as young Walker did, until his
vision comes. Whatever then appears to him is
his supernatural friend, his Manitou. Of course
the abnormal mental excitement is caused primarily
by the lack of food, but everywhere among primitive peoples it is ascribed to a possessing divinity.[1]

A very certain though unsavory bit of evidence
of the negro's primitive state is found in the great

[1] Cf. Spencer, "Principles of Sociology" (1–1), p. 239 f.

gulf still fixed in his consciousness between religion and morality. Average ecclesiastical leadership is not yet skilful enough safely to bridge the abyss. It was only recently that the following was published in a Southern newspaper over a negro bishop's name.[1] " But through His death and resurrection we may commit sins of lying, stealing, Sabbath breaking, getting drunk, gambling, whoring, murdering and every species of villany, and then come to God through our resurrected Christ and enter heaven in the end."

This great gulf is revealed especially by the absence of sexual virtue to so marked a degree, and by the overpowering propensity to petty theft. The wide prevalence of the crime of lynching among the whites of the South testifies eloquently to the reign of lust among the blacks, and as for petty thieving, it is so common as often to excite only humorous comment. A colored house-girl, " seeking religion " under the guidance of a colored "mother in the gospel," will abstract a pound of butter from the day's churning of her employer, and carry it as a compensation to her " mother " for helping her to " come through," without a glimmering of the real nature of her act. This appears to be unmorality rather than immorality. Long ago the great Englishman Jowett spoke of the " ages before morality," by which he meant the time when ethics in the modern sense of the relation of man to man was not born, although

[1] Cf. *The Outlook*, July 30, 1904, p. 745.

religion was born and was flourishing. And the
negro still lives in those ages, and has the undeveloped ethical sense.

I have been speaking of the American negro
type, and not of all negroes. Wherever the
influence of Hampton and Tuskegee and other
institutions has permeated, the leaven is at work
that will some day no doubt regenerate the whole
lump. There is something intrinsically noble in a
race which has manifested such an original genius
for beautiful music. Nothing like it has appeared
in any other population element on American soil.

CHAPTER VI

ONE of the most famous of the religious revivals in America occurred in the state of Kentucky in and about the year 1800, among a population predominantly Scotch-Irish. More than half a century afterwards, in 1859, a similar movement took place in the original home of this population in the north of Ireland. The object of discussing the two movements in successive chapters is to set side by side some points of likeness and some of contrast. The Scotch-Irish were a mixed people in the north of Ireland, as their name indicates. The large influx of Lowland Scotch in the seventeenth century was decisive in fixing their ethical and religious character. But in their blood from ancient time was both the Teutonic and the Celtic strain. Long before the Anglo-Saxon invasion of Britain, long before the Roman invasion, a very early wave of Teutonic migration had swept across the North Sea, through the Highlands of Scotland and into the north and east of Ireland. And in their character the Scotch-Irish combine the shrewd, practical common sense and intelligent purpose of the Teuton with the strong emotionalism of the Celt, and the former element has been held to predomi-

nate on their native heath. On the whole they have
probably shown a superior intelligence when compared with their fellow-countrymen to the south.
They have been less superstitious. They have been
better trained educationally than the rest of the Irish
people. They have been Protestant to the core and
have shown an amazing fondness for theological argument. It is of them that one of their pure Celtic
countrymen wittily remarked that when the potato
crop failed, they lived on the shorter catechism.

During the first half of the eighteenth century
these people began coming to America in considerable numbers. Most of them entered at the port of
Philadelphia and worked slowly down the long valleys of the Appalachian Mountains into Kentucky
and Tennessee. Many of them, however, entered
at the port of Charleston. Long before, the low-
lands of Virginia and the Carolinas had been occupied by the Cavalier planters, and the Scotch-Irish
immigrants passed on to the higher ground in the
back country, and ultimately over the Blue Ridge
into the rich valleys of the Green River, the Tennessee and the Cumberland. These two branches
of the same stock came together on this border-
land, "took root and flourished, stretching in a
broad belt from north to south, a shield of sinewy
men thrust in between the people of the seaboard
and the red warriors of the wilderness." [1]

It must be remembered that the men who came
voluntarily from the north of Ireland, or from any-

[1] Roosevelt, "Winning of the West," Vol. I, pp. 104, 105.

where in the Old World during the seventeenth and eighteenth centuries, were usually the result of a fine process of selection. They were the independent, the hardy, the adventurous. Very often in the study which we have before us, these people will not appear at their best. Swept away on a great tide of emotion, they do not exhibit some of their higher qualities. All the more on this account do I pause for a word of appreciation of this magnificent strain in the nation's blood. The descendants of these people have done much for America, and will do more when the millions of their belated kin in the Southern mountains are brought under the influence of twentieth-century enlightenment and culture. For what they have already done they deserve a statue in the nation's hall of fame with the Huguenot, the Hollander, the Cavalier and the Puritan. In those early days they showed not only a daring but a capacity for progress that are beyond eulogy. These were the men who "long before the first Continental Congress had assembled had lost all remembrance of Europe and all sympathy with things European, and had become Americans in speech, thought and character,"[1] who were the first to declare for independence, and who, in the war of 1812, saw more clearly than New England the necessity of the struggle, and were for it, through and through, when New England held back because of commercial interest and unpatriotic sloth. The decisive victory of

[1] Roosevelt, "Winning of the West," Vol. I, p. 108.

General Jackson of New Orleans was largely won
by the few hundred clear-eyed, straight-shooting,
backwoods riflemen from Tennessee. And the
fact that the very heart of American democracy
beats to-day in the great central west is partly due
to the sane instinct and the moral stamina of these
Scotch-Irish pioneers.

It is possible to form a rather definite notion of
their type of mind about the year 1800. They
were already quite different in many respects from
their kinsmen remaining in the north of Ireland.
In the first place they were a selected population,
fitted for a border life, and their forceful motor
traits appeared in their children. The new environment, too, had put its stamp upon them.
There was necessarily some disintegration of
intellectual elements. The professional classes,
who at home were great centres of self-control,
were comparatively few in number in this pioneer
community. These people were in a new, wild
country, where neither conventionality nor law held
its accustomed sway. The rational restraints of
religion were many and strong in their native
land, but were largely absent in the wilderness.
They came to live more and more in what they
knew to be open violation of the law of their own
consciences, and of that stern but strongly ethical
religion in which they and their forefathers who
followed Knox and Calvin had been reared.
Furthermore, the circumstances of their daily
living developed in them a quick response to

stimulus. They were obliged to be ever on the alert against attacking savages. And the slightest alarm would bring together every man and boy in the settlement who could use a rifle in defence of the women and the children. They lived in an environment of fear, though they were of such sturdy stuff that they grew in the very midst of it to be utterly fearless and even reckless of danger that they could understand and measure. Nevertheless, the new experience of rational inhibitions removed, of a strange and dangerous environment, developed in them to a high degree the motor and emotional tendencies which were already in the blood of their kind. The primitive surroundings once more fanned into flame the primitive traits. They were not only a sturdier but a far more excitable and sanguine population in 1800 than their brethren in the north of Ireland, and when at last there was brought to bear upon them in the course of events that most powerful species of psychological "crowd," a protracted religious camp-meeting, and they were suddenly halted and aroused by the most fervid, imaginative and reiterative appeals to a sense of their apostasy and their everlasting doom if they should not repent, there resulted as perfect a combination of conditions for the propagation of influence by imitation and the production of nervous and mental infection as the world has ever seen.[1]

The emotional epidemic attained greater violence,

[1] Cf. Bacon, "History of American Christianity," p. 238.

also, because in this population there was still
another important class that we have not yet mentioned. The vehemence of any form of impulsive
social action is always increased by the presence
of a relatively large number of the criminal and
degenerate type in a community. And the border
had very many of this class in the pioneer days.
" There was a large influx of people drawn from
the worst immigrants that perhaps were ever
brought to America, the mass of convict servants,
redemptioners and the like who formed such an
excessively undesirable substratum to the otherwise
excellent population of the tide-water regions in
Virginia and the Carolinas. Many of the Southern
crackers, or poor whites, sprang from this class,
which also in the backwoods gave birth to generations of violent and hardened criminals and to
an even greater number of shiftless, lazy, cowardly
cumberers of the earth's surface." [1] The presence
of this stratum in the Kentucky revivals was very
often alarmingly and dramatically evident in the
attacks of mobs upon the religious camp-meetings,
which were so often repulsed under the vigorous
leadership of such magnificent physical and moral
specimens of the backwoods preacher as Peter
Cartwright and Finis Ewing.[2] And it is interesting, too, to observe how often individuals of this
same stratum were the first to be laid low by
the sturdy spiritual blows struck later by these

[1] Roosevelt, "Winning of the West," Vol. I, p. 130.
[2] Cf. "Autobiography" of Cartwright, p. 90 f.

stalwart champions of a better order and a better life.[1]

The propagating centre of the revival of 1800 was Logan County in southwestern Kentucky, in what was then known as the Cumberland country. The settlements extended from the Green River on the north to a point in Tennessee south of the Cumberland. The country was beautiful, the climate salubrious, the soil fertile, and, as we have remarked, families and individuals were constantly on the march from Virginia and the Carolinas, as well as from other parts of the Union, to make their abode in this fair Cumberland region. So far as religious belief is concerned, the Presbyterian body was altogether the most numerous in this whole section by 1800. The pioneer preachers who initiated the revival and the camp-meeting were Presbyterians, with one important exception. The beginnings of the movement were among the people and within the bounds of the Transylvania presbytery and the synod of Kentucky. The tendency to revivalism was hotly opposed by the majority of the synod, and eventually some of the leaders of the movement were disciplined for alleged laxity of doctrine and of practice.

This warm evangelistic temper appeared with the Rev. James McGready and others from the Caro-

[1] "Autobiography" of Cartwright, p. 126: "On Sunday night, when such a tremendous power fell on the congregation, my gang of rowdies fell by dozens on the right and left."

linas and Virginia, and can be traced, I think, to
the ministrations of Whitefield in those parts about
the middle of the eighteenth century.   The Rev.
James McGready came from North Carolina to
Logan County in 1796.   His doctrine was a modified Calvinism.   He dwelt upon the necessity of the
new birth and the importance of knowing the time
when and the place where the conversion had occurred.   This was a new note in the Presbyterian
denomination in that section of the world.[1]   But
there was another note in the gamut of his eloquence that was not new.   In New England under
Edwards, and in Old England under Wesley, it had
sounded forth clear and strong and terrible in fearful denunciation of the wrath of God upon impenitent sinners.   A friend of McGready[2] said of him
that he would so array hell before the wicked
that they would tremble and quake, imagining a
lake of fire and brimstone yawning to overwhelm
them and the hand of the Almighty thrusting them
down the horrible abyss.   And it is also recorded
of him that "the fierceness of his invective derived
additional terror from the hideousness of his visage
and the thunder of his tones."[3]   Because of his
remarkable objurgatory talent he was strongly

---

[1] Cf. Crisman, "Origin and Doctrines of the Cumberland Presbyterian Church," p. 26.

[2] Rev. William Barnett.   Cf. "Life and Times of Finis Ewing,"
Cossitt, 1853.

[3] Davidson, "History of the Presbyterian Church in Kentucky,"
p. 132.

urged through the medium of a letter written in blood to leave North Carolina.   He did shake the dust of that locality from his feet — not necessarily from fear, however, but rather because some of his former hearers had moved on to the Cumberland country and invited him to join them in that land flowing with milk and honey.   He became the minister of three small congregations of the Presbyterian Church — Gasper River, Muddy River and Red River societies.   He was now in an environment in many ways suited to his peculiar type of ability, and in many ways deserving, too, his message of doom.   For Logan County was an ugly community.   Peter Cartwright tells us that when his father moved there in 1793, it had the rather unpleasant appellation of " Rogues' Harbor " because of the fact that an actual majority of the citizens was made up of murderers, horse-thieves, highway robbers and counterfeiters, fugitive bond-servants and runaway debtors, who fled there from all parts of the Union to escape the clutches of the law.   If these wretches were ever brought to trial, they either swore each other clear or escaped any penalty because of the lax enforcement of justice. It became a necessity for the better portion of the citizens to unite in a lynching organization known as "The Regulators."   Pitched battles were fought with the "rogues," who at first won, but were ultimately beaten and driven to cover.   And even among the law-abiding people there was a great deal of irreligion, as well as drunkenness and other

forms of vice. As soon as McGready arrived in
the midst of this modern Sodom, a transformation
began. He was terribly in earnest, and his presence and his preaching immediately brought his
own members, at least, to the same frame of mind.
It was said that if you came anywhere upon a
crowd of McGready's older people, they were
weeping and talking about their souls. And if
you encountered his young people, either singly or
in groups, it was the same. They spoke only of
the need of the soul's salvation.[1] In 1797 there
arose a little cloud like a man's hand. In 1798
the heaven was black with clouds and wind, the
chief apparent cause being McGready's thunderous
personality. His reputation attracted great crowds
to all the services and gave his meetings fame far
and wide. And so it happened that in the summer
of 1799 two McGee brothers, William, a Presbyterian, and John, a Methodist, when crossing the
pine barrens into Ohio, determined to turn aside
and visit a sacramental solemnity at Red River,
that they might observe for themselves the remarkable power and influence that everywhere
attended the ministry of this pulpit Boanerges.
What they actually happened upon that day, and
furthered by their presence, was the beginning of
one of the most tremendous religious revivals in
modern history. In narrating the occurrences of
this occasion I am following a letter written in 1820

[1] McDonnold, " History of the Cumberland Presbyterian Church,"
p. 12.

by John McGee.[1] I do this because, while there
is no important variation in the historical accounts,
there is some slight difference of detail, and the
testimony of an eye-witness and participant is
therefore particularly valuable. Several preachers
spoke. First John McGee, the Methodist, and
never, as he says himself, did he preach with more
light and liberty. Then his Presbyterian brother
and the Rev. Mr. Hodge spoke with much animation and power. While the latter was discoursing,
a woman in the east end of the house, unable to
repress the violence of her emotions, gave vent to
them with shoutings loud and long. At the close
of the sermon the other ministers went out, but the
two McGees and the people seemed loath to depart.
" William felt such a power come over him that *he
quit his seat and sat down on the floor of the pulpit,
I suppose not knowing what he did.* A power
which caused me to tremble was upon me. There
was a solemn weeping all over the house. At
length I rose up and exhorted them to let the
Lord God Omnipotent reign in their hearts, and
submit to Him, and their souls should live.
Many broke silence. The woman in the east
end of the house shouted tremendously. I left
the pulpit and went through the audience shouting and exhorting with all possible ecstasy and
energy, and the floor was soon covered with the
slain."

[1] To Thomas L. Douglas, presiding elder of Nashville District,
Tennessee Conference of the Methodist Episcopal Church.

The little cloud no larger than a man's hand had filled the heavens with blackness, and now came the great rain. Or, to change the metaphor, the people from this Red River sacramental service were like fire in dry stubble among their neighbors. Upon the return home, "they rushed into the arms of their friends, shouting and telling what wonderful things God had done for their souls." [1] Elder B. W. Stone, of a congregation in Bourbon County, came not long after to the scene of this remarkable religious excitement and carried the fire to the Cane Ridge country, where it blazed with a fury unequalled in any other section. From there it spread to Ohio and into Washington County, Pennsylvania, where derangement of the nervous system and loss of physical strength were common phenomena. Foote's history of North Carolina and of Virginia is full of thrilling accounts of revival fires lighted by people who returned from McGready's meetings. While in the Cumberland country itself, no opposition, no criticism, could for a long period allay the excitement in the least. From the Green River to the Cumberland, the settlements were full of religious fervor and revival zeal. From distances of forty, fifty and one hundred miles men came with their families in covered wagons, provided with food and bedding, to listen to this group of evangelists who had so stirred the congregation at the Red River sacra-

[1] McDonnold, "History of the Cumberland Presbyterian Church," p. 13.

ment. And thus originated what is known as the first camp-meeting in America at the Gasper River church in the summer of 1800. It certainly is the first known to fame, though it is possible that this extension of the pioneer Presbyterian sacramental service into several days' duration in the open air was an imitation of the quarterly circuit meeting of the early Methodists which for twenty years had been common in America, in Kentucky, Tennessee and Ohio. If not an imitation, it certainly was a growth from the same root of necessity. McGready had advertised this Gasper River meeting as widely as he could, and a great concourse assembled. The little church was far too small, and the neighboring forest was occupied as a temple. The woodsmen worshippers, with their accustomed fertility of resource, were ready for this emergency. They cleared away the underbrush and felled the pine trees for pews. They improvised a platform for the speakers, and the wild woods, which early in the day had rung with the sound of their axes, later in the day rang with shout and song. They had not planned to remain longer than the evening. But when night came they were far from surfeited with religious zeal. The women pieced together the extra sheets and quilts which they had brought with them in the wagons, and the men cut poles over which these coverings were stretched for tents. Some brought straw from the nearest farms and others foraged for provisions. And when the darkness fell, many fires were kindled through the new-made village among the trees.[1]

The meeting lasted from Friday until Tuesday. The preaching, praying and singing continued almost without cessation save for a few hours in the early morning. It was not until Saturday evening, however, that any special outbreak of overwrought nature manifested itself. Then two women became greatly excited, and their fervor was communicated by contagion through the whole multitude. The camp became a battle-ground of sobs and cries, and ministers spent nearly the whole night in passing from group to group of the " slain."

Now imitation began in earnest upon the return of these worshippers to their homes. Ten such camp-meetings were held one after another in the Green and Cumberland settlements. They became the vocation of the people. " Age snatched his crutch, Youth forgot his pastime, the laborer quitted his task," " the crops were left forgotten, the cabins were deserted, in large settlements there did not remain one soul."

The most notorious example of this intense form of the revival " crowd " is furnished by the Cane Ridge camp-meeting of August, 1801, which took place farther north in Bourbon County, Kentucky. The biography of Elder B. W. Stone makes it clear that it was an imitation from Logan County. Elder Stone lived in Bourbon County. Word had

[1] Cf. article on " Red River Revival," *Western Christian Advocate*, April 16, 1902.

come to him of the amazing scenes of excitement and zeal in the southwest, and he made the journey in the spring of 1801 to witness what to him was "new and passing strange." The historians of the Cumberland Presbyterian Church — which by the way was an excellent product of the Logan County revival — have been sometimes wont to contend that the disorder and super-emotionalism which defile the record of these early days, were the output of the Cane Ridge quarter of Kentucky and should not be charged against the settlement in the southwest. On this point the unvarnished tale of Elder Stone reflects some light. By the side of his own Cane Ridge, which he regarded as a dead community spiritually, he set the wonderful work which he saw in Logan County. It baffled description, he says. "Many, very many, fell . . . and continued for hours together in an apparently breathless and motionless state, sometimes for a few moments reviving and exhibiting symptoms of life by a deep groan or a piercing shriek or by a prayer for mercy fervently uttered. After lying there for hours . . . they would rise, shouting deliverance." Then others would fall, under the eloquence of those who rose and related their experience. In addition he saw much which he thought fanaticism, but considered to be the devil apeing the power of God. He returned with ardent spirit to his congregations at Concord and Cane Ridge. The next Sunday morning at the latter place he met a multitude who had gathered to

listen to his recital of his experience of grace at
Logan. There was awful solemnity, and many
wept. At night he spoke in the Concord church
and told the story of what he had seen in the southwest. During that meeting two little girls were
struck down under the preaching "*and in every
respect were exercised as others were in the south
of Kentucky.*"[1] The people were greatly moved,
and not long after a vast host, estimated by a revolutionary officer on the ground to be twenty thousand souls, came together at the Cane Ridge camp.

The remembrance of that fateful gathering lin-
gers in Kentucky after the lapse of a century.
Nothing was lacking to stir to its profoundest depths
the imagination and emotion of this great throng
of men, women and children. It was at night
that the most terrible scenes were witnessed, when
the camp-fires blazed in a mighty circle around the
vast audience of pioneers bowed in devotion.
Beyond was the blackness of the primeval forest,
above the night wind and the foliage and the stars.
As the darkness deepened, the exhortations of the
preachers became more fervent and impassioned,
their picturesque prophecies of doom more lurid
and alarming, the volume of song burst all bonds
of guidance and control, and broke again and again
from the throats of the people, while over all, at
intervals, there rang out the shout of ecstasy, the
sob and the groan. When daylight came, the

[1] Quoted in "The Disciples," American Church History series,
Vol. XII, Tyler.

temper of the assembly was somewhat modified, but there was the same tendency to boisterous emotion.   Men and women shouted aloud during the sermon, and shook hands all around at the close in what was termed the " singing ecstasy." [1] There are many suggestive bits of testimony to the highly overwrought state of these susceptible people.   One of the most careful observers, the Rev. Mr. Lyle, who kept a diary and journal through this whole period, and passed calm judgment in the midst of the wild excitement, to whom we owe the best account of the extravagances and disorders, has described the crowd at Cane Ridge rushing from preacher to preacher if it were whispered that it was " more lively " at some other point, swarming enthusiastically around a " fallen " brother, laughing, leaping, sobbing, shouting, swooning.   If the assembly were languid, he says, a few shrieks and one or two instances of falling would quickly arouse them, and as far in every direction as the people could see or hear, others would be caught in the contagion and would likewise fall.[2]   Children were allowed to preach, a little girl of seven being propped up on the shoulders of a man, and exhorting to the multitude " till she sank exhausted on her bearer's head."

And when we reflect that this mighty crowd did not break up on this occasion until the food gave

[1] Davidson, " History of the Presbyterian Church in Kentucky," p. 138.

[2] *Ibid.*, p. 140.

out, but remained for days an agitated mass of humanity in the midst of such surroundings as these, contemplating the most momentous truths, ascribing every extraordinary nervous contortion to the mysterious agency of the divine, we can well understand how many, very many, would be physically and mentally overwhelmed. The whole body of persons who actually fell helpless to the earth during the progress of the meeting was computed by the Rev. James Crawford, who avers that he endeavored to keep an accurate account, to be three thousand persons, about one in every six. The number who fell in the ghost-dance on White Clay Creek was, it will be remembered, about one out of three. Measured by this test, the Kentuckian of 1800 is certainly entitled to the distinction of being twice as civilized as the savage. Those who fell were carried to the meeting-house near by. " At no time was the floor less than half covered. Some lay quiet, unable to move or speak. Some talked, but could not move. Some beat the floor with their heels. Some, shrieking in agony, bounded about like a live fish out of water. Many lay down and rolled over and over for hours at a time. Others rushed wildly over the stumps and benches, and then plunged, shouting, 'Lost! Lost!' into the forest."[1]

When the frenzy was at its height, these revival crowds were subject to a set of nervous and muscular manifestations probably as varied and terrible

[1] McMaster, " History of the United States," Vol. II, p. 581.

as ever afflicted a population in this world. There is no question of the truth of this sad chapter of pioneer history. The evidence is too over-powering and convincing. There is no question of the reality of the manifestations, though as else-where it is likely there was considerable humbug and deception. But there were many doubters, and the "fallen" subjects were often put to the proof. For instance, our friend the Rev. Mr. Lyle, furnished with a phial of hartshorn by a physician, "applied it to a stout young man who was lying flat on his back, and inadvertently al-lowed some to run into his nostrils. But he took not the slightest notice of it, so much was his attention absorbed by devotional feeling." [1]

With respect to extravagancies and disorders, there are a large number of corroborative refer-ences in Lyle, Peter Cartwright,[2] Lorenzo Dow and other contemporaries. Next to the "falling" exercise the most notable and characteristic Ken-tucky phenomenon was the "jerks." The un-happy victim shook in every joint. Sometimes the head was thrown from side to side with great ra-pidity. Again the feet were affected, and the sub-ject would hop like a frog. Often the body would be thrown violently to the ground, where it would continue to bound from one place to another. Peter

---

[1] Lyle, "Diary," p. 18.

[2] See, for example, Peter Cartwright's "Autobiography," p. 93, where it is recorded that, after a mob was quelled, "three hundred fell like dead men in mighty battle."

Cartwright declares that he had seen more than five hundred persons jerking at once in his congregation. And Lorenzo Dow, writing of a time some years later, when the epidemic again broke out in that section, remarks that on Sunday at Knoxville "the governor being present, about one hundred and fifty had the jerking exercise." It is still a phenomenon in the religious life of that country. I saw mild cases of it in the summer of 1903 among the whites in the Chilhowee Mountains. In 1800 no one was proof against it, saint or sinner, white or black, except, as Lorenzo Dow naïvely remarks, "those naturalists who wished to get it to philosophize upon it, and the most godly. The wicked are more afraid of it than of smallpox or yellow fever."

It became an infectious disease. It passed the bounds of normal imitation and became a morbid contagion, and many a scoffer bit the dust in the midst of his contempt and derision. Peter Cartwright relates a serious instance of this which he vouches for as having taken place in William McGee's congregation. "There was a great work of religion and the jerks were very prevalent." A large man with a bottle of whiskey in his pocket reviled both the jerks and the religion. In a flash the contagion pursued him, caught him, and though he started to run, it was useless. "He halted among some saplings, took out his bottle of whiskey and swore he would drink the damned jerks to death. But he could not get the bottle to his mouth, though he tried hard. At this he became greatly enraged, fetched a very violent jerk, snapped his neck, fell, and soon expired, with his mouth full of cursing and bitterness." [1]

Another phenomenon not so common was the "barking" exercise. The votaries of this dignified rite gathered in groups, on all fours, like dogs, growling and snapping the teeth at the foot of a tree as the minister preached,— a practice which they designated as " treeing the devil" !

When this stage was reached, it is evident that the tension had invaded the brain. It is only natural, then, that we have here again the trance and the vision. The affections of the ghost-dance Indians were duplicated very exactly, so perfectly indeed that it would not be inaccurate to describe the ghost-dance ceremony as a Kentucky camp-meeting run amuck. Many of these camp-meeting folk lay insensible, sometimes for hours, but when they recovered from the swoon it was to relate, in what were called "strains of heaven," experiences of interviews with departed friends and visions of glory not vouchsafed to their normally conscious and less fortunate brethren. They claimed divine inspiration and prophesied of the end of all things. The phenomena of Millerism, spiritualism and faith healing were as manifest here as among the Cherokees or the Shakers of Puget Sound. [2]

[1] " Autobiography," Peter Cartwright, pp. 50, 51.
[2] Cf. Davidson, *op. cit.*, pp. 152, 153; also Cartwright, " Autobiography," pp. 51, 52 f.

When nervous tension had risen to the maximum, it is interesting to mark its fall towards the minimum in the changed character of the phenomena. When a year or two had elapsed, the milder hysterical forms of muscular action began to display themselves in certain quarters, until, in 1803, the "holy laugh" became a feature of the worship. While the minister was preaching, the members would burst out one after another, and then in chorus into what was regarded as a solemn laugh. The manner was devout even when the laugh was boisterous.

There were grave charges, also, such as were commonly heard in former times with respect to camp-meetings in many parts of the country, of the extraordinarily free companionship of the sexes. And these allegations were made not by the ungodly, but by prominent ministers of standing and courage who inaugurated plans for night watches "to reconnoitre the camp and the stand." [1] While we may admit that there has been some exaggeration of this evil in the literature of revivals, we must remember that the human love passion and the spiritual love passion appear to modern psychology to be delicately interwoven, particularly in the case of young people between fourteen and twenty-five, and the kind of spiritual excitement which a super-emotional revival generates is likely to be more harmful than helpful to the self-control

---

[1] Lyle gives some shocking instances of indecency in his "Diary." Cf. Davidson, *op. cit.*, pp. 163, 164.

of the individual as exhibited in both his sexual and spiritual activities.

There appeared also in Kentucky those more moderate forms of disorder which we shall see distinguishing the Edwards and Wesley revivals. I refer to such evidences of the absence of ordinary rational deliberation as are indicated by the singing of different hymns at the same time, the vociferous praying of many at once, and the loud ejaculations of approval.

These phenomena, some of them curious and some of them dreadful, were far more common than they are often believed to have been. The Rev. James Gallagher was the editor of an early Presbyterian publication, "The Western Sketch-book." He was also a witness and a close student of these peculiar physical exercises. In referring to the grosser forms of them, he declares it to be his judgment that of the professors of religion who were in that country at the time, perhaps one-half became subjects of these bodily disorders.[1] They ranged all the way from the normal imitation of the "holy laugh" to the morbid contagion of the "jerks" and the blackness of insanity.[2] Even so enthusiastic an observer as Peter Cartwright, who regarded the "jerks" as the judgment of God to bring sinners to repentance, was at one time ap-

[1] Cf. McDonnold, "History of the Cumberland Presbyterian Church," p. 37.

[2] For illustration of this latter affliction, cf. Cartwright, "Autobiography," pp. 86, 87.

palled by "the fearful tide of delusion that was sweeping over the country."[1]   It is not wonderful, therefore, that rational control of this mighty sympathetic movement was for a long time impossible. At the inception, there were men in the synod of Kentucky who set themselves against the wild extravagances.   But their power to resist the tide was lessened by the fact that they attacked the revival preachers perhaps more vigorously for certain alleged aberrations of doctrine than for the disorderly methods and the practical vagaries.   And when the movement was well under way, the very momentum of it swept all criticism before it, and any minister who put himself in the path did so at the peril of his reputation and his influence.   It was not till the summer of 1803 that the abuses were opposed with any degree of success.   Then Lyle preached a sermon which attracted wide attention from the text — "God is not the author of confusion but of peace."   Father Rice, an old white-haired preacher of commanding intelligence and sound judgment, insisted upon better regulations and a guard around the camp, " and exhorted powerfully against noise and false exercises."[2]   The path of opposition was sometimes thorny.   An editor at Lexington arose and insisted that some ladies who had fallen needed air and nothing else, but the " ladies themselves, on being asked, professed the contrary, and the editor slunk away ashamed."

[1] Cartwright, *op. cit.*, p. 53.   [2] Lyle, " Diary," p. 44.

This difficulty of control was accentuated by the very considerable measure of ignorance, superstition and fear that actually existed in the population. They had firm trust in signs and omens. Peter Cartwright relates an amusing illustration, showing how inbred was the belief in magic. Two fashionably dressed young women, attended by their brothers with loaded horsewhips, came to one of his meetings in 1804. Cartwright was feeling somewhat ill, and, before he preached, took a small bottle of peppermint from his pocket and sipped a little. During the sermon which followed the two young women became afflicted with the "jerks," to their great mortification. At the close of the meeting the brothers were waiting for the preacher with the horsewhips. Cartwright professed innocence of any intention to influence the sisters after this fashion, but the brothers hotly affirmed that he need not deny it, for they had seen him take the phial out of his pocket in which was the substance that had "tricked" the young women.[1] And this same rugged pioneer preacher, who had a fine vein of sanity in him, has also told us of the thousands of people who crowded into membership in the churches from mere fright during the period of the severe earthquakes of the Mississippi Valley in the year 1812.[2]

I think that we may wait with advantage until a later chapter for an estimate of the social value of such a movement as has here been described. I

---

[1] Cartwright, *op. cit.*, p. 49.   [2] *Ibid.*, p. 180 f.

will not refrain, however, at this point, from pay-
ing a tribute to the splendid worth of the typical
pioneer preachers of those days.   As a class they
were ignorant in matters of learning, but shrewd
and thoroughly trained in the practical experience
of living — narrow with respect to the wearing of
ruffled shirts and jewelry, but in general very
broad in their charity.   Some were not so well
balanced as others, but as a type they were
admirable — utterly fearless, sturdy and honest.
Finis Ewing was a man of this stamp.   Peter
Cartwright was another.   No novel is more interesting than his autobiography.   Preaching with
marvellous eloquence to thousands, repelling mobs
with the vigor of his fists, setting himself like flint
against the worse extravagances and giving great
offence thereby, he stalked through Tennessee and
Kentucky and later through Illinois with the tread
of a giant.   He was a great lover of his country
and of his kind, always as vitally concerned for
the life of the nation as for the life of the church.
The real ethical and spiritual power of some of
these men explains the other side of the Kentucky
revival, and the other side of pioneer religious
activity in general.   For it must be remembered
that the revival of 1800 was only a remarkable
episode in a half century or more of pioneer
preaching.   In spite of an unbridled religious
method which gave free rein to human weakness
and human passion and which did an incalculable
amount of harm, there were still enforced in a

very large number of cases true rational principles of living. And it is due to the straightforward manliness and moral sanity of many of these rugged pulpit personalities that a multitude in their day and generation did not sink to the level of the savagery with which they were surrounded, but were saved to add their moral vigor to democracy and all the higher life of the nation. And this was a great gain. But on the other hand there is much reason to believe that the habits of impulsive social action, developed and fostered in the early years of the century by the Kentucky revivals, and imitated at intervals ever since, have played their unworthy part in rendering that section of our country peculiarly susceptible to highly emotional outbreaks of prejudice, passion and even of criminality.

CHAPTER VII

THE SCOTCH-IRISH REVIVAL IN ULSTER IN 1859

THE later Scotch-Irish revival in Ulster presents no new principles and few new facts, and its importance to this study therefore will not warrant our lingering long upon it. I recommend it, however, as an excellent example of the normal working of the laws of impulsive social action. In the first place it was an imitated revival. Intelligence of the great religious movement of 1857 in America had spread to the north of Ireland, and a considerable number of self-controlled and excellent ministers wished for a spiritual shower upon their own thirsty vineyards, prayed for it and planned for it. But when the shower came, it burst first upon the Connor district of county Antrim as the result of a fellowship meeting held in a butcher shop. The butcher was an ignorant man who two years before did not know the alphabet. There were several day-laborers present, including a stone-cutter and a blacksmith's boy. There was also a stone-breaker, one of four brothers. His mother was the sister of a notorious pugilist, to whom she had been a bottle-holder, and she was watched as a thief when she entered a shop in that community. Her sons bore a bad name.[1] I mention this not to the discredit of these persons, who were groping for something better in character, but only to illustrate the law of origin. It is not remarkable, therefore, that from the outset there were physical manifestations, singular and violent. They acted like a shock upon the community and were imitated far and wide.

Men from the Connor meeting journeyed from place to place in praying bands. The revival spread next to Ahoghill, then to Ballymena, three miles distant from Ahoghill. Here the laws of imitation and of origin revealed themselves once more. A man fell on his knees in the market-place and aroused the people on all sides "by loud and desperate cries expressive of the most appalling agony, such as might be expected from a man who felt himself suddenly attacked and sinking under the repeated and deadly blows of an assassin." [2] A great spread of the revival in Ballymena followed. Next the movement spread northward three miles to the village of Brougshane. Several young women were affected with prostrations in a spinning factory. The mental excitement became so intense that within an hour "twenty or thirty persons of both sexes were laid prostrate," and the business of the factory was interrupted for several days.[3]

[1] Gibson, " The Year of Grace," p. 45.
[2] *Ibid.*, p. 58.   [3] *Ibid.*, p. 75.

We read at once of great congregations in this community, several thousand gathering in the open air and remaining all day in prayer and praise.

Thence the revival spread to Coleraine in northern Antrim, where it produced most startling effects and seems to have reached its maximum.   In this community it swept nearly the whole population under its sway.   The figures of speech in sermon and song reflect the condition.   Winter is over in a moment, and the time of the singing of birds has come. The favorite hymn, "What's the news?" represents the revival as spreading as the news spreads, swiftly from lip to lip.   The Rev. William Arthur, an English Wesleyan minister, remarks incidentally that among the common people the movement was spoken of as a disease.   "He took it," "he caught it," and similar phrases were common.   The revival invaded the local newspaper office, and compositors were struck down so that the publication of the *Chronicle* was delayed. It was at Coleraine on the 9th of June, 1859, that nearly one hundred persons who were suffering from the prostration of religious meetings were carried into the town hall and sheltered until morning.   These are the same people, we see, whose kin were at Cane Ridge; and also at the Cabin Creek meeting, Kentucky, when on the 22d of May, 1801, on the third night, men and women by the score were carried into a church near by "to prevent their being trodden upon, and were laid out on the floor as so many corpses." [1]

Next it spread to Belfast and the surrounding country as the result of a visit of a band of young men from Coleraine, thence through county Armagh. By this time there had developed a large number of cases of passive manifestation. Around Belfast there were many victims of the delusion that " stigmata " had appeared upon their bodies, and the Rev. William Brakey, of the town of Lisburn, who was sceptical about it, encountered great opposition among the common people, who fully believed in the existence of these divine marks. In this vicinity there were also a considerable number of "sleeping " phenomena, the religious subject falling into slumber at will and waking several days afterwards at the time which he himself had set, to relate his experience of divine revelation. These caused great excitement until Dr. McCosh vigorously attacked both the deluded and the impostors with the proposition that the Orientals could perform the trick far better. In county Armagh were many instances of visions, dumbness and blindness, the hysterical action having invaded the centres of sight and speech.

It was on the whole a revival, like that of 1857 in America, marked by much prayer among the people and in the congregation, rather than by the violent pulpit demonstrations of the Kentucky days and the periods of Edwards and Wesley. But in

[1] McMaster, " History of the United States," Vol. II, p. 580 f.

many sections, such preaching as there was
shocked whole communities into a sense of frightful personal danger, and pictured as faithfully and
as vividly as did the old pioneers the fiery hell
yawning at the feet of the impenitent.   It was the
crushing sense of sin, the awful apprehension of
impending doom, the looking forward to judgment, the fierce wrestling with the Evil One, which
were everywhere the exciting conditions of the
paroxysms.

The movement from the beginning was under
far better control than in Kentucky.   The number
of rational leaders among the professional classes,
the clergymen and others, was of course much
larger than could be found on the border in 1800.
But the yawning gulf of possible convulsion in the
population had opened, and it was not an easy thing
to close it again.   Dr. Gibson, the historian of the
revival, speaking in Belfast, attempted to avoid, if
possible, all disorder and extravagance of emotion.
And so he began, he says, "in a most unimpas-
sioned strain," avoiding every allusion which might
cause disturbance.   But there was no help for it.
He had not proceeded far before a woman sank
with a despairing cry and had to be borne out.
She was succeeded by another and another, until
he was obliged to suspend his address and engage
the audience in singing until they were all disposed
of by their friends and the ushers.   The general
assembly which met in July of that year threw its
influence with the party of control on the interest-

ing ground that "a desire to experience prostrations was being raised all through the north of
Ireland."

And so the influence of better counsels extended
itself in every direction. In county Down the
prostrations, which had been many, practically
ceased after the first few weeks, and there were
communities in Ulster where the work of moral
transformation went on with hardly a single instance of "striking down."

I wish in closing this chapter to call attention to
the difference in type of the automatisms of Kentucky and Ulster. In Kentucky the motor automatisms, the voluntary muscles in violent action, were
the prevailing type, although there were many of
the sensory. On the other hand, in Ulster the
sensory automatisms, trance, vision, the physical
disability and the sinking of muscular energy were
the prevailing type, although there were many of
the motor. I do not mean that I can explain it.
It may be that as the Charcot and Nancy schools
of hypnosis brought out by chance, each in its own
field, different kinds of hypnotic phenomena, which,
when known, spread by imitation in the respective
localities and under the respective influences, so in
Kentucky and the north of Ireland by chance there
appeared different types of physical manifestation
which were then imitated in the respective countries. But I have a belief that this is not the whole
of the matter, but that the type of automatism will
be found to be correlated with the type of mind of

the population. The Kentucky of 1800, though exhibiting many higher elements, was also a strongly motor community, and motor manifestations were as natural to it as were the sensory to the settled, peaceful, and less physically progressive people in the north of Ireland in the middle of the century.

CHAPTER VIII

THE NEW ENGLAND AWAKENING ORIGINATING WITH JONATHAN EDWARDS

THE religious interest which began at Northampton, Massachusetts, in the winter of 1734–1735
under Jonathan Edwards, culminated in what is
known as the Great Awakening under George
Whitefield and other revival preachers. But the
latter movement was far more extended in time
and space. The Great Awakening belongs at least
to the whole decade from 1740 to 1750, and ranged
over the whole eastern sea-coast from Maine to
Georgia. I propose in this chapter to discuss
briefly only the New England section of the Great
Awakening in its inception under Edwards and
in its extension under other men. I make this
segregation both because the limited field will sufficiently abound in material for our purpose, and
also because we shall thus be able to observe the
influence of a great sympathetic religious movement upon quite a different type of mind than any
we have hitherto studied. The New England
population of the first half of the eighteenth century was not a primitive population within any
sound meaning of the word. It was not even any

longer living in a strictly pioneer environment which might bring out in relief certain latent primitive traits, as was the case with the Scotch-Irish in Kentucky. During a large part of the century preceding, it had been *conquering* a primitive environment, that is true, — and the effect of this it is possible to trace into the mental prepossessions and characteristics of the New Englander of the eighteenth century. He was not by any means the same type of personality as his forebears in the eastern counties of old England. But the conquest was practically over. The stony soil had yielded to the plough and harrow, and the savage had succumbed to superior intelligence and the firearm. The conquerors had made peaceful settlement upon farm or village. Harvard and Yale were shedding the light and warmth of higher education far and wide. And above all the Puritan pulpits were, in the main, centres of intellectual, moral and spiritual virility. The propositions of the now practically extinct Puritan theology were argued with a vigor and with a stern helpfulness to the mental and moral life of the community that we can scarcely measure in our time. Here is a population of stability, one would say, that could not under such restraint be easily swept from the moorings of rational control.

But there is another side. The environment of a hundred years had left its mark upon them. The immediate ancestors of these people were a homogeneous group. They had come from the eastern

counties of England, where the blood of the Saxon
and the Dane was the leading strain. They had
come in response to the same desire to be free from
the bonds of religious and political oppression.
They were so much alike that for a long time they
could not brook any variation from the type. They
established anew the principle of oppression, and
held out the hope of personal freedom only to those
who believed with themselves in theocratic uniform-
ity. Of course I am referring to the Puritans of
Massachusetts Bay, and not to the Pilgrims of Plym-
outh, who were happy indeed in a wider human experience and the leadership of John Robinson in their
formative period. The New Englander shows the
influence of selection in the abnormal development
of religious emotion in those early days, and also
in the lack of variety in his intellectual interests.
Theological problems were the chief food of his
thinking. This is because Puritan migration was
first of all religious in character, and the men who
thought and felt strongly in matters of theological
distinction were the men who came to America.
And they were men in whose minds not only tra-
ditions of personal religious freedom, but the very
images which their system of theology invoked,
were extremely vivid and powerful. They were
men of profound religious imagination and deep religious emotion. And they remained in this highly
specialized state long after a wider range of intellectual interests had powerfully affected the Englishman at home. They had a well-marked vein

of melancholy that revealed the strain of Danish blood, and from out the gloom of New England skies and forests, from out the burden of New England hardships, and above all under the depression of Puritan theology, the melancholy Yankee emerged. To relieve his sad estate, nature gave him a peculiar flavor of humor, certainly "extra dry," but Celtic in its genesis, too, it may be, for the Yankee was not altogether Teuton. Even in the eastern counties of England the Celt was not wholly driven out or exterminated. The strain was still perceptible if not strong.[1]

Surely this description does not fit exactly the Englishman of the period, although these Yankees were all English one hundred years before. Social selection and environment had given stability to something approaching a new human variety. This variety was on the whole of the dogmatic-emotional type of mind, as distinguished from the merely sympathetically emotional type of the negro, or the motor-emotional type, with strongly dogmatic elements, which we observed in eighteenth-century Kentucky. But it must be remembered that this dogmatic type, which profoundly cherishes beliefs, which is austere in morality, which may be deduc-

[1] An excellent piece of work upon the Yankee type, which has been very helpful to me in the preparation of this chapter, is contained in a " Study of Provincial Massachusetts," — a Seminar paper in sociology at Columbia University, by Mr. Samuel P. Hayes. Cf. also his "Study of the Edwardean Revivals," *American Journal of Psychology*, Vol. XIII.

tive and logical to a considerable degree, is capable of tremendous outbursts of emotion when belief and imagination combine to open the sluice-gates. And with the eighteenth-century New Englander they did so combine — as will be shown, I think, in the pages that follow. Nowhere that I know of do we find such frightfully vivid images of sin and hell and the wrath of God as existed in the mind of Puritan minister and layman and found expression in the Puritan hymn and sermon and later in the New England theology. We shall have ample illustration of this matter soon from the sermons of Jonathan Edwards and others, but an example or two now will indicate how readily this powerful imagery fell into Puritan poetry and hymnology. Michael Wigglesworth's " Day of Doom " was very popular in New England at this time. Lowell says of it that it was " the solace of every fireside, the flicker of the pine knots by which it was conned perhaps adding a lively relish to its premonitions of eternal combustion." Thus doth it image forth the tender doctrine of everlasting punishment !

> " For day and night in their despite,
> Their torment's smoke ascendeth.
> Their pain and grief have no relief,
> Their anguish never endeth,

> "Who live to lie in misery
> And bear eternal woe.
> And live they must while God is just,
> That He may plague them so."[1]

[1] Pancoast, "American Literature," p. 64.

When Margaret Deland wrote her first novel, I think it was, she put into the mouth of one of her characters this stanza of an old New England hymn:—

> "My thoughts on awful subjects roll,
> Damnation and the dead.
> What horrors seize a guilty soul
> Upon a dying bed!"

The critics of the book asserted that she must have composed it for the purpose, but I know at least one man who has a distinct recollection of sitting in a New England prayer-meeting as a boy and listening to his grandfather as he rolled forth this stanza to a melody which was fully as comforting and inspiring as the hymn. It was this sort of a religious consciousness, which had an awful reverence for God and a dreadful fear of His wrath combined with a profound trust in His righteous, sovereign will, that gave birth on the one hand to the very vigorous and original thinking of the New England theology, and on the other to the burst of religious emotion which characterized the Edwards revival and the Great Awakening.[1]

That there was in this population an immense amount of superstition we need no further evidence than the witchcraft delusion, but I think when we take into account how much there was in their physical and religious environment to generate superstition, the wonder is that there was not after all a

[1] Cf. Hayes, "Study of the Edwardean Revivals," *American Journal of Psychology*, Vol. XIII.

great deal more of it. " That there was so little of
it is the strongest testimony possible to the hard
sense, robust character and sharp intelligence of
the New England people."[1]

With respect to the passional element of the
Edwards revival, I think it may be said that no
such effects as are there visible could have been
produced even with the aid of the shocking appeals
to terror employed by the preachers of that period,
if there had not been in the population a tremendous amount of latent fear. It seems paradoxical
so to speak of a community which had conquered
its foes and overcome every hardship. One would
say that there must have been in this population
a remarkable development of fearlessness. And
so there had been. The New Englander of the
eighteenth century no longer felt conscious fear of
starvation and the savage. He was master in the
presence of the powers of evil whose ability to do
him harm he could measure. But after all, fearlessness and fear are only opposite sides of the
same shield. Professor William James defines fear
as a "reaction aroused by the same objects that
arouse ferocity."[2] Fearlessness and fear dwell
together in the same bosom. With the New Englander it had been a century of terrors — and now
the time of reaction had come. He no longer
dreaded known danger, but the latent fear of a
century rose up now to reënforce the emotion of

[1] Lodge, " English Colonies in America," p. 436.
[2] James, " Psychology, Briefer Course," pp. 407, 408.

terror aroused by the *unseen* and the *unknown*
peril by which his attention was extraordinarily
arrested in the time of revival — fear of the devil,
fear of hell, fear of the infinite wrath of an infinite
God. And in the face of this most dreadful of all
terrors, the courage born of a century of conflict
with foes without and foes within stood him in
little stead. He was in the same plight as the
tiger of one of Henry Drummond's discourses, in
the time of a great inundation in India. There
was a bungalow on an eminence of small area
which arose above the flood. In this shelter a
group of human beings had gathered, and also
several comparatively harmless wild animals had
escaped thither. Suddenly the current bore a
royal Bengal tiger in that direction, and he crawled
under the roof, so paralyzed with terror at this new
and frightful experience that one of the men in the
company had no difficulty whatever in stepping up
to him, thrusting the barrel of a rifle to his head,
and blowing out his brains. Utterly fearless of
danger which he could measure, the brute was
entirely overcome by the unknown peril suddenly
brought to bear upon him.[1]

One need not wade very deeply into the mass
of literature descriptive of the period just before
the New England revival without finding that lan-
guage has been practically exhausted in depicting
the sad state of morals and religion. We read of
the luxury and frivolity of the royal province

[1] Cf. James, "Varieties of Religious Experience," p. 262.

which had now supplanted the Puritan theocracy, of the increase of tavern haunting and pro-
fanity, of irreligion among the young, of the
decline of orthodoxy among the mature and the
growth of heterodoxy and even of foreign infidelity.
The venerable Pastor Stoddard of Northampton
and his Half Way Covenant, admitting to the
Lord's Supper those who had not made a profession of personal piety, are widely believed to have
reflected faithfully the utterly lax ethical and
spiritual standards of the time. And so no doubt
in part they did. But I cannot resist the conviction that the total amount of existing wickedness
has been considerably exaggerated.[1]

The early thirties of the eighteenth century compare quite favorably, I think, with the period
about eighteen hundred when Lyman Beecher
wrote his famous sophomore reminiscences of
immorality and impiety at Yale, when the religious lethargy of fifty years, which followed partly
as a reaction after the excitement of the great
revival, had cast its pall over New England, and
when political matters connected with the Revolution engrossed the attention and consumed the
energy of the colonists. It is easy to see how the
exaggeration has come about when we reflect upon

[1] Since writing this paragraph, I have had my attention called
to the fact that Hutchinson, the historian of Massachusetts, "with
an almost contemporaneous knowledge of the time," reënforces
what seems to be a fair sociological interpretation. Cf. Allen,
"Jonathan Edwards," p. 52 f.

the censoriousness which was so marked a feature
of the revival.   Even Whitefield, as we shall see
later on, was greatly addicted to it, and many of
his confrères in the movement far exceeded him in
vituperative criticism of all who did not agree with
their methods and their opinions.   Their oppo-
nents were unspiritual men, unconverted, unworthy hirelings.   They and those who stood
with them were alleged to be responsible for
the depths into which the Puritan communities
had sunk.   And later the volume of enthusiastic
praise for the good which the revival wrought
not only quite overwhelmed all discussion of the
evil, but produced a too favorable contrast of
the years of refreshing with the years that preceded.   So late as 1904, I read a series of lectures
on the Great Awakening which brought the name
of Chauncy, the foremost critic of the New England revival and a man whose cool judgment and
spirituality it is impossible to doubt, into very
unpleasant juxtaposition with the Scriptural text,
" The name of the wicked shall rot."   In opposition to the view of the lecturer, that Chauncy is
forgotten, a name unheard, I venture the prediction that his name will more and more be heard in
proportion as we attain a really dispassionate verdict upon the events of his period.   There was also,
at the time, a too harsh judgment of the increasing
measure of really sane and searching liberalism in
thought which began to appear in England and on
the Continent in the eighteenth century.

The most that we can say of the conditions that preceded the revival is that they were relatively bad — relative, that is, to the ethical standards of the Puritan *ancien régime*. But we must look elsewhere for anything like a perfect illustration of the theoretically total depravity of the period. There had been changes in government which loosened the restraints upon many of the weaker individuals in the community who had been kept to a higher plane of life by the stalwart disciplinary props of the Puritan theocracy. There was already a revolt against the stern and somewhat monotonous morality of the fathers, and, as ever, this tendency reached toward an extreme. Liberalism had set in, especially in eastern Massachusetts, and the new ways of thinking were not immediately favorable to a warm and emotional type of religion. The pioneer communities were in a rather low state of morals. There was religious apathy. The restraint theocratic and the restraint theological had been removed to a considerable degree, and the pendulum for the moment was swinging too far in the other direction. But there were not wanting after all many proofs of substantial character and righteous living.

However, as measured by the standards of the fathers, morality and the true faith seemed doomed. And Jonathan Edwards, metaphysician and practical human worker, believed that they were doomed unless something were done right speedily to beat back the rising tide. The personality of this great man was doubtless the most notable in the New England of his generation. The quality of his intellect, its perfect courage, its energy, its originality, its marvellous philosophic acuteness, seem to have been a gift of inheritance in the line of his mother's genius. She was a woman of splendid intelligence and indomitable will. As his family name indicates, the ancestors on his father's side were Welsh. And it may well be that the Celtic strain is responsible for that almost oriental imagination and that mystical religiousness of nature which were so characteristic of Jonathan Edwards. Joined with these traits was the practical common sense of the Saxon, exhibited in such a marked manner in his revival activity. The logic of total depravity, unconditional election and irresistible grace, was all against an appeal to men to press into the kingdom. How could a man press into the kingdom except God elect him? And if God elect him, how could man resist Him? But the sound Saxon instinct of Edwards prevailed. Men have called it since the Edwardean paradox, and paradox it was, and Edwards could never satisfactorily explain it. The popular version of it, which has been attributed to that eccentric religious character, Lorenzo Dow, ran as follows : —

> "You can and you can't,
> You will and you won't,
> You'll be damned if you do,
> You'll be damned if you don't."

But Edwards, at the parting of the ways, sanely

followed experience rather than logic, and " press
into the kingdom " became the watchword and
the working principle of the New Light party of
which he was the distinguished head.

Edwards was called to the church at Northampton as a young man, fresh from graduate study
and a tutorship at Yale, to become the colleague
and ultimately the successor of his grandfather,
Solomon Stoddard. Northampton was a prosperous, intelligent and growing community of some
two hundred families. The church was famed in
New England for its long history of mental and
spiritual vigor. The community and church at
this time, however, are declared by Edwards to
have been in a state of theological and religious
decline. And it became his purpose from the
first to foster a warmer and deeper piety, and
to redeem the community from its moral laxity
of walk and conversation. With a tremendous
earnestness, a wealth of imagery, a strength and
weight of logical argument that, his premises being
granted, were irresistible, he so presented the
chief themes of the Christian religion and the
Calvinistic creed that at the end of the winter of
1734–1735 "there was scarcely a single person in
the town, old or young, left unconcerned about the
great things of the eternal world." [1] Beginning
with a single young woman prominent among the
social " company keepers " of the town, who first
became " serious, giving evidence of a heart truly

[1] Edwards, " Works," Vol. IV, p. 23.

broken and sanctified," it overspread the community, until, when springtime came, this little village of two hundred families sheltered "three hundred souls savingly brought home to Christ." [1] From Northampton it spread with great rapidity in all directions, to South Hadley, Suffield, Sunderland, Deerfield, Hatfield, West Springfield, Long-meadow, Enfield, Springfield, Hadley and Northfield. [2] So swift was the movement that there was written of it, " Who are these that fly as a cloud, and as doves to their windows?" The winter's labor and fruit-age were not confined to this section alone, for the news spread afar, especially through Edwards' little book, the "Narrative of Surprising Conversions," which he wrote at the instance of two English clergymen who had read one of his descriptive letters to a mutual friend. And when Whitefield came, in 1740, the seed of the Great Awakening was already sown.

Edwards' method of arousing the sinner had in it very little indeed of the merely superficial art of the orator and rhetorician. There was an extraordinary power of fascination in him, even though his eye never seemed to rest upon his audience, but flashed continually from his manuscript to the opposite wall. And this strange personal fascination, which was a family characteristic, appeared in an evil form in Edwards' grandson, Aaron Burr. But, in general, his influence was something

[1] Edwards, "Works," Vol. IV, pp. 18, 28.
[2] Edwards, "Thoughts on Revivals," p. 14 f.

far more profound. By dint of prodigious intellectual strength, by the wonderfully vivid imaging forth of premises which seem absurd to us but were as fundamental to his auditors as their own being, by the masterly marshalling of terrible argument, he wrought out an appeal to the fears of his hearers which stirred them to the very depths of their souls. They wept, they turned pale, they cried aloud. Some fainted, some fell into convulsions, some suffered thereafter from impaired health and some lost their reason. Of course he preached upon other themes, but the sermons which he himself says were remarkably blessed, which truly awakened his hearers, were ever those in which he pictured "the kind of hell an infinite God would arrange who was infinitely enraged against a human being who had infinitely sinned in rejecting God's infinite love." [1]

The proof of this is usually presented in the form of Edwards' famous Enfield sermon of July 8, 1741, upon the theme, "Sinners in the hands of an angry God"; but it abounds elsewhere, for instance in a discourse of May, 1735, entitled, "Wrath upon the wicked to the uttermost," or of April, 1739, upon "The eternity of hell torments," or of April, 1741, demonstrating the future punishment of the wicked to be unavoidable and intolerable. Other subjects are : "The justice of God in

[1] Hayes, "Study of the Edwardean Revival," *American Journal of Psychology*, Vol. XIII. The ten points of the Enfield sermon are from the same source.

the damnation of sinners," — " The torments of the wicked in hell no occasion of grief to the saints in heaven," — " Wicked men useful in their destruction only."

The Enfield sermon [1] is typical of those of an imprecatory character, and we know the circumstances of it perfectly, for Eleazar Wheelock heard it and wrote a description of it to the historian Trumbull. The audience of New England farmers had gathered carelessly without thought of the avalanche of woe that was to sweep down upon them from the pulpit. And when it came, many cried aloud for mercy till the preacher could not be heard, and convulsively grasped the benches to prevent themselves from slipping into the pit. His text was from Deuteronomy xxxii. 35, " Their foot shall slide in due time." His thesis was that there is nothing that keeps wicked men at any one moment out of hell but the mere pleasure of God. He argues this in ten propositions. (1) There is no want of power in God to cast wicked men into hell at any moment. (2) They deserve to be cast into hell; therefore divine justice never stands in the way. It makes no objection against God's using his power at any moment to destroy them. (3) They are already under a sentence of condemnation to hell. (4) They are now subjects of that very same anger and wrath of God that is expressed in the torments of hell. (5) The devil stands ready to fall upon them and seize them as his own at what

[1] " Works," Vol. IV, p. 313.

moment God will permit him. (6) There are in the souls of wicked men those hellish principles raging that would presently kindle and flame out into hell fire if it were not for God's restraint. (7) This is no security to wicked men for one moment that there are no visible signs of death at hand. (8) Natural men's care and prudence to preserve their own lives, or the care of others to preserve them, does not secure them for a moment. (9) All wicked men's pains and contrivances which they use to escape hell . . . do not secure them from hell for one moment. (10) God has laid himself under no obligation by promises to keep any natural man out of hell one moment.

He played upon the chords of dread and doom in such passages as this: "The unconverted are now walking over the pit of hell on a rotten cover, and there are innumerable places in this covering so weak that they will not bear their weight and these places are not seen."

Those in his audience who may think themselves in peace and safety are warned that God is more angry with many of the living, even with many in the Enfield church that day, than He is with many who are already in hell.[1] And the terrible conclusion runs as follows : —

"If we knew that there was one person and but one, in the whole congregation, that was to be the subject of this misery, what an awful thing it would be to think of ! If we knew who it was, what an

[1] Cf. Allen, "Jonathan Edwards," pp. 128, 129.

awful sight it would be to see such a person! How might all the rest of the congregation lift up a lamentable and bitter cry over him! But, alas! instead of one, how many it is likely will remember this discourse in hell! And it would be a wonder if some that are now present should not be in hell in a very short time, before this year is out. And it would be no wonder if some persons that now sit here in some seats of this meeting-house, in health and quiet and secure, *should be there before to-morrow morning*."

When we remember that the major premise of his argument was that "the greater part of men who have died heretofore have gone to hell," that it was his constantly reiterated belief that in every generation those who were saved were in the minority,[1] it is possible to understand with what crushing weight the message fell upon any particular congregation. The chance of the throw was against every man before the sermon began, and the God of the universe was under no obligation to save him even after prayer and crying strong. It was then with almost the desperation of despair that he struggled for his possible chance of life as over against his probability of eternal death. According to this system, spiritual growth could follow only upon spiritual convulsion. There was no such process in Edwards' theology as blossoming into the kingdom of heaven. The symptoms of deliverance from evil were tragic and appalling.

[1] Cf. Allen, *op. cit.*, p. 124.

There was the sense of awful danger and of agonizing fear, the intolerable burden of sin and the apprehension of divine wrath, and the realization of utter and almost abject dependence upon a higher will for salvation.

The imagery with which Edwards was accustomed to clothe his propositions of everlasting judgment is illustrated sufficiently by such quotations as follow from his sermons : —

"You have often seen a spider or some other noisome insect when thrown into the midst of a fierce fire, and have observed how immediately it yields to the force of the flames. There is no long struggle, no fighting against the fire, no strength exerted to oppose the heat or to fly from it.   Here is a little image of what you will be in hell, except you repent and fly to Christ."[1]

Or this : —

"The bow of God's wrath is bent and the arrow made ready on the string, and justice bends the arrow at your heart, and strains the bow; and it is nothing but the mere pleasure of God and that of an angry God . . . that keeps the arrow one moment from being made drunk with your blood."

Again, in discussing hell torment, he says: —

"We can conceive but little of the matter; but to help your conception, imagine yourselves to be cast into a fiery oven, or a great furnace, where your pain would be as much greater than that occasioned by accidentally touching a coal of fire as the heat is greater.   Imagine also that your body were to lie there for a quarter of an hour, full of fire and all the while full of quick sense.   What horror would you feel at the entrance of such a furnace.   How long would that quarter of an hour

[1] Edwards, "Works," Vol. VI, p. 103.

seem to you.   And after you had endured it, for one minute, how overpowering would it be to you to think that you had to endure it the other fourteen.   But what would be the effect upon your soul if you must lie there enduring that torment for twenty-four hours.   And how much greater would be the effect, if you knew you must endure it for a whole year.   And how vastly greater still, if you knew you must endure it for a thousand years.   Oh! then how would your heart sink if you knew that you must bear it for ever and ever — that there would be no end, that for millions and millions of ages, your torments would be no nearer to an end and that you never, never would be delivered.   But your torments in hell will be immensely greater than this illustration represents."

Or read this description of the tormenting devils that peer through the gloom that shrouds the bedside of the dying sinner.

"If we imagine to ourselves the feeling of the little child that had been pursued by a lion, when it is taken hold of and sees the terrible creature open his devouring jaws to tear it to pieces. I say if we could have a perfect idea of the terror and astonishment which a little child has in such a case, yet we would have but a faint idea of what is felt in the departing soul of the sinner, when it falls into the hands of those cruel devils, those roaring lions which then seize upon it."

The combination of such a personality and such a message upon the population of New England at that period was psychologically if not theologically predestined to produce much mental and nervous disorder.   And I do not see how Edwards can escape in some measure the responsibility for it.   It is a great tribute to the essential mental strength and stability of New England that no worse effects were produced by so mighty a cause.

I have sometimes pondered with dismay upon what
might have happened in a Kentucky camp-meeting of half a century later if a Jonathan Edwards
had appeared upon the scene and delivered the
Enfield sermon!   Surely there would have been
none left but the preacher of the occasion to bear
away the "fallen" and the "slain."   I know that
Edwards did not regard many of the bodily affections which occurred under his own ministry as
the highest proofs of divine grace.   They were only
incidental to it.   He was far too keen a student of
the human spirit to blunder so.   And he never
could abide "impulses" and "impressions."   But
he was an ardent apologist for the messages of
terror and for many of the unhappy influences that
followed in their wake.   For years he was by no
means sufficiently apprehensive of the dread results
of the encouragement of the many manifestations
of mental and nervous disorder.   He often spoke of
this overwhelming of soul and body by a sense of
the awful majesty and infinite terribleness of the
wrath of God as if it were a natural and healthful
and divine phenomenon.   The sympathetic propagation of strange nervous affections which he witnessed in his own meetings, especially among the
young, he looked upon with complacency.[1]   Of
course the nature of such disorder was not then
known, and we have no right to censure Edwards
too severely.   On the whole, he stood for order

[1] Cf. Hodge, "Constitutional History of the Presbyterian Church
in the United States," Vol. II, p. 51.

and wholesome restraint. In later years he seemed
to lament that he had not in the earlier stages of
the revival taken a more decided stand against delusion of every form, and in 1746 he published
that classic treatise on the religious affections that
has gone far to establish his reputation for sound
discretion. For its time, it exhibited rare judgment and rational discrimination. Of course it
could not be expected to anticipate the more radical scientific view of modern psychology. In this
work he refers to the imagination as the devil's
grand lurking place, the very nest of foul and delusive spirits, and affirms that " when the affection
arises from the imagination and is built upon it as
its foundation, instead of spiritual illumination and
discovery, then is the affection, however elevated,
worthless and vain." And in passages of surpassing insight and power he lays bare the principle
that is entirely acceptable to the most modern psychology of religious experience that, though the
affections are the tap-root of true religion, yet the
test of any one of them is not at all in the quality
or character of the emotion or in anything else save
the results that are manifest in life and conduct.
As Professor William James has put it, by their
fruits ye shall know them and not by their roots.[1]

But years before this treatise was written, the
powerful social and psychological forces which
Edwards had called into action were at work all
through New England, and the momentum of the

[1] James, "Varieties of Religious Experience," p. 20.

movement was too great to be restrained by any calm philosophic discussion. However, the revival ran its natural course in the face of a fire of criticism that must have checked its excesses in many quarters and have furnished some considerable measure of control. Not only Edwards, in his days of calm afterthought, but many others stood as breakwaters against the ever increasing tides of fanaticism and delusion that rose and fell in connection with the general movement. The most notable of these personal centres of rational control was Dr. Charles Chauncy, pastor of the First Church in Boston. He was a graduate of Harvard, sixty years a minister of the gospel, a man distinguished both for learning and spirituality, withal an ardent patriot, — he lived through nearly the whole span of the eighteenth century, — and it is especially remembered of him that his last days were given almost entirely to devotional exercises.[1] This is not the picture of a "pharisee," a "hypocrite" or an "unworthy hireling," but I suppose no man of his generation would have been selected so quickly by the radical friends of the revival as the original model of each of these ignoble characters. This would probably have been Whitefield's opinion, and James Davenport would have proclaimed it from the housetops. For Davenport was Chauncy's special aversion, and with good reason. The "Rev. Mr. James Davenport" of Southold, Long Island, a descendant in the direct

[1] Cf. Tyerman, "Whitefield," Vol. II, p. 125.

line of the famous John Davenport of the New Haven colony, was the most prominent and the most uncanny spirit of that whole group of extremists who, lacking the brain and balance of Edwards, urged to such lengths the movement which he inaugurated that judicious men to this day find it difficult to decide whether there was in it more of good than evil, whether the very many transformations of character and conduct which appeared to be genuine and normal were not after all purchased at too great a social cost. The other notorious members of this company of extremists who shared Davenport's spirit and method were Barber, Pomeroy, Wheelock, Allen and Bliss. At this point Chauncy is the most important contemporary source. He was a great protagonist of order and righteous conduct as over against "the things of a bad and dangerous tendency," of which he wrote in his famous sermon published in 1742, and his more pretentious work of 1743 entitled "Seasonable Thoughts on the State of Religion in New England." The radical strictures of this book upon the revival as a whole we may not be prepared to accept in their entirety. Chauncy needs comparison with Jonathan Edwards. Chauncy argued that the revival must be of the devil because it worked out into so great extravagance and excess. Edwards contended ultimately that while the peculiar emotional "affections" in themselves were nothing, they might coexist with a real work of grace. But abundant evidence of the prevalent irrationality and disorder appear in the writings of both these observers, though they received the more powerful portrayal in Chauncy. And with respect to this important group of New Light extremists of the Davenport persuasion, Chauncy was thoroughly right in his main contention. The extremists practically believed that enthusiastic emotion is ever a certain sign of the presence of the divine spirit, a clear proof that God's saving grace is at work in the heart. Therefore, they always had a simple test of their own conversion, and of the regeneration of their fellow-men — especially of their fellow-ministers. In their eyes, an enthusiastic emotional experience speedily discriminated the hireling from the shepherd. And it was only a step, as it has always been, from this doctrine to a belief in their own direct inspiration. Dreams, visions, impulses, scriptural texts suddenly occurring to the memory — what were they but the mind of God directing them as to what they should speak and in what path they should move? And of course the violent shriekings, faintings, tremblings under this stress of emotion were indubitable evidences of divine indwelling. Against such blind heresy of ignorance Chauncy spoke out trumpet-toned. And it was well for New England in such a crisis of delusion that he and others did so speak.

The personality of the above-mentioned James Davenport, as I have said, especially attracted Chauncy's opprobrium. It is somewhat disconcerting to find the said Davenport lauded in

Whitefield's journal as one of the most godly and useful men whom he met in America. But it is comprehensible, after all. Whitefield was of much better mental and moral balance than Davenport, but the two men had similar beliefs with respect to "impulses" and "impressions," and were considerably alike in their censorious estimates of others. On the whole, Chauncy's view of the man fits the evidence much better than Whitefield's. This Mr. Davenport was especially noted for his power to produce agony and distress, fallings, faintings, tremblings and shriekings. He would thus address himself to a congregation: "You poor unconverted creatures in the seats, in the pews, in the galleries, I wonder you do not drop into hell. It would not surprise me if I should see you drop this minute. You Pharisees, hypocrites, now, now you are sinking into the pit." And then he would leap and clap his hands and shout, "The war goes on, the fight goes on, the devil goes down." Visions, trances and impressions were his guide to conduct. He believed that he had the power of discerning spirits, and when he entered a town, he first hied himself to the house of the minister to observe whether he was really converted. And if the poor man were disinclined to grant him free access to the pulpit, or in other respects did not attain to the measure of the stature of Davenport's lofty zeal, he would publicly denounce him as a wolf in sheep's clothing and seek to draw off to another camp the faithful who would follow, leaving the "ungodly" sometimes in consternation and dismay in the clutches of their formerly revered pastor. He believed that he had the gift of healing and attempted to exercise it on a dumb, mentally unbalanced woman in a parish next to his own. He spent a day of fasting and prayer with her in the company of a group of his admiring brethren, prophesying that on a certain day she would recover.[1] As it happened, the poor woman died on that day. When this was brought to Davenport's attention, he responded that his faith was verified, "for that she was delivered by being received to heaven." · He soon became such a public nuisance that he was haled before the General Assembly of Connecticut, and among other things it was proved against him that "he endeavored by unwarrantable means to terrify and affect his hearers, by pretending some extraordinary discovery and assurance of the very near approach of the end of the world, by an indecent and affected imitation of the agony and passion of our blessed Saviour, and also, by voice and gesture, of the surprise, horror, amazement of persons supposed to be sentenced to eternal misery, and by a too peremptory and unconditional denouncing of damnation against such of his auditory as he looked upon as opposers, vehemently crying out that he saw hell flames flashing in their faces."[2] The Assembly took the magnanimous ground that he was the victim of enthusiastic impulses, but or-

[1] Chauncy, "Seasonable Thoughts," p. 190.   [2] *Ibid.*, p. 98.

dered him deported from the colony. He now regarded himself as in the happy company of those who are persecuted for righteousness' sake, and it was not long before he was under indictment by the grand jury in the city of Boston for a breach of public order. One of the witnesses testified that, on one occasion on Copp's hill, he had heard him offer this prayer — "Good Lord, I will not mince the matter any longer with Thee. Thou knowest that I know that most of the ministers of Boston and of the country are unconverted and are leading their people blindfold to hell." [1] The crowning act of his erratic career was performed in New London in 1743. He professed to have received it from the Lord in a dream that his adherents should put away from among themselves everything in which they delighted — " wigs, cloaks and breeches, hoods, gowns, rings, jewels and necklaces must all be brought together into one heap into his chamber that they might by his solemn decree be committed to the flames." The collection of "idols" also included some choice books of devotion by distinguished and saintly men. It is recorded that Davenport fell ill just before the time of conflagration came and that his followers relaxed their principles in the matter of the wearing apparel, but did burn the volumes, solemnly assuring the assembled audience "that the smoke of the torments of such of the authors of the above-said books as died in the same belief as when they set

[1] Tracy, "The Great Awakening," p. 247.

them out, was now ascending in hell, in like manner as they saw the smoke of these books arise." [1]

The delirium had now run its course with Davenport, who soon after publicly recanted and apologized for his irrational procedure. His colleague, Barber, went still further in his claims of immediate impression by the Spirit. He became an itinerant exhorter, "took no money with him, neither change of apparel nor shoes, but was shod with boots, and as he passed along . . . he publicly declared that he had laid aside all study and forethought of what he should deliver . . . and depended wholly on the immediate direction of the Holy Ghost." Finally he settled down in one hapless community, "where he abode some months; neither could he be persuaded to remove thence, but led an inactive, idle life until he was grown very fat and ragged, alleging in his justification that he had received no direction from the Spirit to remove thence, and must remain stationed there so long as the cloud abode upon the tabernacle." [2]

The doctrines and the methods of these men became a menace not only to common law and order, but to intellectual integrity and moral decency. Learning and the schools were mocked at, and even licentiousness was practised by some under the sanction of a "revelation," as it was later on under the same species of emotional excitement in spiritualism and Mormonism.

After enumerating the many and dreadful effects

[1] Chauncy, *op. cit.*, pp. 220–223.   [2] *Ibid.*, p. 184.

of fear and vagary, such as falling on the ground and lying for a time speechless and motionless, convulsions, screaming, besides unmentionable indecencies, Chauncy affirms that they did not seem to be accidental nor peculiar to any locality, but to have been very general. " Numbers in a congregation — ten, twenty, thirty, would be in the same condition at the same time ; nay hundreds in some places, to the opening of such a horrible scene as can scarce be described in words." [1] It is easy to read between the lines the influence of hypnotic conditions and of suggestion. "I have been present," he says, "when an air of seriousness reigned visibly through the whole congregation. They were all silent and attentive, having their eyes fastened on the minister as though they would catch every word that came from his mouth. And yet because they did not cry or swoon away, they were upbraided with their hardness of heart, and every topic made use of, with all the voice and action the minister was master of, to bring forward a general shrieking in the assembly." The effect was often increased by the indirect suggestion of the wonderful results wrought by the same sermon elsewhere, the congregation having been speedily melted and dissolved, and so overpowered that they fell down as if struck dead. [2]

A friend, whose character and capacity for making observations Chauncy declares can be relied upon, wrote a letter, a part of which is published in

[1] Chauncy, *op. cit.*, p. 76.   [2] *Ibid.*, p. 93.

the "Seasonable Thoughts."[1] He tells of the terror and consternation which reigned in the audience under the influence of the terrible manner and message of the exhorter, "which sometimes spread through a large part of the assembly in a few minutes from its first appearance. I have seen the 'struck' and distressed brought together by themselves from the several parts of the assembly . . . the poor creatures fainting, screeching and bitterly crying out." On another occasion "about half a score of young women were thrown into violent hysteric fits. I carefully observed them. When the preacher grew calm and moderate in manner, though the things delivered were equally awakening, the young women by degrees grew calm and still. When he again . . . spake like thunder, the like violent strugglings immediately returned upon them. Sometimes he put the emphasis upon little unmeaning words, and delivered a sentence of no importance with mighty energy, yet the sensible effect was as great as when the most awful truth was brought to view." Of course this same phenomenon can be seen again and again under negro preaching in the South, where the continued violent enunciation of the word "Mesopotamia" has been known to throw an audience of blacks into the wildest religious excitement.

Chauncy reprints also a bit of evidence from the *Boston Postboy*, pointing to the conclusion that the attempt of the many itinerant preachers and

[1] Chauncy, *op. cit.*, p. 94.

exhorters who were suddenly developed under the stress of the revival, was to terrify the imagination and heighten the effect of their speech by the suggestion of the extraordinary things that took place where recently they were, and by affirming that the audience now before them is made up "of the last hardened wretches that stand out, that this is the last call that ever they are likely to hear, that hell fire now flashes in their faces, that the devil stands ready to seize upon them — and they will often times repeat the awful words, 'damned! damned! damned!' three or four times over."

It would be possible, if there were need of it, to adduce other evidence to the same effect from other sources.   Whitefield himself, with his splendid power, and, on the whole, sane influence over the emotions of all classes of society, drew at times the unsparing criticism of thoughtful and earnest men on this side of the water.   He was imaginative, superstitious, much given to "impressions," a man of impulse rather than of judgment.   Jonathan Edwards cautioned him against some of his weaknesses, as other true friends had done before, but it seemed to the great Northampton preacher that Whitefield "liked him not so well for opposing these things."[1]   When the bodily agitations suddenly appeared so vigorously under Wesley in England, Whitefield opposed them with vehemence, but soon grew very mild in his disapproval.

[1] Quoted in Bacon, "History of American Christianity," p. 169.

And in a number of instances, notably in Kilsyth, Scotland, and at Nottingham and Fogg's Manor in this country, he gave every evidence of encouraging these manifestations. When the people cried out all about him so that they drowned his voice and fainted here and there, he says he never saw a more glorious sight.[1] He also became very vain and critical after his successes in America. He does not escape Chauncy's lash for his censoriousness and the aid and comfort which he lent to all manner of fanaticism. In fact, Chauncy declares that the censorious spirit which developed to such a hateful extent in Davenport and the other extremists appeared first in Whitefield, who seldom delivered a sermon " but he had something or other in it against unconverted ministers, and he expressed his fears in his journal of New England that ' many, nay the most that preached, did not experimentally know Christ.' " [2] Gilbert Tennent imitated him, and rash and bitter judging became very common in New England, " parents condemning their children and children their parents, husbands their wives and wives their husbands, masters their servants and servants their masters, ministers their people and people their ministers." [3] The excellent David Brainerd fell somewhat under the malign influence of Davenport, and was expelled from Yale for attacking the piety of the college

[1] Cf. Hodge, " History of the Presbyterian Church in the United States," p. 84 f.

[2] Chauncy, *op. cit.*, p. 140 f.　　　　[3] *Ibid.*, p. 169.

faculty.[1]   And so it went on all over New England.
Whitefield opened fire upon Yale and Harvard.
"Their light has now become darkness," he said in
his journal.   He had been invited to preach before
Harvard on the occasion of his second visit to this
country, but when he came, in 1744, the faculty of
that college branded him in a published statement as
"an uncharitable, censorious and slanderous man."
There is little doubt that in this direction Whitefield
exerted a baneful influence, but it should be said to
his everlasting credit that he afterwards met these
and other charges in most beautiful temper, defended himself against some misrepresentations
with much success, and confessed humbly that his
censorious onslaught had been a grievous wrong.
It is a clear case of overexcitement of enthusiastic
impulses by the revival.   It was not native to the
man.

In seeking to strike a balance of the evil and the
good in this religious movement, we are confronted
with much divergent testimony.   On the one hand
we have the record of the rather large increase
of one hundred and fifty regular Congregational
churches in New England between 1740 and 1760.
Upon the testimony of Rev. Ezra Styles, afterward
president of Yale, these were none of them separa-
tist churches created by the deplorable divisions
which characterized the revival, and the number at
least indicates that religious interest for a time
kept pace with the increase of population and

1 Tracy, " Great Awakening," p. 237.

perhaps somewhat outstripped it. We have also the statement of Edwards and others that great numbers of persons were so alarmed as to "immediately quit their sinful practices,"[1] and we may well believe that a new centre of character became sovereign in a relatively large number of instances. And the imprecatory Edwards was by no means the whole man. Through the abolition of the Half Way Covenant, he laid in New England the foundation of the separation of church and state which became a basal principle for the nation. He enunciated and defended such enduring and uplifting theological beliefs as the sovereign immanence of God and the immediate action of the divine spirit upon the human. Out of the theological debates of the Old Lights and the New, there grew up in the years that followed a much modified Calvinism which made it a vastly more useful tool in religious practice. The post-Edwardean church became a better instrument of social reform, just because it gave fit recognition to the element of emotion, without which as a driving force social betterment never comes. It was Hopkins, the pupil of Edwards, who led the movement for the abolition of slavery in New England. Through the religious enthusiasm of other individual leaders, such as Wheelock, who founded Dartmouth, there were important contributions made to education.

On the other hand, we have the sad record of churches rent and torn by faction. There were the

[1] Edwards, "Works," Vol. IV, p. 31.

Old Lights, who were unalterably opposed to the
revival on grounds both doctrinal and practical.
And of the New Lights there were two divisions,
the Edwards group and the extremists. It is an
interesting comparison that whereas in Kentucky
the revival gave birth to new sects, which have
long maintained their independence,— the Cumberland Presbyterians[1] and the Disciples among others,
— in New England the lines of cleavage were
mainly in theological thinking and practical method
which time has largely obliterated.

We have, too, the disheartening chronicle of
mental and nervous disorder ranging from the
swoon to the suicide. The atmosphere of morbid
suggestion which was developed in the awful tension of the revival would seem incredible, if we did
not have Edwards' word for it. In the month of
May, 1735, after the first winter of the awakening
in Northampton, a man, well and favorably known
in the community, suddenly developed melancholia
and cut his throat. Let Edwards relate the sequel.
"After this, multitudes in this and other towns
seemed to have it strongly suggested to them and
pressed upon them to do as this person had done.
And many that seemed to be under no melancholy,
some pious persons that had no special darkness
or doubts about the goodness of their state, nor
were under any special trouble or concern of mind

---

[1] While this is being written, there are overtures which indicate the possible return of this denomination to the general Presbyterian fold.

at anything spiritual or temporal, yet had it urged upon them, as if somebody had spoken to them, 'Cut your own throat! Now is a good opportunity. Now! Now!' So that they were obliged to fight with all their might to resist it, and yet no reason suggested to them why they should do it." [1]

On the unfavorable side of the ledger, too, we have the reign of religious terror, the fanaticism, the delusion, the censoriousness, the immorality. And we have something more. We have melancholy evidence of the profound reaction that set in at once and continued for a half century. And the evidence is the strongest at the very centre of impulse of the whole movement, namely Northampton. We have the facts and figures of the rise and fall in Edwards. During the winter of 1734–1735 more than three hundred persons were received into the church as "true converts." [2] In 1736 the number of communicants was almost coextensive with the adult population of the town. In 1740–1742 there were still other additions, and the work was esteemed by Edwards singularly free from unworthy and extravagant "affections." And yet in 1744 Edwards writes : " There has been a vast alteration within two years. God was provoked at the spiritual pride and self-confidence of the people and withdrew from them. Iniquity abounds, and the love of many has grown cold. Multitudes of fair and high professors have back-

[1] Quoted in Allen, " Jonathan Edwards," p. 159.
[2] Edwards, " Works," Vol. IV, p. 28.

slidden, sinners are desperately hardened, experimental religion is more than ever out of credit with far the greater part."[1]

From 1744 to 1748 the church was utterly dead to spiritual things, not a single application being made for admission to membership.[2] And notice what follows. In the fall of 1748, when Edwards had been twenty years a pastor, and the flame of revival had had so full and free an opportunity to purify the church, what happened? Not only his own membership but the neighboring churches turned against him in sufficient numbers to cast him out of his pastorate by a majority of one vote in the council, and exile him to Stockbridge and the Indians, where he wrote the "Freedom of the Will," and whence he was called to the presidency of Princeton. And this was done in an atmosphere of acrimony most bitter and slander most gross. These were the same people who a few years before had held a solemn service of thanksgiving, and had made public vows of many things, especially to refrain from evil speaking, and from everything that feeds the spirit of bitterness, to do nothing in the spirit of revenge.[3] But because this man Edwards took them at their word, and attempted to set up a fair standard of religious purpose and profession, their vows were disclosed as Prince Rupert drops, which broke as soon as they were

[1] Dwight, " Life of Edwards," p. 467.
[2] *Ibid.*, p. 438, quoted in Hodge, *op. cit.*, p. 74.
[3] *Ibid.*, p. 166 f.

cooled. It is a very perfect bit of testimony that the influence of the revival, even at its healthiest centre, had not sunk very deeply into character. It reminds us of many another piece of impulsive social action, whose retiring wave left little trace of good behind.

And what of the next fifty years in New England? It is doubtful if that section of the nation ever touched a point nearer the low-water mark of popular indifference to the religious and moral life. There was more than one reason for this. Matters military and political absorbed the energies of the people. But I think we should not fail to include among the causes of religious lethargy, the revolt against the excesses and the reaction against the stormy excitements of the "great revival."

CHAPTER IX

JOHN WESLEY AND ENGLISH SOCIAL EVOLUTION IN THE EIGHTEENTH CENTURY

WE have seen that the Scotch-Irish revival in Ulster was imitated from America. It would be far too much to say that the Wesleyan revival was an imitation of Edwards. The germinating centre of the great English revival was the little group who met as the Holy Club at Oxford, and particularly the foremost genius of that group, John Wesley. But it is perhaps not idle to observe that Jonathan Edwards and the somewhat earlier New England religious interest may have had an influence. Edwards' account of the Northampton revival of 1734–1735 found its way at once to England and attracted much attention there. Wesley has told us in his journal that he read it with profound thankfulness and emotion during a walk from London to Oxford in 1738. The wonderful "bodily effects" which Edwards described had not yet occurred in England, although they followed soon under Wesley, and there had been at this time no such outburst of emotional enthusiasm as later came to pass.[1]

[1] Cf. note bottom p. 134, Allen, "Jonathan Edwards."

However, the English movement had not only
an originating personality of its own, but antecedent
conditions of its own.   The England of the eighteenth century is in many ways a lamentable spec-
tacle, but there was no country in Europe, after all,
in which there was such a measure of liberty.
And as prosperity is always the offspring of liberty,
England was prosperous; she was growing in trade
and commerce, her ancient towns were strengthened
and new towns rose within her borders.   But increased prosperity brought a largely increased
population, and England was neither socially,
politically nor religiously ready to care for the
added multitude of her children.   The small
governing class was benevolent enough in its
purpose towards the great mass below, would not
wittingly have oppressed them, but it never really
lifted a finger for their elevation, their enlightenment, their progress.   There was an utter neglect
of schools and mental training.   The universities
themselves were in a state of intellectual decay.
Public order and social discipline were pitiably
weak, as is evidenced by the great activity of
mobs on the one hand and the extreme severity
of the laws on the other.   The small farmers
were bearing a weight of pauperism that, later
on, well-nigh crushed them.   And the multitudes,
who knew no other pleasure, took to the drinking
of gin, with which intoxicant the country had
recently become familiar.   In 1736 it is affirmed
that every sixth building in London was a gin-shop,

and the keepers thereof promised on posted placard to get a man drunk for a penny, dead drunk for twopence and furnish him with a straw pallet in the cellar upon which to sleep off his debauch.[1]

And as for the state on its ecclesiastical side, namely the church, this arm of social control had utterly withered from disuse. It may almost be said that the church was absolutely without power or influence in the upper or lower ranks of society. It was only a feeble appendage to the state in the early eighteenth century. Not by the addition of a single parish had the increase in population been met. It was an age of political prelates, of absentee bishops and fox-hunting parsons. Montesquieu crossed the channel during that period and remarked of the fashionable ladies and gentlemen whom he met, "Every one laughs if one talks of religion." To make the matter far worse, the upper ranks were unintelligent, and immoral and vulgar, too, beyond anything ever known in England.

And the lower ranks? Never a ray of vitalizing warmth and light permeated them from the stratum overhead. They were in a worse than primitive condition. They were ignorant and brutal, it is true. But they were also in the shadow of that cold, opaque body of political and religious aristocrats above. They were neglected. They were hardened. They cared for the satisfaction of

[1] Cf. Green, "A Short History of the English People," Vol. IV, p. 1610 f.

appetite and passion and for naught else, either in this life or that to come.

It is clear that this is not a case of relative badness. The evidence is cumulative and overwhelming that England was in a glacial epoch of her political, ethical and religious life. There was perhaps nothing that characterized this period more precisely than a dampened enthusiasm, an emotional deadness. The dread of political and ecclesiastical strife and passion was bred in the bone of the ruling classes, as the result of the experiences of Puritan revolution in the preceding century. It was not rational control of emotion. It was an irrational and systematic repression of moral enthusiasm. But let no man believe that this unnatural psychological condition could be maintained forever in a fresh and growing population. There were powerful instincts and needs of human nature that craved satisfaction. There were great slumbering passional forces that demanded an outlet. And nothing could permanently have restrained them. But it was given to one man, above others, to awaken suddenly these slumbering energies of the human spirit, and direct them in channels of national helpfulness and the social weal. It was the great privilege of John Wesley to have been endowed with such genius for leadership over seemingly inert multitudes of men, such practical sense of what was lacking in the life of the nation, such capacity for action, that he was able to exercise profound influence upon the social evolution of the English people.

Ultimately, the whole establishment of church and state felt the inspiration of the religious movement of which he was the embodiment, but his work primarily was done with and for the masses of the population from the lower middle class downward. Not only the plain people of the trades and the towns, but the neglected and hardened wherever he and his followers could find them — the colliers of Kingswood, the wreckers of Cornwall, the profligate soldiers of the king, the neglected, the vicious, the brutal — there was breathed upon them all the breath of a new and larger life. Wesley's appeal was to the divineness in the human soul, the bit of godlikeness that in his belief was never absent from man made in the Creator's image. Like Luther he would set the individual free, and like Edwards he would hold to the immediate action of the divine upon the human spirit. And every man shall know that he is free and that God hath unbound his fetters.[1] Wesley's preaching and practice were not without extravagances, and some of his followers were under far more grievous bondage in this respect than he, but in the main his message was sane and hopeful. It was a long step in advance of the

[1] In a letter written in 1768, Wesley made the distinction between the full assurance of the few and the ordinary assurance of the average man subject to doubt and fear. When the average assurance was lacking, he believed it to be the result of "disorder of body or ignorance of the gospel promises." Letter to Dr. Rutherforth.

" abstract inhumanity " of Edwards, who affirmed again and again that each generation must present the major portion of her sons and daughters as an offering to the Moloch of damnation, and that it was likely that many of every congregation to which he spoke would remember his discourse in the midst of torment intolerable and everlasting.

John Wesley was the soul of the great movement which bears his name. We shall, therefore, do well to examine into the nature of his distinguished personality. And the first thing that impresses us is its strange contradictions. The credulous and the critical, the superstitious and the rational, fanaticism and sound judgment, were well-nigh inextricably commingled. But this is only another way of saying that he was a thoroughly eighteenth-century human. There were others more or less like him even among the intellectual geniuses of the age.

Dr. Samuel Johnson is an example. But Wesley outdid Johnson. His mind early suffered an abnormal twist in the direction of belief without adequate evidence, especially in matters that had to do with the mysterious and the unseen. While he was absent at school, there were strange noises under the paternal roof at the Epworth rectory. They continued for the space of two months, and consisted of rappings, the moving of feet and of furniture and the lifting of latches. It is interesting to note that Wesley's mother and sisters heard them first and his hard-headed father last of all.

Samuel Taylor Coleridge's comment upon the incident is also illuminating : " All these stories — and I could produce fifty at least equally as well authenticated, and, as far as the veracity of the narrators and the single fact of their having seen such and such sights and sounds is concerned, above all rational scepticism — are much like one another, as the symptoms of the same disease in different patients. And this indeed I take to be the true and only solution — a contagious nervous disease, the acme or intensest form of which is catalepsy."

Of course we know now that it may not even be a disease, but an indication of overwrought imagination and nervous instability, which may or may not be pathological. There was much made of these mysterious noises in the family letters and the family records, and they never lost their power over the mind of Wesley. The belief of the age in ghosts, in witches, in mysterious and malign spirits, was confirmed in him from his youth. His journal has a generous collection of tales of the preternatural which would not bear a moment's scientific sifting. He implicitly believed the stories related by his friends of halos both bright and gloomy hovering over the faces of the dead. He would have been the last to class them, as modern psychology does, with hallucinations of the sane. The belief in witchcraft, which was dying out in England, was still vital with him. He held that many who were clearly overcome by his own personality in the pulpit were "possessed of Satan"!

If one were to look only at this side of his nature, one would think at times that he had an almost infinite capacity for believing incredible things. He carried the doctrine of special providence to a limit which has probably never been surpassed. He opened his Bible at random, and the text at the top of the page was his guide in the critical hour. One day his head was aching and his horse was lame. "I thought — cannot God heal either man or beast by any means or without means? Immediately my headache ceased and my horse's lameness in the same instant." Again his carriage was stoned by a mob. But he experienced no harm, for, as he writes, with no suspicion of the delicious humor of it, "a very large gentlewoman sat in my lap and screened me so that nothing came near me."

I do not mean that there was any arrant dogmatism about all this. He did not ask others to believe it. They might disbelieve it entirely without giving any offence to him. He was very tolerant in this and all other matters of opinion, and this is the reason, I take it, why he did not actually fan into a mighty flame the latent superstition of the primitive people to whom he preached. But that his own conviction in these matters, together with the excitement of the revival, did exert to a considerable extent a reactionary influence, I think there can be little doubt. England and Europe in

his day were coming over to the scientific view of
" demoniacal possession " and phenomena of that
character. Wesley himself observes the change
and solemnly protests against it as an evidence of
the religious scepticism of the time.   " The English in general, and indeed most of the men of
learning in Europe, have given up all account of
witches and apparitions as mere old wives' fables.
I am sorry for it. . . .   With my last breath will
I bear testimony against giving up to infidels one
great proof of the invisible world.   The giving up
of witchcraft is the giving up of the Bible."   It is
likely that the saner scientific judgment found
little favor with the many thousands who fell under the spell of such vehement assertion as this.
And it would indeed be strange if Wesley's influence did not make it more difficult at a later day to
storm the citadel of primitive superstition in the
English population.   Substantial evidence for this
view is found also in the outbreak of reflex phenomena, which occurred first under Wesley and
were encouraged by him in the face of wiser coun-
sel.   The superstitious explanation of these events
which he so clearly sanctioned one hundred and
fifty years ago has not yet entirely faded from the
thinking of his followers.

After what has just been said, it may seem a
paradox to affirm, as I do, that one great secret of
Wesley's power was his possession to a remarkable degree of the superb practical sense of the
Saxon race.   Jonathan Edwards had a saving meas-

ure of it, but John Wesley had it in abundance. In all matters which were neutral, in which he was not directly and personally interested, which did not immediately concern his own friends and his own cause, he was capable of the most discriminating scepticism. About 1740 a sect of religious "Jumpers" arose in Wales. Wesley visited them and described their extravagances dispassionately. Their vociferous singing of hymns over and over again, their posturing and their leaping, seemed to him only a species of religious drunkenness or madness. "They are honest," said he, "but understand little of their own natures." Early in the eighteenth century the sect of French Prophets appeared in England. They had been driven out of France and had already spread the well-known phenomena of nervous instability through Germany and Holland. They were subject to trance, vision and violent bodily agitation. Wesley sounded a sturdy note of warning against them. Their inward feelings, their revelations, their tears, their physical contortions, were in themselves absolutely untrustworthy. They had no validity until put to an external practical test. He prepared a trenchant criticism of Swedenborg. He began the investigation "with huge prejudice in his favor." His conclusion is that Swedenborg "is one of the most ingenious, lively, entertaining madmen that ever set pen on paper," that he was subject to delusion, that his religious visions are many of them "silly and childish to the last degree . . . palpably absurd, contrary to all sound reason." He had an instinct for historical criticism. The ancient tales of the Amazons and the Argonauts fared ill at his hands. " Many allegories and prophetic fables," he says, " have been mistaken for real histories." [1]

In spite of his superstition of opening the Bible in a fortuitous manner to ascertain the will of God, he was much more akin to Edwards in his distrust of impulses, impressions and inward feelings than to a man like Whitefield, for example. At least this was thoroughly true of his later years. It is somewhat disquieting to observe that when he re-published in London in 1745 Edwards' work on the Northampton revival, he carefully abridged it by excluding the strictures on " impulses and impressions," and including the wonderful record of " bodily effects " to which Edwards at that time gave something approaching unqualified approval. But we may be doing violence to Wesley's motive. A quarter of a century later he was charged with believing that the mind has an inward sense that enables it to discern the source of psychical manifestations, whether they be of God or not, and even from which person of the Trinity they come. Wesley replied that if any of his disciples believed it, they had never learned it of him, that for forty years his doctrine of inward feelings had been that no man could discern whether they were divine or not except by external test, and that in this matter

[1] Cf. article " Criticisms of John Wesley," *New York Christian Advocate*, J. M. Buckley, July 9, 1903.

one could be inwardly conscious of nothing save that the Scriptural fruits of the Spirit are being exemplified in his life. And he closed the letter of defence [1] with an expression of disgust at the excesses into which the heated imagination of some of his followers had led them, and tells of the discipline that had been visited upon them in expulsion from the ranks of his society.

But the conservative practical sense of the man was still more obvious in administration. It is at this point that he has won encomium from every great student of the period. He was a true Englishman in his dislike for change, as well as in the promptness with which he accepted the new when the old way was no longer useful. He fought every step of departure from ecclesiastical precedent, from field preaching to separation from the church of England, and yielded every step except the last, which was consummated after his death. Macaulay, Buckle, Lecky, and Leslie Stephen have vied with one another in bearing tribute to this genius for cautious judgment and for practical action.

In the quality of pure intellect, by which is usually meant, I suppose, the power of abstract thinking, he was manifestly inferior to Edwards. Perhaps it would be fairer to say that he was of another type than Edwards, for Wesley had fine intellectual endowment. But he was not a speculative genius — only a strong, plain, deductive logi-

[1] To Dr. Rutherforth, *op. cit.*, 1768 ; quoted in *New York Christian Advocate*, July 9, 1903.

cian, with what has impressed Lecky and others as an "exaggerated passion for reasoning." He had the best university training of his time, and exhibited refinement of scholarly taste and breadth of culture. Contrary to a quite generally received opinion, he laid great emphasis upon reason throughout his career. If there was one thing above another that he could not endure among his followers, it was unintelligent faith. A distinguished antagonist once asserted that it was a fundamental principle of his societies that all who went into them should renounce their reason. "Sir," said Wesley, "are you awake? Unless you are talking in your sleep, how can you utter so gross an untruth? It is a fundamental principle with us that to renounce reason is to renounce religion, that reason and religion go hand in hand, and that all irrational religion is false religion." And this was not the sudden burst of impassioned debate. He exhorted his disciples frequently in his journal, in his appeals, in his sermons, to use all the reason they had if they really sought true religion.[1]

He was very firm, even domineering, in the personal government of his societies, and strong in conviction with respect to what he regarded as the essentials of faith in its simplicity. But he was exceedingly broad in his charity for the beliefs of other people in all matters which did not fall within the range of these essentials. And in this

---

[1] See, for example, his "Calm Appeal," 1743.

L

respect there was, I think, a perceptible mellowing to the end of his long life. He published for his disciples the biography of a very excellent Unitarian, Thomas Firmin. "The arch-heretics of history, — Montanus . . . Pelagius . . . Servetus . . . — he declared that in his opinion they were all holy men, who at the last, with all the good men of the heathen world, — Socrates and Plato and Trajan and Marcus Aurelius, — would come from the east and the west and sit down in the kingdom of heaven."[1]

Proof of the essential liberalism of the man can be produced in plenty, but I know no passage in his collected writings which more perfectly sets it forth than the following paragraph from a letter of advice to his people in 1745 : —

"Lay so much stress on opinions that all your own, if it be possible, may agree with truth and reason ; but have a care of anger, dislike or contempt towards those whose opinions differ from yours. You are daily accused of this (and indeed what is it whereof you are not accused ?) ; but beware of giving any ground for such accusation. Condemn no man for not thinking as you think. Let every one enjoy the full and free liberty of thinking for himself. Let every man use his own judgment, since every man must give an account of himself to God. Abhor every approach, in any kind or degree, to the spirit of persecution. If you cannot reason or persuade a man into the truth, never attempt to force him into it. If love will not compel him to come in, leave him to God, the Judge of all."[2]

[1] Professor C. T. Winchester, in a brilliant bicentennial monograph, "John Wesley the Man."

[2] Wesley, "Works," Vol. V, p. 253.

There is no brilliant speculative treatise associated with his name as there is with that of Edwards. He lived all his days in a world of action, and not in the atmosphere of philosophy. And he could not have rivalled his New England contemporary in that domain. He was lacking in the lofty poetic imagination which was at once the glory and the peril of Edwards. His style, "plain and nervous," as he calls it, was very useful for the practical purpose of instructing the thousands of his converts, but it is wanting in richness and picturesqueness just because its author was wanting in imagination. As a consequence, his sermons, letters and appeals are not widely read by posterity. It is the opinion of a very competent critic,[1] however, that his journal is one of the three or four most interesting books of the eighteenth century, and that, except for its lack of humor, it would be a work which no intelligent man could leave unread. As it is, the surpassing record of human action which it contains lends to it its chief charm.

Still contrary to a widely prevalent popular apprehension, Wesley's personality could in no proper sense be characterized as emotional. Whitefield was an emotionalist, — so were others who were connected with the movement, — but not Wesley. I do not mean that his nature was so frigid as some of his biographers have found it. Love of humanity was strong within him. There was also a

[1] Professor C. T. Winchester, *op. cit.*

vein of sentiment, even of sentimentality, in the
man somewhere, as appears from his unfortunate
matrimonial hazard, and his clear preference for
the sentimental and romantic in literature.[1]   But
leaving out of account his love affairs, it would be
difficult to name a man who all his life long exhibited such mastery of passion and emotion.   He
conquered many a mob by his absolute self-possession.   There was the look in his calm gray eye of
a man who never knew fear.   There was very little
that was sensational in his sermons.   He had no
love for " the amorous style of praying and the
luscious style of preaching."   For the most part
he urged the claims of a new life, a new experience,
a new character, in a quiet, unenthusiastic, straightforward, but terribly impressive manner.   Although
Moravian mysticism influenced him at the outset
of his career, Wesley was no mystic.   There was
too much of the stolid Saxon about him.   He was
not given to tears.   He never would have wept
throughout a sermon of Whitefield's as Jonathan
Edwards did.   I do not know how the contrary
impression of this man has so gotten abroad.   It
may be due partly to the likeness of Wesley in
his old age, which has usually been printed to
image forth his person to posterity.   It is a portrait which combines a look of rare saintliness with
feeble physical vitality, and it has not appealed as
forcibly as perhaps it should have to the unregen-
erate popular mind.   But the Didsbury College

[1] Professor C. T. Winchester, *op. cit.*

portrait of Wesley while he was still young reveals a face similar to Cromwell's in firmness and
strength, but more kindly. The misapprehension
about the man may also be due to the fact that
after all he really gave the impulse to what was
essentially a tremendous outburst of emotion. He
tapped the sources of it in the population, and so
mighty was the flow that for a century and a half
his followers on two continents have been carried
onward by the rush of it. They are only now getting back that rational balance that was in their
founder, and many of them do not yet understand
that their Magna Charta of intellectual liberty and
temperamental sanity is to be found in the principles and the practice which governed Wesley's
own mental and spiritual life.

A question arises at this point which it is not easy
to answer. How is it that this sort of a personality
could be the exciting cause of such a profusion of
reflex phenomena as are recorded and even described
in detail in the journal? Whitefield addressed
great audiences of the common people with all the
persuasiveness and magnetic eloquence which he
could command, but reflex phenomena never appeared under him until they had first appeared under
Wesley and spread by imitation and contagion. But
they were very common under Wesley during the
early years of his itinerant ministry. Before we attempt an explanation of this somewhat mysterious
circumstance, let us turn the pages of the journal
and scrutinize the particulars of the phenomena.

April 17, 1739. At Baldwin Street after the preaching Wesley called upon God to confirm His word. A woman "that stood by (to our no small surprise) cried out aloud with the utmost vehemence even as in the agonies of death." Soon after, at the same meeting, "two other persons, well known in the place as laboring to live in all good conscience toward all men, were seized with strong pain and were constrained to roar for the disquietness of their heart."

April 21. "At Weaver's hall a young man was suddenly seized with a violent trembling all over, and in a few minutes, the sorrows of his heart being enlarged, sunk down to the ground."

April 25. At Newgate, at the close of his sermon, he called upon God to bear witness to His word. "Immediately one and another and another sunk to the earth. They dropped on every side as thunder-struck." These appear from the context to have been women.

April 26. "All Newgate rang with the cries of those whom the word of God cut to the heart."

April 29. Still at Newgate, a woman was so affected that great drops of sweat ran down her face, and all her bones shook.

May 1. "At Baldwin Street my voice could scarce be heard amidst the groanings of some and the cries of others. . . ." "A Quaker who stood by . . . not a little displeased . . . was biting his lips and knitting his brows, when he dropped down thunder-struck. The agony he was in was even terrible to behold."

May 2. "John Haydon, a weaver, who was at Baldwin Street the night before . . . a man of regular life and conversation, one that constantly attended the public prayers and sacrament, being informed that people fell into strange fits at the societies, came to see and judge for himself. . . . We were going home, when one met us in the street and informed us that John Haydon was fallen raving mad. It seems he had sat down to dinner, but had a mind first to end a sermon he had borrowed on 'Salvation by Faith.' In reading the last page, he changed color, fell off his chair and began screaming terribly and beating himself against the ground. . . . I came in . . . the room being full of people. . . . Two or three men were holding him as well as they could. . . . He immediately fixed his eyes upon me, and . . . cried, 'Ay, this is he whom I said was a deceiver of the people. But God has overtaken me!' He then roared out — 'Oh, thou devil! Thou cursed devil! . . . Thou canst not stay. Christ will cast thee out. . . .' He then beat himself against the ground again, his breast heaving at the same time as in the pangs of death and great drops of sweat trickling down his face. We all betook ourselves to prayer. His pangs ceased. . . . His voice was lost and his body as weak as that of an infant. But his soul was in peace."

May 19. "At Weaver's hall a woman first and then a boy about fourteen years of age was overwhelmed with sin and sorrow and fear."

The exceeding abundance of the phenomena in the vicinity of Bristol by this time aroused the spirit of inquiry and opposition. Wesley was evidently not at once convinced that they were supernatural, for his brother Samuel says that John doubted at first and examined into the ecstasies, and he endeavored to warn the great preacher against fanaticism, in the following letter: " I have my own reason as well as your authority against the exceeding clearness of divine interposition here. Your followers fall into agonies — I confess it. They are freed from them after you have prayed over them. Granted. They say it is God's doing. I own they say so. Dear brother, where is your ocular demonstration? Where indeed is the rational proof? Their living well afterwards may be a probable and sufficient argument that they believe this — but it goes no farther." [1]

Soon Wesley gave the clearest encouragement to the manifestations. In a reply to a persistent objector,[2] he affirms that God works these effects in this very manner of swoons and outcries. And as for visions, " I know several persons," he says, "in whom this great change was wrought in a dream, or *during strong representation to the eye of their mind, of Christ either on the cross or in glory.*" [3]

---

[1] Quoted in Southey's " Life of Wesley," Vol. I, p. 282.

[2] " Journal," Vol. I, p. 134.

[3] Italics here, as elsewhere in this book in quotations from the journals of religious leaders, are my own.

And his comment at the same time makes it very clear that he regards God as suffering these miraculous effects at a critical time in order that the inward change may be made manifest to the dull eye and ear of a froward generation. The contagion needed no further encouragement. The last restraint was gone when this calm master of assemblies gave full rein to these extravagances, sympathetically regarding them as throes of the new birth. The credulous element in Wesley's nature rose into full sovereignty for the hour.

May 21. "To-day our Lord answered for Himself" those opposers who believed that the fainting was simulated or caused by the closeness of the air in the crowded room. God made bare His arm before two thousand witnesses in the open air. "One and another and another were struck to the earth, exceedingly trembling at the presence of His power." There were loud and bitter cries of raving and suffering. The excitement was so intense, the suggestibility of his hearers so great, that he would scarcely begin speaking before they would fall on every side. In the evening he was interrupted at the beginning of his sermon by one who was "pricked at the heart," and strongly groaned for pardon and peace. "Another person dropped down, close to one who was a strong asserter of the contrary doctrine. While he stood astonished at the sight, a little boy near him was seized in the same manner. A young man who stood up behind, fixed his eyes on him and sunk down himself as one dead, but soon began to roar out and beat himself against the ground so that six men could scarcely hold him. Meanwhile many others began to cry out . . . in so much that all the house, and indeed all the street for some space was in an uproar."

By the middle of the following month he was in the vicinity of London.

June 15. "While I was earnestly inviting all sinners to enter into the holiest, many of those who heard began to call upon God with strange cries and tears. Some sank down and there remained no strength in them, and others exceedingly trembled and quaked. Some were torn with a kind of convulsive motion in every part of their body, and they were so violent that often four or five persons could not hold one of them." Wesley encouraged these poor creatures to believe that they were torn of Satan, asserting that he had seen many hysterical and epileptic people, but they were not as these. "One woman was offended greatly, being sure that they might help it if they would, and was got three or four yards when she also dropped down in as violent an agony as the rest."

In a short time he was back again at Bristol and Kingswood, in an atmosphere congenial to strange mental and nervous manifestations. He found that in the eight days' absence Satan had gained great advantage. Disputes had crept into the little society, so that the love of many had waxed cold. The French Prophets had been busy sowing the seeds of dissension. The rational in Wesley rises toward the surface again in the presence of these interlopers. He warns the people that dreams, visions, revelations, tears, involuntary effects, are of a doubtful, disputable nature. They may be from God and they may not. One gains a faint impression, however, from the journal that if the French Prophets cause them, they are not to be relied upon. If they occur under his own preaching, they are more likely to be trustworthy. There is little evidence just at this time of any attempt to sift the tares from the wheat. They are allowed to grow riotously together, pending the harvest.

June 22. "While I was speaking, one before me dropped down as dead and presently a second and a third. Five others sank down in half an hour, most of whom were in violent agonies."

June 24. "In the evening a girl and five other persons, . . . with sighs and groans, called upon God for deliverance."

June 25. "At ten in the morning, J——e C——r, as she was sitting at her work, was suddenly seized with grievous terrors of mind attended with strong tremblings."

June 26. "Three persons terribly felt the wrath of God abiding on them at the society this evening."

July 1. "A young woman sank down at Rose Green in a violent agony of both body and mind, as did five or six persons in the evening at the new room, at whose cries many were greatly offended. The same offence was given in the morning by one at Weaver's hall, and by eight or nine others at Gloucester-lane in the evening. The first that was deeply touched was L—— W——, whose mother had been not a little displeased a day or two before when she was told how her daughter exposed herself before all the congregation. The mother herself was the next who dropped down, and lost her senses in a moment."

Up to this time Whitefield's ministry had never been attended by these manifestations, and he wrote to Wesley expressing his repugnance at such occurrences and admonishing him against lending them such powerful encouragement.[1] Twelve days later Whitefield passed through Bristol, and Wesley's time of triumph came. To his amazement Whitefield found that the effects were now produced under his own preaching. He had no sooner begun to invite sinners to repent than "four persons sunk down close to him almost in the same moment. One of them lay without either sense or motion. The second trembled exceedingly. The third had strong convulsions all over his body, but made no noise unless by groans. The fourth, equally convulsed, called upon God with strong cries and tears." And Wesley adds, not, it seems, without a touch of haughty asperity and sense of conquest over a weaker brother, "from this time, I trust, we shall all suffer God to carry

[1] *Methodist Magazine*, 1849, p. 165.

on His own work in the way that pleaseth Him." [1] It is suggestive of the type of Whitefield's mind that he was convinced not only by the exemplariness of the conversation of the converts in common life, which was well enough, but also by their loud and repeated "Amens"—both of which, as he says in his own journal, show that they had not received the grace of God in vain.

Still at Bristol: —

July 30. "Two more were in strong pain, both their souls and bodies being well-nigh torn asunder." At this point a woman opposer "was struck through as with a sword, and fell trembling to the ground. She then cried aloud, though inarticulately, her words being swallowed up. In this pain she continued for twelve or fourteen hours and then her soul was set at liberty. But her master (for she was a servant till that time at a gentleman's in town) forbid her returning to him, saying he would have none in his house who had received the Holy Ghost."

August 11. "In the evening two were seized with strong pangs as were four the next evening, and the same number at Gloucester-lane on Monday — one of whom was greatly comforted."

Charles Wesley now took his brother's place at Bristol, and John went to London. Charles did not agree with his brother's interpretation of the "signs and wonders," and discouraged them, and they seldom occurred under his impassioned

[1] "Journal," Vol. I, p. 144.

preaching even when the tendency to morbid imitation was at its height. But he could not entirely
escape them at Bristol. On one occasion a woman
screamed for mercy so as to drown his voice, and
on another, "he heard on all sides the sighing of
them that were in captivity." In the meantime
his brother John on Kennington Common and in
Moorfields was preaching to great multitudes of
the poor of London, with comparatively few
demonstrations of an uncanny nature. But when
he got back to Bristol in October, these strange
responses to the stimulation of his personality
broke out afresh.

October 11. "In the evening our Lord rose on
many who were wounded . . . one of these showed
the agony of her soul by crying aloud to God for
help . . . she continued in great torment all night,
but while we were praying for her in the morning,
God delivered her out of her distress."

October 12. "We had fresh occasion to observe
the darkness which was fallen on many who lately
rejoiced in God." The presence of Wesley, however, wrought its effect, and a "cloud of witnesses"
testified at the morning meeting to a sudden return
to faith.

The mental and nervous strain of the revival
excitement soon became so intense that some individuals were on the verge of insanity. Wesley
was under concern for one or two who were "tor-
mented in an unaccountable manner and seemed
indeed to be lunatic." But he received an answer

from the word of God that all was well. "Soon after I was sent for to one of those who was so strangely torn by the devil. . . . We prayed God to bruise Satan under her feet. Immediately we had the petition we asked of Him. She cried out vehemently, 'He is gone, he is gone.'"

October 23. "I was exceedingly pressed to go to a young woman in Kingswood. I went. She was nineteen or twenty years old, but it seems *could not write or read*. I found her on the bed, two or three persons holding her. It was a terrible sight. Anguish, horror and despair, above all description, appeared in her pale face. The thousand distortions of her whole body showed how the dogs of hell were gnawing her heart. The shrieks intermixed were scarce to be endured. But her stony eyes could not weep. She screamed out, as soon as words could find their way, 'I am damned, damned, lost forever. Six days ago you might have helped me. But it is passed. I am the devil's now. I have given myself to him. His I am. Him I must serve. With him I must go to hell. . . . I must, I will, I will be damned.' She then prayed to the devil. We began, 'Arm of the Lord, awake, awake!' *She immediately sunk down as asleep*, but as soon as we left off, broke out again, with inexpressible vehemence: 'Stony hearts, break! I am a warning to you. I am damned that you may be saved.' She then fixed her eyes on the corner of the ceiling, and said: 'There he is, ay there he is, come, good devil,

come. Take me away. You said you would dash
my brains out. Come, do it quickly. I am yours.
. . .' We interrupted her by calling again upon God,
on which she sunk down as before — and another
young woman began to roar out as loud as she had
done. . . . We continued in prayer until past
eleven, when God in a moment spoke peace into
the soul, and they both joined in singing praise to
Him who had stilled the enemy and the avenger."

October 25. " I was sent for to one in Bristol
who was taken ill the evening before. She lay on
the ground furiously gnashing her teeth and after
a while roared aloud. It was not easy for three or
four persons to hold her, especially when the name
of Jesus was named. We prayed. The violence
of her symptoms ceased, though without a complete deliverance." Wesley was sent for again in
the evening, but was loth to go after the earlier
experience of the day. However, having con-
sulted the oracle — his Testament chanced to
open at the words, "I was afraid and went and hid
thy talent in the earth " — he stood reproved and
went. " She began screaming before I came into
the room, then broke out into a horrid laughter,
mixed with blasphemy, grievous to hear. *One
who from many circumstances apprehended a preternatural agent to be concerned in this*, asking,
' How didst thou dare to enter into a Christian ? '
was answered, ' She is not a Christian, she is mine.'
Then another question, ' Dost thou not tremble at
the name of Jesus ? ' No words followed, but she

shrunk back and trembled exceedingly. 'Art thou not increasing thy own damnation?' It was faintly answered, 'Ay! Ay!' which was followed by fresh cursing and blasphemy . . . with spitting, and all the expressions of strong aversion." And the second day after, Wesley called and prayed with her again — "All her pangs ceased in a moment, she was filled with peace, and knew that the son of wickedness was departed from her."

October 28. "I was sent for to Kingswood again to one of those who had been so ill before. . . . Just at that time, the woman (then three miles off) cried out, 'Yonder comes Wesley, galloping as fast as he can.' When I was come . . . she burst out into a horrid laughter and said: 'No power, no power; no faith, no faith. She is mine; her soul is mine. I have her and will not let her go. . . .' *One who was clearly convinced this was no natural disorder* said, 'I think Satan is let loose. I fear he will stop not here,' and added, 'I command thee in the name of the Lord Jesus to tell if thou hast commission to torment any other soul?' It was immediately answered, 'I have — L——y C——r and S——h J——s.'" These two persons lived at some distance and were then in perfect health, according to the journal. But the atmosphere of the community was so electric with suggestibility that they did not long remain so. They were evidently made acquainted with the prediction of the "demon," for Wesley called next evening at Mrs. J's. in Kingswood. He found both the unfortunate girls there. Was he curious, or even anxious to know whether this supernatural proph- ecy would be fulfilled? It seems so, and that he himself was the centre of suggestion. For "it was scarce a quarter of an hour, before L——y C——r fell into a strange agony, and presently after, S——h J——s. The violent convulsions all over their bodies were such as words cannot de- scribe. . . . We poured out our souls before God, till L——y C——r's agonies so increased that it seemed that she was in the pangs of death. But in a moment God spoke — she knew His voice, and both soul and body were healed. . . ." A little later S——h J——s recovered from the paroxysm.

Wesley appears here in the rather unlovely rôle of a pagan exorcist. If he was not the "one who" actually conducted the conversation with the demon, he was clearly an assistant and in full sym- pathy with the method employed. The medicine- man or priest always treated the many cases of possession which occurred in primitive communi- ties by just this process. He would attempt to drive the evil spirit out by his own impressive personal power, and by invoking friendly super- natural aid.[1] Here are also several instances of the emergence of the "double personality," a phenomenon so common in the Shantung prov- ince of China during similar paroxysms. Of course the intelligent observer perceives in a

[1] Cf. Spencer, "Principles of Sociology" (1–1), p. 241 f.

moment that the key to the explanation of these things is not in demon possession at all, as Wesley clearly believed. Some of the cases of alleged possession were no doubt purely pathological. But so far as they occur in normal health, as they appear to have done in the west of England under Wesley and very frequently in Shantung under the observation of Nevius, they indicate a rudimentary stage of mental and nervous evolution. In a primitive and nervously unstable population, full of mythical notions with respect to the easy entrance of evil spirits into the body, any considerable stress of excitement, especially if it be religious, will bring these phenomena to the surface. They have no more causal connection with the supernatural or with Christianity than they have with the phases of the moon. And not only the relief which Wesley obtained for his subjects, but the state of exaltation which ensued, have been duplicated times without number in the experience of pagan priests and savage exorcists, and by native missionary assistants in heathen lands.[1]

Observing these phenomena closely, as well as others which occurred in the same year, we shall be impressed at once with the grouping in time and space. Although there were sporadic instances in London and elsewhere, — a considerable number of them on the whole, — yet most of the striking cases gather about the neighborhood of Bristol

[1] Cf. Nevius, " Demon Possession," p. 13 ; also pp. 30–35.

and Kingswood when Wesley's personality first broke upon the population in 1739. Tyerman, who carefully collated the phenomena,[1] noted also the grouping which, he says, adds to the strangeness and mysteriousness of the facts, but he offers no explanation. It is not far to seek. Bristol and Kingswood at this time contained a population the most primitive, brutal and ignorant in all England. Wesley himself spoke of the colliers as "a people, famous from the beginning hitherto for neither fearing God nor regarding man, so ignorant of the things of God that they seem but one remove from the beasts that perish, and therefore utterly without desire of instruction as well as without the means of it."[2] They were outcast, ignorant, neglected, sunk in vice and bitterness and envyings and strife, and were like tinder to the revival flame. It was in this population that the revival was kindled, and it is exactly what we should expect according to the law of origin. And from what we know of the primitive nature of man unmoulded by experience and civilized environment, where more certainly would the peculiar phenomena be likely to appear in the England of the eighteenth century than in the neighborhood of Bristol and Kingswood? If, while he was still seeking an explanation, Tyerman's eye had lighted upon a page of the journal of 1743, I am sure it would have been to him very interesting reading. After

[1] Cf. Tyerman, "Life and Times of John Wesley," Vol. I, p. 255 f. [2] "Journal," Vol. I, p. 170.

a lull of four years in the storm of phenomena, they suddenly appear again in great abundance near Newcastle at a place called Chowden, which Wesley characterizes as " the Kingswood of the north." As he entered the village for the first time, twenty or thirty wild children ran round him, staring in amazement. They were neither clothed nor quite naked. A girl of fifteen, for example, had a piece of ragged, dirty blanket hung about her and a cap on her head of the same cloth and color. The people received him as if they would have swallowed him up. It was the very abode of savage ignorance and wickedness. Wesley undertook a course of visiting to study the cases of the many who had cried aloud every night in the week during the preaching. He found that, without exception, they were persons in perfect health and had not been subject to fits of any kind until they were thus affected, and that the manifestations had overcome them very suddenly under the preaching or in meditation upon it afterwards. They at once dropped down, lost all their strength and were seized with violent pain. Some said they felt as if a sword was running through them, others that they were being squeezed down by a great weight. Some were choked, others in imagination torn to pieces. With some, their minds were overwhelmed, stunned and confounded. With others there was great fear of the wrath of God. And it seems that it was at this point, when something whispered to them that there was no hope, that they were lost forever, that the pains of the body occurred and wrung from them the loud and bitter cries.[1]

There is material here for an interesting study in religious psychology, but I let it stand for the present simply as further illustration of the fact that the burst of phenomena occurred among the primitives of England, in the Kingswood of the west and the Kingswood of the north. Experience and environment had never developed the inhibitions of civilization, and they were ripe for the effects that were actually produced.

But why did the coming of Wesley first arouse the manifestations in these primitive people? Whitefield preached first to the colliers of Kingswood until, we are touchingly told, "the tears made white gutters down cheeks blackened from the coal-mine." They gathered in the fields, in thrilling, enthusiastic audiences of five, ten, fifteen thousand people, but there were no strange "signs and wonders" till Wesley came. Was it the character of his message? Wesley was indeed still under bondage to the terror theology of his age. I happened the other day upon this passage in one of his sermons.[2]

"What is the pain of the body which you do or may endure to that of lying in a lake of fire burning with brimstone? When you ask a friend who is sick how he does — 'I am in pain now,' says he, 'but I hope to be easy soon.' That is a sweet mitigation of the present uneasiness. But how dread-

---

[1] "Journal," Vol. I, p. 281   [2] Vol. II, sermon on "Hell."

ful would his case be if he should answer, 'I am all over pain, and I shall be never easy of it. I lie under exquisite torment of body and horror of soul, and I shall feel it forever!' Such is the case of the damned sinners in hell."

This is not cheerful preaching, and it measures up very well with the worst of Edwards'. But I think one cannot look his journal and sermons over without being convinced that impassioned appeals to terror were uncommon with Wesley. I do not mean that he did not lay bare the sins of his generation and of the audiences before him with an unsparing hand and make very plain to them the proximity of the pit toward which their feet were sliding. He did that with great power. I only mean that the awful messages of woe which the theology and the rich imagination of Edwards made it possible for him to produce, were not the chief exciting cause of the strange effects under the ministry of Wesley. Wesley believed in everlasting torment for the wicked as really as Edwards, but here was the difference. The English leader proclaimed every man free from the law of sin and death who in the untrammelled exercise of his will should turn to God. Edwards' belief led him to consign to perdition the majority of each passing generation. Every man was exhorted to be violent for the kingdom of heaven, but the chance of his obtaining it was by no means as hopeful and inspiring as that which Wesley held out to men. Fear of eternal retribution was no doubt one reason for the crushing weight which fell upon the souls of the colliers of Kingswood and the north. But Whitefield spoke that message, and the brother Charles, — yet there were no strange phenomena till Wesley initiated them.

Fear and other strong emotions aroused in a susceptible population may be regarded as important predisposing conditions. The exciting cause of the reflex phenomena was the man Wesley. It was the quality of his personality more than the quality of his message that produced the effects. Wesley was in manner the antithesis of Whitefield, whose action in the pulpit he regarded as too violent.[1] But in spite of the perfect outward calmness and self-possession, he was probably the most terribly impressive preacher that England ever knew. It would be hard to mention a man whose influence over an audience can be so perfectly described by the term " awful." If it were not such a hateful word when applied to so complex and noble a personality, one would say that it closely approached the hypnotic. And I think there was a strong element of this in his nature. There were few men, or mobs either, for that matter, that did not surrender to the look of his searching eye. He says in his journal that he found it best always to face a mob. His usual method was to single out the leader and bring all the calmness, courtesy, dignity and strength which he possessed to bear upon the one man. And it

[1] " Journal," Vol. II, p. 498.

seldom failed. On one occasion there was a concerted plan to disturb an evening meeting at Long-lane, London. A violent and notorious woman was the leader. Wesley says that the very instant she broke out he turned full upon her and declared the love God had for her soul, and then prayed for God to confirm the word. "She was struck to the heart, and shame covered her face. From her I turned to the rest, who melted away like water, and were as men that had no strength."[1] And this is no isolated circumstance. We meet its like frequently in the journal. Such was the overwhelming influence of the man that those who were not ready to submit to his will and his message were afraid to listen to him.[2] It was the same in his private life. A half-superstitious dread of the man affected even his brother Charles. And his brother-in-law, Mr. Whitelamb, who had known him from the old Oxford days, preferred to write to him about a matter rather than run the gantlet of a personal interview. "I am at a loss how to behave," he said in his letter; "your presence creates an awe, as though you were an inhabitant of another world."

Whitefield was emotional, sympathetic, magnetic, but Wesley was overpowering. Whitefield had a vivid imagination, and his wonderful word-pictures and his eyes suffused with tears drew outward the emotions of his auditors, and they wept with him.

[1] "Journal," Vol. I, p. 191.
[2] Cf. Buckley, "History of Methodism," Vol. I, p. 329.

The energy of the organism, set free by the stimulation of his preaching, followed this particular channel. Wesley's example of calm self-possession thwarted the outflow in the form of the quieter and saner emotions, while the shock of his dominating and fascinating personality, his plain and searching speech and his demand for instantaneous decision fell with terrific force upon the plastic mental and nervous organization of his hearers. The pent-up energy found vent in almost every conceivable form of muscular reflex action, and finally into cries and groanings and terrors of impending judgment.[1]

I am not speaking of the results of all this, which were often salutary, contributing to real transformation of character. I am speaking of the process. Whitefield's was certainly as divine as Wesley's. The difference in the immediate effect of the two processes, the population remaining the same, is certainly to be accounted for by the difference in the personality of the two men. The power of fascination and suggestion appears usually to accompany a high quality of will. Did ever Cromwell or Napoleon exhibit to the world finer volitional fibre than Wesley?

The reader will not make the mistake of supposing that I believe the whole secret of Wesley's influence is to be found in this extraordinary power of impression and suggestion which he possessed. The human personality is a marvellous

[1] Cf. "Journal," Vol. I, p. 281.

complex, and that there were elements of the highest ethical, intellectual and, in the best sense,
religious power in John Wesley, I do not doubt.
To say that these qualities did not reënforce the
great influence of impression and suggestion which
he exerted upon men, would be absurd. They
were even in combination with it at all times.
But they do not account for that mysterious influence which differentiated him from Whitefield and
from other religious leaders.

These grewsome happenings under Wesley's
own preaching attained their maximum of intensity within a year or two, and after 1740 he manifested in his own spirit a healthy, well-balanced
religious experience, and until the close of a further
half century of tireless toil there is evidence that
he gave less encouragement to the spread of the
"signs and wonders" than in the early period.
Certainly they were far less common than when in
the year 1739 the shock of his personality was first
felt among the colliers of Kingswood. Like Edwards, however, he cannot escape a measure of
responsibility for the wild excesses of some of his
followers. No community ever saw more terrible
scenes of mental and nervous disorder than are
described in the journal as having occurred under
the preaching of one Berridge and one Hicks in
the vicinity of Everton, almost under the shadow
of the University of Cambridge. Wesley had the
facts from the journal of an eye-witness. It is a
horrible account of a reign of terror under the

preaching of these men, who were passing sentence of death upon the souls of suffocating multitudes who filled the church to listen. The picture of the agonies and contortions of body of many little children, the loud breathing of men and women half strangled and gasping for life, the outcries, the bitter anguish, the faces turning red and then almost black, the sinking in silence, the convulsions, the awful morbid contagion that swept over the stifled crowd, the numbers carried into the parsonage house, where they struggled or lay as dead, the breaking of pews and benches, the dropping in a heap on the road home, the trance, the demoniac shrieks, the emergence of the second personality, the uncontrollable laughter, the child seven years old and her visions, the woman rolling on the ground and tearing up the hard-trodden grass with her hands, the almost limitless superstition of Berridge and his people — that picture will never fade from the memory of the man who has once read the description.[1] The experiences in trance were as irrational as ever floated through the untutored brain of an African savage. One girl, who had "come through" after shrieking and insensibility and violent distortion of face, related that in the swoon she thought herself on an island and saw Satan in a hideous form just ready to devour her, hell all around open to receive her and herself just ready to drop in. But just as she was dropping, the Lord appeared between her and the gulf and

[1] See "Journal," Vol. II, p. 25 f. and p. 34 f.

would not let her fall.   And one John Dennis lay
on a table stiff and motionless as a statue, his very
neck as if made of iron, looking steadfastly up to
heaven and praying aloud with a melodious voice
and with great intelligence.   Berridge assured the
assembly that they needed no better preacher, for
none could unfold the truths of the gospel more
clearly.   When the subject came out of the fit, he
was in perfect health, but declared he knew not a
word of all he had spoken.

And this was in 1759, twenty years after Kingswood, and still Wesley was not entirely ready to
give over the manifestations.   But his judgment
was shaken somewhat by the sudden dying away
of the trances, convulsions and visions in Everton,
although the religious interest remained strong.
And, true Englishman that he was, he could modify
his former belief, but could not wholly change it.
He thinks there was danger at one time of regarding the extraordinary circumstances as essential.
He thinks perhaps now the danger may be of condemning them altogether, of imagining that they
are a hindrance, with nothing of God in them.
The truth is, he says, that God in the former time
did visit lost sinners with such conviction that the
natural consequence was outcry and convulsion,
that he favored several of them with divine dreams
and others with trances and visions.   But after a
while there was some "nature" mixed with grace,
and finally Satan stepped in and imitated the work
in order to discredit it.   It was originally wholly

from God; it is partly so still, but Satan is now responsible for a share.[1] In Leslie Stephen's phrase of comment — "a singular coöperation between God and the devil!"

If the discussion of these phenomena appears to fill too large a space upon the horizon of my theme, I regret it. They are important to the student of a great sympathetic religious movement, for they frequently accompany it and lay bare its social character and conformity to social law. Sympathetic social action lifts the inhibition from the individual, and reveals the nervous instability, the mental plasticity, the suggestibility, if you will, of primitive man. But when we recall how dim the light of science shone in the eighteenth century, we need not fear that these phenomena and the superstitious explanation of them will cloud a fair name. They are an incident in the life and a single blot upon the fame of a great and useful man.

And I revert finally to what was basal in him when I say that, take him all in all, his whole life through, England had no more sane, conservative, statesmanlike spirit within her borders in his century. He grew to be the very embodiment of the sound sense of the Saxon, his controlling emotion came to be the love of his fellow-man and he gave himself throughout a long life with the utter abandon of unselfishness to the cause of the English people. For years before he died he was per-

[1] "Journal," Vol. II, p. 49.

haps the best-known and, at least among the masses, the most honored man within the circuit of the three kingdoms.

It seems the irony of circumstance that one of his temper should have been mobbed as a revolutionist so often and so long. There was nothing in him of the political radicalism of the Roundhead or the Covenanter. For the democracy of the state within the constitution he cared not at all. The polity of his own organization was autocratic in the extreme. "If by arbitrary power," he said to his critics, "you mean a power which I exercise simply without any colleagues therein, this is certainly true, but I see no hurt in it." His giant blows were struck for the ethical and spiritual vivification of the state behind the constitution. We can best measure his influence, not by the number of the converts, although their name was legion. The rôle of the truly good is nowhere fully and accurately kept upon this planet. But we have a test in the new life which he summoned into consciousness and sent throbbing through the pulses of the nation. His greatest service was not to the church, but to democracy. He was first of all a champion of the new life spiritual, but he aroused also in the vast human area which he influenced an intense aspiration for the new life mental, social and political. The very gathering of such masses of men with a common purpose was in unconscious sympathy with the drift of the age. Its like had never been known before in

England. The fundamental democratic right of assembly was not yet evolved. Legal permission had still to be obtained from some administrative officer of the crown. The religious revival broke that barrier down, and gave the great body of the English people their first sense of latent, aggregate power. Wesley's system of printing and distributing letters of advice and appeal to the thousands of his converts was consciously or unconsciously imitated in the politics of the late eighteenth and early nineteenth century. The great mass meeting, the platform speech, the political pamphlet freely and widely distributed — these were the very organs of public opinion in the democratic movement, and they were in large measure the outgrowth of the revival.[1]

England escaped a French Revolution. Such a method of securing liberty and progress is not thoroughly in accord with the English mind, although not entirely contrary to it. Neither was the wrong so deep, the burden so grievous on the island side of the Channel. But nevertheless, there was vast social unrest which might easily have been stirred to disorder and disruption. In certain places and at certain times the revival did arouse primitive instinct and irrational reflex action

[1] Cf. Ostrogorski, " Democracy and the Organization of Political Parties," p. 25 f. ; also Jephson, " The Platform," p. 6 f.

The pamphlet had been employed in the time of the Restoration and earlier, but had never been so general and so powerful an instrument of appeal as in the Wesleyan and the democratic movements.

after a fashion to be deplored. But in the long
range of the years of Wesley's leadership and
labor, slowly another result emerged. Brutal
passion was softened to an extraordinary degree.
The released volume of emotion rolled into the
channel of inspiring religious song. Scores of
thousands of men all over the nation were bound
together by the bonds of sympathy and brotherhood, not only for their own class, but, in a measure, for every class. And a French Revolution,
improbable in any event, was rendered impossible.

The revival was strong in the towns. And when
the industrial disturbances of later days reached a
maximum of intensity and peril, the labor movement
was to a marked extent leavened by the chapel and
class meeting of Wesley's societies. In them work-
ingmen for two generations had been trained not
only in sympathy, but in organization, in financial
administration, in methods of communication. The
local preacher and the labor leader became for a
long period almost synonymous terms. And it is
impossible to doubt that at least one of the sources
of the sanity and intelligence of the trades-union
movement in Great Britain is the Wesleyan revival.

Even when a kind of Puritan asceticism, manifesting itself in distrust of adornment and other
forms of pleasure, set in to narrow somewhat the
outlook and consequently the spirit of Wesley's
followers,[1] in society at large the movement was

[1] Cf. Ostrogorski, *op. cit.*, p. 25 f.

still a force making for the freedom and the broadening of human personality, and a better environment for all classes of the English population.
For more than fifty years Wesley himself ranged
the three kingdoms, a mounted herald of social
regeneration. Everywhere he preached the gospel,
not only of righteousness and temperance and
judgment to come, but of intelligence, thrift, clean-
liness and good manners. He was a philanthro-
pist to the extent of distributing the whole of his
substance among the needy. There was not a
practical reform mooted in eighteenth-century
England which he did not further with his voice
and with his pen. He advocated a more equitable
system of taxation. His arguments for juster Par-
liamentary representation were made seventy years
before the reform was accomplished, but they were
as strong as any that were advanced on the eve of
its fruition. He lent active aid to the cause of the
prisoner, the lunatic, the debtor and the slave. In
all these matters he was only an evangel. The
reforms were demanded by the spirit of the age,
and more potent and active agents than he were
directly concerned in their fulfilment. But the
spirit of the movement which he inaugurated
strongly reënforced the spirit of the age. It is due
to this capacity for what has been happily called
"the statesmanship of salvation" [1] that the movement which he inaugurated presents the aspect not
of an injurious recoil, but rather of a great purify-

[1] President Woodrow Wilson.

ing social force working steadily for the evolution and regeneration of society. And it is this eminent service to his country and his century which entitles him to be known as the social figure, par excellence, among modern revivalists.

CHAPTER X

THE TRANSITION PERIOD IN THE UNITED STATES —
NETTLETON, FINNEY AND MOODY

THE fifty years of popular indifference to religion which followed hard upon the New England
awakening were destined to be succeeded by a
surprising recrudescence of revival interest and
activity in all parts of the United States in the
early nineteenth century. Not only in the new
settlements of the southwest, but throughout the
northern and eastern sections of the country, and
especially in western New York, the revival fires
burned unrestrainedly and long. In New England
the spirit and method of Edwards were renewed
in the personality and practice of Asabel Nettleton.
Nettleton enjoyed the vivid religious experience of
Edwards, and accepted the Edwardean doctrine as
an explanation of his own spiritual struggle and
triumph. He was thus naturally led to adopt the
Edwardean method of practical effort for the salvation of men. It was his custom to awaken sinners
by the able and fervid proclamation of God's
sovereignty and His law, with its dread sanctions
and solemn claims. Here he was at one with
Edwards. But as soon as the first blows were

struck and the influence of them was passing away, and there seemed danger of the sinner settling down in presumptuous confidence that the Spirit was already working in his heart, and that he need only employ the means of grace and bide God's time — then Nettleton declared the doctrine of election with super-Edwardean zeal. He stood ready to press home the utter vanity of any attempt of man to save his own soul, even to the point of stirring rebellion in the sinner's heart against " a God that commands sinners to do what it requires Almighty power to cause them to do." Fear of hell and a partial conviction of sin were thus deepened into despair and a sense of absolute helplessness. This terrible agony must not be lessened, dut increased the rather and allowed to weigh upon the rebellious soul until real conversion come and joy and peace succeed to trouble and distress.[1] But in one important respect Nettleton marked an advance upon Edwards. It was indeed true that he played upon the chord of fear, but he was from the beginning a most vigorous opponent of all uncontrolled outbursts of emotion. He was the foe of sensation, of mere physical and mental excitement, even of publicity. He endeavored to instil the spirit of meditation, of deep and quiet reverence, in his hearers. He was an individualist in his methods. He advised his converts to retire to their homes without converse with the crowd, and, entirely apart from its influence, to

[1] Hayes, *op. cit.*, seminar paper on the New England revivals.

reflect in the companionship of their Maker alone upon the things they had heard. He visited the awakened from house to house, and the personal touch of the man combined with his careful system of sifting and instruction wrought a permanent influence upon many lives.

Probably the leading evangelist of the first half of the nineteenth century in America was Charles G. Finney, a contemporary of Nettleton, though he survived him many years. With Finney came the strong common-sense reaction in revival philosophy and sentiment against the hyper-Calvinism of the earlier day. He could not disentangle himself completely from the notion of election; for ever, according to his view, it was God who, in the last analysis, pressed the truth home to the conscience and induced the sinner to turn into the way of righteousness. And he was no more successful after all than Edwards in harmonizing human responsibility with the doctrine of the absolute sovereignty of the Supreme Being. But he stood at the turn of the tide, and with all the strength of a really vigorous intellect he repudiated the theological concept of the total depravity of humanity, and espoused with vehemence the notion of moral agency, that the will of man is free to choose between the motives that come to it through reason and emotion.

The field of his labor was the entire eastern United States, but the propagating centre of his influence and the locality of his greatest successes was the pioneer community of western and central New York. It would be a profitable study to determine the strange mixture of elements which must have entered originally into the remarkable population of the western New York section particularly. There seem to have been two periods of migration thither, with two vastly different qualities of human stock. The second decade of the nineteenth century brought to the Palmyra country settlers from Vermont of rather unsavory fame, represented notably by the tribe of the Smiths, from whose loins sprang Mormonism. In the third decade came a young, virile, intelligent, industrious people from eastern New York and New England. They are responsible for that strain of intellectual, moral and industrial strength which has especially characterized the Rochester country. But the mixture of elements has given to that section a psychological history of its own. It has been a hot-bed of fanaticisms as well as a centre of sane and progressive social movements. The earliest agitation which helped to reveal the unfortunate strain in the blood was the crusade against the Masonic Fraternity in 1826, originating in a widespread belief, unconfirmed by sound evidence, that one Morgan had been foully dealt with at the behest of the Order whose secrets he was accused of revealing. A single and mighty wave of indignation nearly obliterated the fraternity from that part of the United States. In the early forties the Rochester country was one of the two chief centres of the propaganda and excitement associated with the predictions of the Vermont farmer, William Miller, with respect to the approaching judgment and the destruction of the world. In western New York it became a thoroughly irrational epidemic. Men and women forsook their employments and gave themselves over to watchings and prayer. They hardly slept or ate, but in robes of white awaited the coming of the bridegroom. The result in very many cases was utter physical and mental exhaustion, ending in the horrors of insanity.

The tendency to outbursts of religious fanaticism was especially marked in this population. In the late forties the delusion of spiritualism entered upon its epidemic course with the "Rochester rappings" of the Fox sisters. It spread by imitation to New England, and thence to Europe, and many of the phenomena attending it — the trance, the vision, the convulsive movement, the involuntary dancing, the many indications of mental and nervous instability — had closest affinity to the extraordinary revival effects which we have everywhere observed.

It is important to notice that for many years during this early period an unbridled revival activity characterized the ordinary religious life of western New York. Before Finney's personality issued upon the scene, before any particular individual assumed the leadership, this fanatical restlessness, this tendency to spiritual commotion, was in the mind of the population, and periodically broke forth in fantastic and exciting revival. There were whole stretches of country in those parts that for generations were known as the "burnt district," and which Finney found so blistered and withered by constant revival flame that no sprout, no blade of spiritual life, could be caused to grow. Only the apples of Sodom flourished in the form of ignorance, intolerance, a boasted sinlessness and a tendency to free-love and "spiritual affinities." I speak of this in the first place to indicate the primitive character of a large element of the population within the environment of western New York and its vicinity in the early decades of the nineteenth century, and thus furnish a factor in the explanation of Finney's remarkable career. When he began to preach, the border of that part of the country was still a western wilderness, the farms had to be burned out of the forests, the Indians were on the frontier, the possibilities of education were meagre and the means of communication were few.[1] But I speak of it also because I wish to remark upon one other strange and base spiritual product of this unique population. Of course it is generally known that Mormonism had its beginning in this region, but it is not so generally understood, I think, that Mormonism was literally born and bred in the unhealthy revival atmosphere which has just been described. In fact the sect of so-called Latter-Day Saints might never have existed

[1] Cf. President Timothy Dwight's "Travels in New England and New York," 1822, Letters II and III.

except for the extraordinary mental agitation
about religious matters which pervaded western
New York in this period. Mormonism has two
main roots, the one to be traced into the mental
and nervous characteristics of the personality of
Joseph Smith, Jr., the other into the revival environment in which he lived and moved — and
neither is a sufficient explanation without the other.
Smith inherited from an illiterate, restless, credulous, nervously unstable ancestry a well-marked
tendency to visions, hallucinations, revelations.
The Book of Mormon, even if considered to be the
intellectual product of Smith, is understandable in
terms of his imaginative, emotional personality, with
its trancelike states and revelations, its hallucinations and belief in miraculous cures. The book is
an irrational mixture of prevailing ecclesiasticism
and liberalism, native in its historical aspects to the
New York wilderness which was its author's home.

And it is especially noteworthy that the whole
panorama of the visions of the Smiths, father and
son, springs out of the environment and arises in the
midst of the mental perturbation of the community.[1]
The revival methods of religious work in this locality
at this time had been directly imitated from Kentucky and Tennessee. It is exceedingly significant
that when the attention of this population became
fixed upon the great religious movements in the
southwest, the seriousness and excitement in New
York State began in Palmyra, Joseph Smith's own

[1] Cf. Riley, "The Founder of Mormonism," Chapters I and II.

town, and nearly all the youth and children of the community at once sought religion. The mental tension of the "protracted meetings" is indicated by the testimony of a prominent Mormon of a later time who took part in them. " A continual stream of glorious truths passed through my mind, my happiness was great, and my mind so absorbed in spiritual things that all the time the meeting lasted, which was about fifteen days, I scarcely ate or drank anything. . . . The spirit of the Lord so operated on my system that I felt full all the time." [1] And young Joseph Smith himself has borne witness that his first great psychic experiences were aroused by revival. His " First Vision " came about in this wise. " Sometime in the second year after our removal to Manchester, there was in the place where we lived an unusual excitement on the subject of religion. . . . During this time . . . my mind was called up to serious reflection and great uneasiness. . . . I attended there several meetings as often as occasion would permit." And he proceeds to relate that one clear spring morning, in the year 1820, under the influence of the spell which bound him, he retired to a secret place to wrestle with God in prayer. Immediately he was seized by some power which entirely overcame him so that he could not speak. Thick darkness gathered around him, and he seemed doomed to sudden destruction. " Just at this moment of great

[1] Benjamin Brown, "Testimonies for the Truth," 1853, p. 5 ; quoted in Riley, op. cit.

alarm," he says, " I saw a pillar of light exactly over my head, above the brightness of the sun, which descended gradually until it fell upon me. It no sooner appeared than I found myself delivered. . . . When the light rested upon me, I saw two personages, whose brightness and glory defy all description, standing above me in the air. One of them spake unto me. . . . When I came to myself again, I found myself lying on my back looking up into heaven." [1] Under these auspices and out of these environing conditions arose the prophet and the sect of the Latter-Day Saints. And the early spread of the Mormon gospel, with all its vagaries, was made possible because the locality itself possessed a large population element which was in the highest degree primitive and credulous, fairly hungering for the occult and the marvellous. And the influence of the early revival experiences can long be traced in the plastic body of Mormon believers. When they were gathered at Kirtland, Ohio, under the magnetic preaching of Sidney Rigdon, very many were "strangely handled by the spirits." There were instances of demoniac possession, some prophesied, others had the heavens opened to their view, there was the swooning, the disfigurement of countenance, the bodily contortion, and the ecstasy which had appeared in the protracted meetings in western New York. There

[1] " Pearl of Great Price," pp. 84–98, extracts from the history of Joseph Smith, written by himself in " Times and Seasons," Vol. III; quoted in Riley, *op. cit.*, p. 50.

was also the gift of clairvoyance, of "interpretation " and of " tongues." The acute suggestibility
was so marked that when the hands of the elders
were laid on the heads of the converts, they would
sink instantaneously in utter prostration of body
and of mind. "Many would fall upon the floor,
where they would lie for a long time, apparently
lifeless. Thus they continued these enthusiastic
exhibitions for several weeks. The fits usually
came on during or after their prayer-meetings, which
were held nearly every evening. The young men
and women were more particularly subject to this
delirium. They would exhibit all the apish actions
imaginable, making most ridiculous grimaces, creep-
ing upon their hands and feet, rolling upon the
frozen ground, going through with all the Indian
modes of warfare, such as knocking down, scalping,
ripping open and tearing out the bowels. At other
times they would run through the field, get upon
stumps, preach to imaginary congregations, enter
the water and perform all the ceremony of baptiz-
ing. Many would have fits of speaking all the
different Indian dialects, which none could understand. Again at the dead hour of the night, the
young men might be seen running over the fields
and hills in pursuit, as they said, of the balls of
fire and lights which they saw moving through the
atmosphere." [1] The strongly hypnotic personality

---

[1] Ezra Booth's letters to the Rev. Ira Eddy from Nelson, Ohio,
September, 1831; published in the *Ohio Star;* quoted in Riley, *op.
cit.*, pp. 267, 268.

of Smith and of Rigdon and of other leaders was always an important factor in the production of these physical and mental effects of the early period as well as in the growth in numbers of the body of the " Saints."

I have made this rather long detour to convince the reader of the immense amount of primitive instability as well as of pyschological distemper which existed in the population of western New York and its vicinity in the first half of the nineteenth century. There was a large element of highly neurotic people who demanded strenuous excitement, and who were accustomed to look for it particularly in religious movements.   And it was this class which first fell under the potent sway of Finney and of the great revivals with which his name is associated.   But it is only just to say at once that Finney was so thoroughly intellectual in his preaching, in the main so strong and well balanced a personality, that the time came soon in his ministry when not only the primitive people heard him gladly, but all classes flocked to him for instruction and for leading.   But there is little doubt that it was this primitive element which furnished the tinder to sustain the revival for so long a time at white heat.

Finney's own conversion was not under direct revival excitement.   It was wrought out in secret with tremendous earnestness and will power and intelligence.   But when it became known in Adams, Jefferson County, New York, that this brilliant young student of the law was to become a Presby-

terian missionary, revival interest began at once
and spread all over the town, and from Adams as
a centre through nearly all the communities of the
county. This was in the early twenties of the
nineteenth century. The first appearance of the remarkable ascendency which Finney exercised over
an audience came at Evans Mills when a Miss G——,
who had been a member of the church for eight
years, became convinced, during the progress of
Finney's sermon, that she had never known the
true God, and the effect of the man and of the
message was such that she had to be carried to her
home, where she lay in anguish and without the
power of speech for about the space of sixteen
hours.[1] Previous to this outbreak, Finney had
been considerably discouraged at the seeming
stolidity of the people, but now at once there ensued throughout the community a state of wonderful conviction of sin and alarm for the safety of
souls.

The law of origin and of imitation was exemplified frequently in these early days of his ministry, —
for instance in a little village of Germans not far
from Evans Mills. The settlement turned out *en
masse* to hear him. While a mother in Israel was
testifying to religious faith, another woman arose,
crowded her way in the presence of the packed
congregation to where the first woman was relating
her experience, threw her arms around her neck,
burst into tears and said, " God bless you, my sister,

[1] Finney, " Autobiography," p. 66.

God bless you." Such a scene as followed, Finney
found it difficult to describe in words. The whole
congregation responded, the simple childlike people fell on each other's necks and were melted
into tears. In a few days the whole settlement
was under conviction.[1] The evangelist passed on
to Rome, and that whole community was shaken
from centre to circumference. From Rome the
movement spread in every direction,— to Utica, to
Lowville, to Auburn, — and finally attained a very
high point of intensity and usefulness in the city of
Rochester in the winter of 1830–1831. There are
not wanting many infallible proofs that a remarkable change followed in the direction of decency and
order in that community of youth and enterprise
but of moral and social laxity.

Finney's methods were purposely fashioned to
gain the attention of the unawakened, and to impress them with the necessity of an immediate
decision. He was far more dramatic than Nettleton — far more sensational, to use a popular term.
He publicly prayed for sinners by name. He was
accused of irreverent familiarity with God in prayer.
He made free use of the "anxious seat" and other
such devices for separating the penitent from his
fellows. He was an emotionalist in manner. He
believed that exciting preaching was needed to
arouse an unfaithful generation, and he would not
listen to the remonstrances of the school of Nettleton. He did not, however, believe in the saving

[1] Finney, "Autobiography," p. 73 f.

quality of unrestrained emotion. Personally he held himself constantly under the control of the higher processes of reason and will. When he was engaged in revival at Bolton, England, he was assisted by a number of ministers, who became very much overwrought when the crowds poured forward to the "anxious seat." These helpers would pound the benches and invoke the throne of grace with great tumult, several at once but by no means in unison. Finney refrained from criticism for a season, fearing that he might disturb the movement of penitents and lead them to "grieve the Spirit." But the confusion became so pronounced that he finally expostulated with the brethren on the ground that the people should have more opportunity to *think* than was possible in such an environment, that they needed the instruction of one voice in prayer, and that calmness of spirit was essential to intelligent conversion.

Without pity or abatement he appealed to the selfish emotion of fear. He held that whoever comforts the sinner does him an injury "as cruel as the grave, as cruel as hell," for it is calculated to send him headlong to the abyss of everlasting fire. His sermon from the text, "The wages of sin is death," depicted the place of punishment as a bottomless pit upon whose walls were written in gigantic letters the words, "Wages," "Wages," "Wages," so that the condemned through all eternity might be reminded of the sort of remuneration which comes to men for rejection of

Christ. He once spoke in a schoolhouse in the neighborhood of Antwerp, in the state of New York, where, up to that time, there had been no preaching of any sort, from the words, "Up, get you out of this place, for the Lord will destroy this city." At the end of a quarter of an hour the people began to fall from their seats in every direction. "If I had had a sword in my hand," says Finney, "I could not have cut them down as fast as they fell."[1] The Rev. Mr. Nash, his helper at Gouverneur, believed thoroughly in his master's method of driving the sinner "from all his refuges in lies and misconceptions." In Finney's presence he thus addressed the "brazen-faced and stiff-necked" youth of the community: "Now mark me, young men, God will break your necks in less than one week, either by converting some of you, or by sending some of you to hell. He will do this as certainly as the Lord is my God." The leader of the young men was very soon overcome, and at Finney's suggestion exhorted his companions to turn to the Lord while there was yet time. And before the days of probation promised by the prophet Nash had expired, nearly all had taken their stand on the side of safety and reconciliation.[2]

No explanation of Finney's career would be at all sufficient which did not take into account the almost preternatural influence of suggestion which he exercised over men's minds. His power to compel individuals and audiences to his will and

[1] Finney, "Autobiography," p. 103.   [2] *Ibid.*, p. 123.

purposes was, it seems to me, the most extraordinary that appears in any great evangelist. As he preached on from hamlet to hamlet and from city to city, his fame in this particular preceded him, and whole sections of country would be in trepidation at his coming and congregations would immediately fall under his sway. Under the first sermon he preached at Rome a young man swooned away, and the next morning the whole town came together at the hotel to an inquiry meeting. On this occasion some of the strongest men had to be taken home by their friends. A physician undertook to examine the pulse of one subject who had fallen in great agony, when he, too, was obliged to grasp a pillar in order to keep himself in an upright position. Five hundred conversions were reported in a short time in Rome, and Finney testifies that the work was with such power that even a few words of conversation would make the stoutest men writhe in their seats. It came to pass at last that no oratory, no factitious methods of creating excitement, were necessary — the mere presence of the evangelist was enough.[1] This unusual influence was partly the mere outgoing of an imperious will. For example, in a series of meetings at Western, Oneida County, New York, a young woman came under conviction, but was not happily converted because of trouble at home. Her parents were not in sympathy with the change which seemed likely

[1] Finney, "Autobiography," p. 161 f.

to occur in the daughter. Finney went at once to the home, called in the father from the field where he was at work, told both the father and mother they must have family prayers on the instant. And he would not leave the house until they repented and established the family altar.[1]

But it was something more than imperious volition. There was an amazingly strange psychic influence which, all his life, he exercised over those with whom he came in contact. At Evans Mills a powerfully built and very evil man went to one of the meetings with a loaded pistol, with a plan to shoot the evangelist while he was preaching. But instead he was so transfixed by the personality which confronted him that he sank down, shrieking in an agony of terror. Next morning Mr. Finney met this man on a street of the town. "Good morning," he said to the would-be murderer, "how do you feel in your mind this morning?" The man related to Finney his experience during a sleepless night. He had wrestled with God in prayer, but with no sense of relief. He had even lost the conviction of sin which was present in his mind the evening before, and had come away from the place of unsuccessful communion with the Almighty. "*But*," said he, "*when I saw you, my heart began to burn and grow hot within me, and instead of feeling as if I wanted to avoid you, I felt so drawn that I came across the street to see you.*"[2]

[1] Finney, "Autobiography," pp. 151, 152.   [2] *Ibid.*, pp. 69, 70.

At New York Mills, near Utica, there occurred an incident which also lets the light in upon the hidden sources of purely natural power which this man possessed. After having preached at a night meeting with powerful effect, he went next morning with one of the owners to inspect a large textile factory which was in operation at that place. As he passed through, he observed a great deal of agitation among those who were busy at the mules and looms. In one of the apartments where a great number of young women were weaving, he saw two of them eyeing him and speaking very earnestly to each other. Finney's own circumstantial account of what followed is worth preserving as a bit of illustration in the psychology of hypnotism. " I could see that they were a good deal agitated, although they both laughed. *I went slowly towards them*. They saw me coming and were evidently much excited. One of them was trying to mend a broken thread, and I observed that her hands trembled so that she could not mend it. I approached slowly, looking on each side at the machinery as I passed, but observed that this girl grew more and more agitated and could not proceed with her work. When I came within eight or ten feet of her, I *looked solemnly at her*. She observed it and was quite overcome and sunk down and burst into tears. *The impression caught almost like powder, and in a few moments nearly all in the room were in tears*." The owner was so affected by what he saw that the machinery was stopped, a large meeting was put in operation at once, and nearly every girl in the mill in that hour professed conversion.[1]

In the Antwerp, New York, revival to which reference has been made, there was a very striking case of instantaneous recovery from insanity under the potent spell of Finney's personality. A woman who was the victim of mental aberration and despair over her religious life was in the audience. When Finney began to preach, she struggled to get out, but was restrained by friends in the same pew with her. The evangelist, who knew of her condition, sought to influence her in the course of the sermon by powerful suggestions as to boldness in faith and hope in the mercy of God. At first she held her head very low, but as Finney proceeded, she began gradually to raise her head and look out from within her long black bonnet. As the evangelist's power over her increased, she stood upright and gazed into his face with intense earnestness. Suddenly, at the climax of the discourse, she startled the congregation with a loud shriek and cast herself from her seat, trembling violently. As Finney concluded, she gradually came back to a sitting posture, " with face wonderfully changed, indicating triumphant joy and peace." As an application of mental therapeutics it was manifestly very helpful, but there may well be grave doubt if in this instance, or in other similar ones which occurred in Finney's experience,

[1] Finney, "Autobiography," p. 183.

there was a trace of the purely supernatural influence to which the evangelist attributed the cure. At their best, they are simply more refined methods of expelling evil spirits than the exorcisms of John Wesley among the English miners, of Joseph Smith, Jr., among the Mormons or of the Shaker enthusiasts among the Indian tribes.

This quality of a very high hypnotic potential cannot fail to impress the student of Finney's mind and method as revealed in his autobiography. It is gratifying, however, to have one's own view confirmed by direct and positive testimony from an unimpeachable source. I was in conversation not long ago with a cultivated business man of excellent scientific training and habit, who resided for a short time in Finney's household, who was intimately acquainted with the evangelist and his family and thoroughly familiar with his unique personality and who entirely corroborates the opinion expressed here with respect to his remarkable power in suggestion. He related to me the following incident as he heard it from Finney's own lips. The evangelist was conducting a series of revival meetings in the old Chatham theatre in New York. A certain woman came night after night and occupied a seat near the front, evidently with the fully formed purpose of resisting the religious appeal. Her attitude of cool insolence became perfectly clear to Finney, and he skilfully planned an attack upon the citadel of her opposition. He prepared a sermon especially for her, in which the guilt and danger of the sinner, the reality of hell as a place of everlasting punishment for the wicked, were painted in colors vivid and terrible.   He pictured the devil as a huntsman with a long bow, threading the forest paths of the nether world, seeking the lost, not for succor but for destruction.   At the point of highest dramatic interest, Finney drew the bow and let the arrow figuratively fly straight at the recalcitrant woman, crying out as he did so, "Thus will his arrow smite thee, O sinner, except thou repent!"   The woman fell senseless into the aisle.   I do not wish to convey the impression that Finney was guilty of any hypocrisy.   He believed implicitly that it was the power of God working through his own spirit that struck the woman down that He might subdue her to Himself.   But of course no scientific student of the human mind would for a moment admit any such assumption.   The woman was probably overcome by a force as natural as the stroke of the lightning or the blow of a club.   The gentleman just mentioned above called my attention also to the marvellous eye which Finney possessed.   By its aid, mob after mob of riotous men parted and allowed him to pass through, and he was able in a few moments to melt them into weeping.   After he became president of Oberlin, there were many students in that institution who would cross the street rather than meet him face to face.   It was partly because of the unpleasant questions he was in the habit of asking.   It was also because they felt that there was something veritably uncanny about this extraordinary man.

But just as no explanation of Finney's career would be sufficient which did not take into account this almost preternatural power of suggestion, so no explanation would be at all sufficient which did not recognize his higher ethical and spiritual qualities, and especially the possession of a very clear and vigorous intellect. It was this splendid quality, in combination with others, which finally came to modify, in Finney's career, the usual law of origin in impulsive movements. Indeed, as he preached on, the time came when merchants, judges, lawyers, physicians, — educated men of all the professional classes, — were the first to receive his message. In 1842 he was invited to Rochester by a petition signed by practically every lawyer in the city. There was already a religious interest in progress, under one Jedediah Burchard, which drew off the common people, and Finney's audiences were composed of the intellectual elite of the community, including the lawyers who were the sponsors of the movement. As Finney spoke on from night to night, the interest deepened, and finally he was requested to deliver a sermon expressly to the legal profession. At the conclusion of his address a judge of the court of appeals walked up the narrow stairway to the pulpit and said, "Mr. Finney, pray for me by name, and I will take the anxious seat." Immediately the whole body of lawyers arose in the centre of the

house and crowded into the aisles toward the " anxious seat," wherever they could find a place to
kneel.

In the winter of 1855–1856 Finney was again in
Rochester at the request of the lawyers, who asked
of him a course of lectures on "the moral government of God." On this latter occasion, also, many
of the natural leaders of the city's population were
brought into the membership of the churches.
The seed evidently fell here on good ground, for
it is asserted by judicious investigators that the
very unusual religious history of Rochester was
moulded and fashioned in those early years by the
personality of Charles G. Finney. Long before
his life's close, he became in many parts of the
United States, as well as in England, the most
conspicuous evangel in his generation of the important beliefs and truths which have given Christianity preëminence, such as the immortality of the
soul, the love of God for sinners, and the glory of
a blameless life.

And now we are getting into modern days. With
Finney the reign of crude irrational fear in revival
preaching came to an end. The violent appeals
to terror which had been so characteristic of the
previous century were losing their power over
men, and the spirit of the age began to be reflected
in Finney. It was not that he ceased to magnify
the guilt of the sinner and the awful retribution
due to sin. He never forsook this line of appeal.
But it was rather in a fresh and vigorous aiming

at the conscience and the will, in a new and larger emphasis upon the love of God, that Finney shows his kinship with the modern age.

The revival of 1857, so extended as to be fairly national in its proportions, was the connecting link between the old days and the new, between the former and the latter half of the century in its religious aspect.   Cradled in an atmosphere of financial fear, this revival speedily threw off its swaddling clothes and became a quiet, deep and sane spiritual movement which pervaded and invigorated the higher life of the American people. It was a revival characterized not by preaching but by prayer, by an intense desire on the part of a great multitude of people for personal communion with Him who is invisible and eternal.   The influence of impassioned hypnotic harangue and of appeal to baser instinctive emotion is therefore not so clearly traceable as in the earlier time.

In the latter, half of the nineteenth century there is one name that stands above every other in religious evangelism, — that of Dwight L. Moody. He was as truly a peerless organizing genius in the religious world as any man who can be described in such terms in the industrial or political world.   He was not only a great and successful leader of popular revival movements for many years, but his superior constructive and administrative ability is shown in the various educational enterprises which he established upon secure foundations — the Bible school at Chicago, the boys' and girls' preparatory institutions at Mount Hermon and Northfield, and the summer assemblies for college men and women. And none of them are so much schools of theology as of practical education and especially of practical training in religion. Moody was not a theologian. His life was too busy for the study of philosophy, and his doctrinal views were simply taken over, truth and error together, from a bygone age. But theological necessity never manacled him. When it came to a crisis, theology went by the board, and religious experience and common sense were his guides. He would have subscribed to the substitutional theory of the atonement, that Christ suffered and died in our place to appease God's wrath. But no man could deal this monstrous doctrine a more deadly blow than he when he said: "I used to think of God as a stern judge on the throne, from whose wrath Jesus Christ had saved me. It seems to me now that I could not have a falser idea of God than that. Since I have become a father, I have made this discovery, that it takes more love and self-sacrifice for the father to give up the son than it does for the son to die."

With Moody, religious evangelism is emancipated from the horrid spectres of irrational fear. I do not mean that he was blind to the natural law of retribution. As powerfully as Finney he penetrated to the consciences of men and made them understand and feel the effect of sin upon character, both here and hereafter. There was no thoughtless optimism about his preaching of divine justice. But the old emphasis was completely changed. Moody's favorite theme was the love of the heavenly Father. He believed that the lash of terror is for slaves and not for the freeborn of Almighty God. His appeals were no less convincing. Of this any man might satisfy himself by sitting under such a sermon as Moody used to deliver from the text, "The Son of Man is come to seek and to save that which is lost." If he did not always appeal to the very highest that was in his hearers, he came far nearer to it than most revivalists who had preceded him. If the balance of reason and emotion was not always perfect, there was always a saving measure of rational control, and men rarely went away the worse for having listened. The peculiar mental and nervous revival phenomena which were naturally passing away with the broadening of experience and environment, with the growth of intelligent inhibition in the population, ceased almost entirely in the Moody movement with the elimination of irrational fear and gross emotional excitement.

I shall hope not to offend needlessly many good people when I affirm a conviction that one of the secrets of Moody's wonderful success in the field of pure revivalism was his past-mastership in the art of hypnotism. This quality differed from Finney's mainly in its greater refinement. That he was perfectly unconscious of this remarkable gift, I have no doubt. But he possessed it. In the power sharply to arrest the attention of an audience by unique remarks at the opening of the sermon, in the skill with which he could distract their attention from all other concerns and bring about a condition of total inhibition of all other ideas except those connected with immediate salvation, in the ability to arouse the higher emotions, in the discernment of the psychological moment when he should call for an immediate execution of his suggestion of "surrender" on the part of his hearers, he was probably without a peer among the religious leaders of his day and generation. A friend of mine who attended one of his inquiry meetings in the early days solely as a scientific observer, and whom Moody knew to be such, was excluded on the ground that his presence would interfere with the freedom of the meeting. And so it would have, as any student of the phenomena of "crowd" hypnotism knows.

There came a remarkable change in the direction of his fine energies in the later years of Moody's life. Suddenly, at what seemed on the surface to be the summit of his popular successes, he turned aside and devoted himself, not entirely but very largely, to the systematic instruction, training and inspiration of those already Christians, that he might make of them personal centres for the ingathering of fresh converts; and his chief interest seemed to centre in the carefully balanced training, scientific as well as religious, of young men and women. I think the time will come when it will be recognized that Dwight L. Moody never exerted such an influence for the higher life of the nation and the world as he did when he presided over the great conventions of English, Canadian and American college men at Northfield in that long series of summer conferences beginning in the eighties and ending only with the close of his eventful life. Purely psychic impression cut very little figure there, although of course it can never be absolutely eliminated when speaker and psychological "crowd" meet. But Moody had before him some of the best blood of the Anglo-Saxon race, young men trained in liberalism and the critical habit, not easily swept from their moorings by arts of suggestion. They smiled now and then at his syntax and yawned over some of his interpretations of the Hebrew Scriptures, but they believed in him as they did in their own mothers, and respected him as they did the best of their college professors. His rugged sense, his spiritual vision, his powerful proclamation of the gospel of good cheer and faith and love, his catholicity of soul that led him to add Henry Drummond and George Adam Smith to his faculty of summer instruction in spite of the rumble of ultra-orthodox dissent — they saw in all these qualities evidences of a great human spirit that could adapt itself perfectly to experience and environment. And they were not wrong in their measurement of him. From the days of the civil war until his life's end he was an important and inspiring figure in the social and religious life of the nation. And it is simply limitless folly to . depreciate, as I have heard some persons attempt to do, the services and sacrifices of such a man.

I do not know what it was which led Moody to recognize so suddenly the limitations of a religious method so closely associated with revival excitement and the revival "crowd." It may have been the immense shrinkage between the number of professed conversions and ensuing church membership. It may have been the increasing difficulty of making even a passing impression upon the great centres of population which, Moody had the discernment to see, are strategic religiously as well as industrially and politically. The time came when the evangelist's frequent visits to New York City were forgotten almost before they were concluded, and when, according to the statistics of his own manager, it required $7000 of expenditure to gather thirty-three people into the churches — over $200 per capita.

As a matter of fact, revival movements of magnitude have become far less common in the more highly developed sections of the country. The change which Moody experienced is only part of a process over which many devout persons grieve, — the progressive decline of revival in large areas of the American population. Along with the growing practical ineffectiveness in the method has gone moral degeneration in its application. Revival crowds have become not gospel hardened so much as method hardened, and many and absurd are the devices employed to soften hard hearts. Instead of the severe form of separation from the world involved in pressing forward to the "anxious seat," evangelists are quite content if penitents will rise where they are sitting, or, failing in this, if they will signify a change of life purpose by the uplifted hand! I have even heard revivalists request their audiences to bow their heads and close their eyes, that when the hand was lifted no one should see, as one of them phrased it, save "the Lord and myself." Long before this stage was reached, such feeble attempts to enmesh the unwary had ceased to command the respect of thoughtful persons.

And along with moral degeneration of method has frequently gone spiritual decay in revivalist personality. Of course I am not speaking universally, for there are noble and notable exceptions, but peripatetic evangelists as a class have not the influence to which they ought normally to be entitled, in the more intelligent and highly developed communities. The mantle of power has not fallen from Elijah upon Elisha. Rather we have had too many instances in the public view of formal, official, commercial, hypnotic manipulation of revival crowds. It would obviously be indiscreet were I to print illustrative personal material, which is, however, not lacking. In some cases the individuals themselves and in others their near relatives are yet alive. I will content myself with one or

two milder citations from the practices of men very
well known in their time in the sphere of evangelism.   One man was accustomed to close a revival
with a personal statement.   He told the people
that if they were grateful for his services, as many
had expressed themselves as being, nothing would
please him more than to receive their autographs.
He suggested to them that they place a short letter
signed with their own names in an envelope, *along
with the amount they were willing to contribute*, and
deposit the same in the collection plates at the
final meeting.   Somebody who was suspicious of
the plan followed him into the railway car when
he left the city and saw him open the envelopes
and tear up and throw out the letters one by one
without reading.   But he retained the money.   He
evidently was acquainted with the commercial
value of publicity and its stimulation to larger
giving.   One revivalist constantly conveyed the
impression that, after he left the city, there would
be very little chance for the conversion of sinners.
" If you are to go on and lead happy Christian
lives," he would say at the conclusion of his series
of meetings, "you must buy my hymnal.   You
must continue to sing the hymns you sang at the
time you were converted.   My young man will
have them on sale at the door.   A great many have
applied for my photograph, wishing the shadow to
remain when the substance has gone elsewhere.
The young gentleman downstairs will supply
these also at a reasonable price."   Under the

ministrations of this man at this time in a leading city of the West, two or three thousand people were published as converted. Only five hundred and forty of these were taken into the churches. The statistics and the judgment of one of the sanest men I ever knew, who was thoroughly familiar with the facts and in entire sympathy with religious movements, even though strongly emotional, combine to indicate that at least three-quarters of all who were temporarily influenced were not transformed in any sense as to their life purposes. And instances of this sort can be multiplied many times in the annals of hypnotic revivalism. Many other men, whose financial arrangements have been entirely unselfish and above reproach, in their intense desire for large numbers of so-called converts, in their strenuous efforts to stay the tide of decline, have consciously or unconsciously practised so perfectly the arts of suggestion that their revivals have come to be little more than semi-hypnotic seances masquerading in the name of religion.

Several reasons have been urged for the decline of this particular method of bringing men to real repentance and newness of life. Some of them have a bearing upon the true reason, and others are more or less important factors in a true explanation. For instance, it is declared with some justice that we are under the dominion of a too radical evolutionary theory of sin. Evil is only good in the making, and why agonize over it as

the fathers did?   The great process will go on.
The survival of the fittest means ultimately the
survival of the best.   The generations that follow
will be somewhat better than the generations that
are gone, and therefore why stir men's souls to
white heat about sin and righteousness and judgment to come?   And so we have entered the régime
of an ethical and spiritual *laissez faire*.   And revivals have declined because the sense of sin has
been weakened in the population.   It is an argument which is worthy of attention, for whatever its
intellectual faults, the old-time revival did often
make a wicked man *think* of his sin, and agonize
over it, too, until frequently he was ready to throw
all his strength into the struggle against its power.
The indictment of the revival at this point is that
it made no rational discrimination between the
utterly vile, the far less sinful and little children.
All alike were exposed every moment to the wrath
of God.   An awful conviction of sin, which is
either a matter of temperament or of reaction from
a riotous career, was made the *sine qua non* of conversion for every soul.   It was a psychological
absurdity, and the revulsion against it may have
gone too far.   But, however that may be, decline
in the sense of sin has contributed to decline in
revival.   The terrors of the law and the dread
visitation of divine anger upon the children of
disobedience were powerful sanctions.   And they
have passed away, at least in the terms of belief of
the old régime.   This, and other reasons which

have been advanced,[1] such as the increase of material prosperity, the growth of the critical habit, the widening of the range of human motive, the passing of superstition, are only parts of one complete explanation ; namely that large areas of the American population have undergone marked mental evolution under the stress of a complex experience and a rapidly differentiating social environment. The great growth in knowledge through public education, the enormously increased facilities for communication, the very struggle and competition of modern life, especially in the great centres, have developed in the average man an intelligence, a self-control, a power of rational inhibition, that make him far less suggestible, less nervously unstable, less imitative, less liable to be swept away by great gusts of passion or emotion. He is in many respects less of a primitive and more of a highly civilized man, and over him the old revival method has correspondingly lost its power. They who are preaching a revival of old-time revivalism in the highly developed sections of America are fighting against the stars in their courses. Recurring tides of faith there may be for generations to come, but they will steadily change in character from those of the old régime. It will require a more rational method to win men in the modern age.

There is a national decline in revival, even in church going, but there is no parallel evidence of a

[1] Cf. Coe, "The Religion of a Mature Mind."

national decline in morals, however imperfect our industrial and commercial ethics may still be. The public mind of America, as it shows itself in its choice of national leaders, in its criticism of public policies, was never so vitally ethical as it is to-day. As it manifests itself in its attitude towards Cuba, for example, towards the brown people of the Philippines, towards Federal corruption, towards the misgovernment of cities, towards all forms of philanthropy, even towards the rights of negroes and Indians, towards the affording of an equal opportunity to all men, rich and poor, it is ethically far in advance of the national mind of a generation ago. There is no evidence of widespread decline in sympathy, in integrity, in quick conscience, in sense of social responsibility. There is a real enthusiasm for pure and undefiled religion among vast numbers of the people. Far too much of it is unecclesiastical, but it is none the less vital. The institutional methods of the army, the navy, the railroad and the general Christian associations attract and hold increasing numbers of young men who are reverent and loyal to the Christian profession. The religious instinct, instead of being eliminated in the process of mental evolution, has come to its flower within the last quarter of a century in those training schools of intellectual, social and political leadership — the colleges of America. The strength and genuineness of this recent religious movement is unquestioned among intelligent observers. It was not brought about by the old-time methods.   They would have been impotent to accomplish it.

The decline in revival is only partial and confined to certain rather highly developed areas of population.   We have still within our borders many heterogeneous and highly emotional elements.   In the tropical dependencies, among the negroes and Indians, in isolated and backward communities, in those parts of the country where environment and temperament combine to foster emotionalism, the forms of impulsive social action, whether religious, judicial or political, will linger long.   Indeed it is conceivable, though it is unlikely, that our whole people might be plunged into the moral and spiritual condition of eighteenth-century England, when it might be necessary, in one sudden outburst of instinct and emotion, to brave all the evils that follow in the train.   And such a movement might conceivably advance the moral and social order.   But if we remain a sanely progressive people, moving steadily and rationally forward in the path of social evolution, primitive religious habits will be sloughed off, and popular religious movements will assume new forms in harmony with modern development and enlightenment.

CHAPTER XI

A NATURAL EXPLANATION OF CERTAIN REVIVAL PHENOMENA

It will not be necessary to rehearse in detail certain characteristic phenomena which have appeared again and again in our studies of the revivals of a marked type in this country and Great Britain. The violent spasmodic action, the contortions of the body, the shouting, the trembling, the hypnotic rigidity and, at the other extreme, the sinking of muscular energy, the trance and the vision — with all these we have become sufficiently familiar. Everywhere we have come upon evidence of a high degree of nervous instability and suggestibility, of a plastic and susceptible mental and nervous organization. Oftentimes it has been clear that we have been dealing with a population which, without improper stretching of the term, might be classed as primitive in experience and environment. Sometimes, also, it has been as clear that a population far advanced in civilization has been, under certain circumstances, temporarily reduced to a primitive mental and nervous condition by the application of revival methods, by the influence of the revival " crowd." But these strange effects are not peculiar to the religious revivals of America, of England or even of Christendom. They were phenomena of the social and religious epidemics of western Europe in the middle ages, where the perfectly enormous amount of mental and nervous instability in evidence was due not only to special conditions, such as the massing of women in convents, but also to barbaric inheritance. They might have been observed in the frenzy worship of the followers of ancient Bacchus, and they accompany the evolutions and howlings of the modern Mohammedan dervishes. Two factors are essential to their appearance in strength — a season of high excitement and the gathering together of the population in psychological "crowds." They have been most common in times of great religious fervor simply because there are no themes which a population deems so vital to present and eternal happiness as religious themes; there is nothing which has shown itself in history which is capable of creating such powerful emotion as intense and prolonged meditation upon men's relation to God and a world and a judgment to come. These phenomena usually affect not the intelligent and the self-controlled, but the undeveloped, the unenlightened, those who are easily swept away by imagination and emotion and are not subject to the higher rational processes, those in whom primitive mental and nervous instability yet linger. And everywhere they are propagated by suggestion and imitation.

For long ages only a supernatural interpretation of these effects was attempted. In our own country this primitive tendency to ascribe miraculous validity to obscure bodily and mental phenomena first received a real check on its mental side from no less a spiritual prophet than Jonathan Edwards. While yet inconsistently attributing the "bodily effects" to the actual presence and power of the Spirit of God, he came to look upon impulses and impressions, upon prophesyings and speakings with tongues, upon special visions and revelations, as childish things which would cease as Christianity attained its majority. "The glory of the approaching happy state of the church does not at all require these extraordinary gifts. As that state of the church will be the nearest of any to its perfect state in heaven, so I believe it will be like it in this, that all extraordinary gifts shall have vanished away. . . . For my part, I had rather enjoy the sweet influences of the Spirit, drawing forth the holy exercises of faith, divine love, sweet complacence and humble joy in God one-quarter of an hour, than to have prophetical visions and revelations the whole year." [1]

But even Edwards looked upon these phenomena as miraculous gifts for an early stage of spiritual development. And it is only in our own time that this form of supernatural explanation has largely ceased in popular religious thought. Within the

[1] "Distinguishing Marks," etc., Vol. I, pp. 556, 558; quoted in Allen, "Jonathan Edwards," p. 173.

memory of men now living, some of these phenomena have been widely regarded as climacteric attestations of the divine spirit to the work of grace. And there are parts of America to-day where the religious section of the population believes no other interpretation.

Speaking historically, this supernatural theory has assumed two forms. Sometimes God has been made directly responsible for these phenomena, sometimes the devil. Such peculiarly instinctive and animal reflexes could never have been regarded as of deep spiritual import by any moderately intelligent population except for that strange tendency of the uncritical mind to look upon that as most divine which appears to be farthest removed from law and order. The deeply mysterious, the abnormal, yea, the irrational — this is miraculous, this is supernatural. God is in the midst of it, while that which has been reduced to the natural process is empty of and needeth not His presence! When the manifestations have been too dreadful for belief that they were directly caused by a benevolent and intelligent divinity, they have been ascribed to demon possession or to some malign supernatural influence. This form of the theological explanation, practically universal among primitive people and frequently employed in the religious literature of all races, reached its highest logical development in the Miltonic conception of a personal devil who has seemed at times to share with Almighty God the rulership of men.

It was of course this theory which was at the basis of the witchcraft delusion, and it has been employed times without number to explain some of the evils of uncontrolled revivalism. The conviction that there exists an exceedingly powerful personal devil is still strong with thousands of religious and irreligious people alike in America and in other lands. It is only the more thoughtful who have emancipated themselves from the traditional belief. Very slowly the more advanced populations are coming to realize that this is God's world in process of evolution from the animal to the spiritual, that it is not the devil's at all, and that there is not a shred of rational evidence of a purely malign supernatural being in the universe.

The miraculous explanation has been succeeded by the pathological, that the phenomena can be accounted for only by disease and serious functional derangement of the nervous system. Certain sporadic cases can undoubtedly be so explained, but not, I think, the extraordinary and widespread exhibitions of mental and nervous instability which we have studied in the preceding pages, affecting at times a large fraction of the whole community. I venture to suggest that the general explanation of these facts will be found to be grounded in normal individual and social psychology and not in pathology.

Darwin long ago called our attention to the very natural forms of expression of emotion in man and

animals.[1] When the cerebro-spinal system is highly
excited, nervous energy is generated, or at least
liberated in excess, and frequently expends itself,
independently of the will, in channels of action
which are most habitual to the subject; if not
always plainly in habitual muscular movements,
then in other channels of expenditure which are
natural to the subject because of the peculiar constitution of his nervous system. The negro revival
trance, developed under religious excitement, may
be as truly a form of involuntary expenditure of
nervous energy as the Kentucky "jerks." Usually
the habitual muscular routes are followed. The
religious shouter vents the liberated energy through
his respiratory apparatus. The highly motor Kentuckian of 1800 found relief in the use of the
voice, in distortions of the face and by bringing
into vigorous action the upper and lower extremi-
ties. If the customary outlet is insufficient, then
there will be an overflow into the less habitual
channels.[2]

There are still other interesting suggestions of
Darwin in the work to which I have referred
which have, I believe, an important bearing on
what seems to me to be the natural explanation of
these peculiar revival phenomena. For example,
he calls attention to the fact that exciting emotions
in animals seem to require for their relief or

---

[1] Cf. "The Expression of the Emotions in Man and Animals,"
Darwin, p. 66 f.

[2] Cf. Spencer, quoted by Darwin, *op. cit.,* p. 71.

gratification some energetic movement. The anticipation of delights leads in children to loud laughter, jumping, the clapping of hands and other purposeless muscular activity. But of all emotions in men and animals, fear is the most exciting, as well as the most depressing. At first it leads to violent motor reflexes, but at last to the sinking of energy, utter prostration, fainting and convulsions. Some reflexes are not at all serviceable, as when strong excitement interferes with the steady flow of nerve force to the muscles and violent trembling ensues. Other reflexes were originally highly serviceable, having been born of the long and terrible period of the pain economy and struggle for life to which animals and the early races of men have been subject. Some forms of muscular contortion have proved a means of escape from the cause of the suffering, or at least have furnished relief in pain, and so have become habitual. Sometimes the relief takes the form of temporary paralysis, as when the animal becomes motionless as death in the presence of great danger; sometimes, in man, the relief comes through the decline of rational consciousness and the uprush of a sort of subconsciousness, as when in the ecstasy of religious fervor the martyr at the stake becomes insensible to torture.

This tendency to serviceable reflex action is in primitive man no doubt partly the result of an animal inheritance, developed and intensified by habitual association in his own experience. Not to speak of other emotions, then, fear and joy in the human race are naturally accompanied by animal and primitive reflexes, the cruder forms of which disappear only with the growth of the power of inhibition in the midst of a wider and less painful experience and environment.

These facts have application, I think, to the social psychology of the revival. The motor and sensory reflexes are always correlated with strong imagination and emotion. Imagination and emotion, themselves ever in association, are greatly strengthened by intensity of belief or expectation. Now there is no form of gathering among men where the elements of belief, of imagination, of emotion, are more powerfully combined than in the revival "crowd." Just as there are no beliefs which are so momentous as religious beliefs, so there is no form of imagination and emotion so intense as the religious. These factors have been present in power in every typical revival gathering. Their influence has oftentimes been greatly increased by the skilful appeals of preacher and exhorter. Latent imagination and emotion, multiplied by the direct suggestion of the speaker and the reciprocal suggestion of the audience, have produced such excitation of the cerebro-spinal system that the freed nervous energy has expended itself in motor and sensory automatisms of varying kinds and degrees.

To make the matter more concrete, let us reflect that the emotions most frequently excited in the revival are fear and joy. The appeal to joy is in anticipation of the glory and the blessedness that shall follow a life of righteousness. We have seen that the tendency of unrestrained joy is to arouse in animals and primitive man the whole muscular system, producing involuntary dancing, leaping or automatic laughter. The appeal to fear in the revivals of the past has been based upon two forms of this dread emotion. There has been the fear of retribution for sin, produced by the preacher in vivid imaginative pictures of a hell of endless torments and of endless remorse. There is also in the average man a great slumbering mass of fear that he cannot shake off, made up of instincts and feelings inherited from a long human and animal past. This can be awakened in ways that every psychologist understands theoretically and that the skilful revivalist employs practically. Under conditions which will bring men together, sharply arrest their attention, fix their minds upon issues of the gravest import for time and for eternity and distinctly discourage all critical thought, — under these conditions men will be governed chiefly by their feelings, and their action, in general, will be reflex and impulsive rather than deliberative. That is, for the time being, their mental make-up will revert to the primitive type. With few exceptions, each individual's power of inhibition will be swallowed up in the maelstrom, and every wave of emotion, whether of fear or of joy, will sweep the major portion of the audience with it.

Now I hold that the crowd which becomes thoroughly primitive in feeling has a strong tendency also to become primitive in reflexes. No one can appreciate in our day, unless he has made a careful investigation of the records, what a frightful agonizing because of sin the old-time revival developed in its votaries. Fear was the central motive in the religious psychology of the period, and to fear the appeal was made. The wrath of God, the terrors of the law, the doom of the non-elect or of the impenitent, the everlasting torment of the lost, — these beliefs, held as self-evident, were pressed home upon revival crowds with consummate skill and power. And under the weight of spiritual agony and contortion, in the temporary absence of rational inhibition, the ancient primitive reflexes asserted themselves to relieve the strain of dread and danger. It is easy to see now why the more revolting phenomena ceased, as they largely did in the more advanced sections of the country, with the decline of the emphasis upon fear and the rise of the emphasis upon the higher emotions.

Of course the phenomena always affect first the most susceptible in the assembly and then spread by sympathetic contagion and imitation. When these latter forces are operating with intensity, sometimes exceedingly self-controlled persons will be drawn into the current. A friend of mine, who at least in his later years has as perfect mastery of himself as any man I know, at the age of twenty happened one day to be standing as a spectator on the fringe of a southern camp-meeting of two thousand people. He had had no religious experience and at that time did not wish any. The crowd was laboring under great religious excitement, and reflex phenomena were abundantly in evidence. Suddenly my friend found himself with his hands pressed against his lungs, shouting, "Hallelujah!" at the top of his voice. He had been unconsciously drawn into the maelstrom.

Dr. Leonard Woolsey Bacon, in his history of American Christianity,[1] relates a similar instance which came under the personal observation of an able and prominent clergyman of the Methodist denomination, Dr. David P. Durbin. The latter was about to preach at a southern camp-meeting when he observed a young giant of a backwoodsman on the outskirts of the crowd, evidently with full intention of disturbing the meeting. In a little time the young man came under the influence of the environment, and evidently, with a strong determination not to yield, grasped with both hands a hickory sapling close by, "but was whirled round and round until the bark of the sapling peeled off in his grasp." The subject was not at all under the sway of religious sentiment.

It therefore follows that spiritual conviction and peculiar physical and mental manifestation are by no means necessarily correlated. Dr. Archibald Alexander also had an interesting experience in

[1] p. 240, note.

the south which thoroughly illustrates my proposition. The sermon was a very impressive one, and the people were generally attentive, except a few old tobacco planters in the rear of the room, who paid no attention to the discourse, but talked together in a low tone upon subjects connected with their industry. Suddenly the preacher became very vehement and boisterous, and immediately there was a response in the centre of the house indicating strong emotion. A female voice broke forth in a piercing cry. Then the people began to rise, one after another, in different parts of the room, under extreme agitation. The women threw off their bonnets and shouted, as did some of the men, in a most uncontrolled fashion. The sympathetic wave spread from the centre to the circumference, and the whole audience was swayed like a forest in a mighty wind. Dr. Alexander himself is on record as having found it necessary to put forth a conscious effort of resistance in order to hold himself steady in the violence of the storm, and he testifies that the old tobacco planters in the rear, who had not listened to one word of the sermon, displayed tremulous emotion in every muscle of their brawny faces, while the tears coursed down their wrinkled cheeks. A quieting song subdued them all in a moment.

The influence of partial hypnotization is always at work in the crowd which is laboring under the pressure of great religious excitement. The element of full consciousness is present, but is feeble.

Sometimes the power of subtle suggestion emanates from the skilful preacher. Sometimes there is self-hypnotization as the result of prolonged concentration of mind upon a single object or a single subject. Whatever be the form of it, it will never fail to do its work upon those impressionable persons in every audience whose powers of reason and volition are not normally regnant. Under such general conditions any hypnotist, religious or other, can produce prostrations or trances at will.[1]

Hypnotization is a most direct form of the removal of rational inhibition, and then under the influence of simple suggestion in the laboratory, or of the appeal to fear or other strong emotion in the public religious audience, the primitive reflexes reappear. And when once they have manifested themselves in the most susceptible, the terrible apprehension that this mysterious agency may gain possession of their own spirits acts as a powerful suggestion to that end upon others throughout the audience who are less impressionable, but who are nevertheless suddenly overcome.

This is the explanation of the catalepsies that befell many under John Wesley's sermons and that have been widely attributed even in our own day to "the power of the Holy Ghost." For example, it furnishes an entirely adequate explanation of the famous and widely quoted Quaker case. The critical Friend was much offended at what he re-

[1] Cf. the practice of Charcot and Pierre Janet.

garded as simulated manifestations in the Baldwin
street audiences at Bristol.   He was knitting his
brows and biting his lips in displeasure when he,
too, was struck down in a moment as by a bolt
from out the blue.   After prayer by Mr. Wesley,
the Quaker lifted up his head and cried aloud,
" Now I know that thou art a prophet of the
Lord." [1]

The same method is followed among the Puget
Sound Indians.   The chief feature in their converts' meetings is the ringing of bells and the
making of other tremendous noises until they in-
duce-cataleptic states and sometimes chronic convulsions in numerous individuals.   If they can get
a sceptic or scoffer into the meeting, they gather
round him and bombard him with these phenomena
until finally he falls and is thereafter reckoned
among the " converts."

Although the subject is an obscure one and difficult, I think particular application of this natural
theory of explanation may be made at least to certain of the phenomena not heretofore specifically
mentioned ; for example, to revival hallucinations
and visions.   Until recent years, in the judgment
of a very competent observer,[2] a large proportion,
perhaps even a majority, of the converts in revivals
habitually experienced temporary hallucinations
of all sorts, coherent and incoherent, grotesque

[1] Wesley's " Journal," Vol. I, p. 130.
[2] Dr. James M. Buckley, " Faith Healing and Kindred Phenomena," p. 171.

and refined.   They are not now common within the areas of high mental development.   They have disappeared under the solvent of increasing knowledge, a widened experience, a more complex environment.   But attention has already been called to the practical universality of such phenomena in the primitive revival worship of the negroes and Indians in this country at the present time.   And they are very common among the peasantry of all nations.   In all these cases they are evidently the product of a plastic and undeveloped mental and nervous organization.   They appear ordinarily only under mental stress.   They are not necessarily evidences of pathological weakness at all.   There are hallucinations and visions of the sane as well as hallucinations and visions of the insane.   The second only are in the strict sense pathological and abnormal.   This distinction was long ago made by no less eminent an expert in mental disease than Griesinger,[1] who not only cited many cases among highly distinguished and intellectual persons, — Goethe, Walter Scott, Pascal and others, — but expressed the judgment formed from wide observation that they occur not rarely but frequently among men with mental development below the average.   No statistical investigation of this matter has ever been conducted on a sufficiently broad inductive basis, but the negro and Indian populations in America would unquestionably afford a most fruitful field for such an inquiry.

[1] Buckley, *op. cit.*, p. 169.

A. Brierre de Boismont [1] has gone a step farther and distinguished two varieties of hallucinations of the sane, "those which are corrected by the understanding, and those which on account of superstition, sluggishness of thought, love of the marvellous, inability to interpret them correctly, or because the emotions which they excite make calm consideration impossible, are not corrected." That is, that part of the population in which rational inhibition has developed overcome their hallucinations, distrust them, put them under foot, finally banish them altogether, while that large section which is primitive, which is mentally undeveloped, continues to harbor the delusions, and if they be of a religious character, regards them as supernatural evidences of the Spirit's presence or as the divine credentials of conversion. In the South, among the negroes, these illusory trains of images, these purely subjective visions, are even quoted in proof of doctrine or in refutation of an adversary, as indeed they were throughout the middle ages in the church of western Europe.

But it is clear that an hallucination is an hallucination, and a vision is a vision, whether it occur under great religious emotion or entirely apart from it. If it be widespread, it is an evidence of a highly plastic mental and nervous organization and a tendency to primitive reflexes in a population. And under the stress of great excitement, especially in a religious gathering which has been

[1] Buckley, *op. cit.*, p. 170.

brought under the dominion of mental agony and fear, such phenomena may be expected to occur with naturalness and frequency. They will appear also in persons who are by no means good subjects, under the impulse of profound meditation and concentration and especially of strong desire and expectation.[1] Why the outflow of liberated energy should take the sensory rather than the motor channel is a secret wrapped up with peculiar nerve-cell connections and the special constitution of the nervous system in the individual.

The complete lapsing of self-consciousness in the religious trance is a similar product, except that hypnotization plays a characteristic part. Indeed, a strongly volitional individual can produce the dissociation between the conscious and the unconscious self not only in others but in his own personality, entirely apart from association or communication with his fellows. Thus is attained that individual " absorption in the Infinite " which is the spiritual goal of many religious minds. The well-known " sleeping cases " of the Irish revival were developed through this process of auto-hypnotization. They attracted wide attention among the common people and were deemed miraculous. The subjects of this phenomenon had the power of inducing slumber in themselves for a considerable period and of waking at a specified time. Dr. McCosh, it will be remembered, effectually pricked this bubble of marvel by citing the instance of the

[1] Buckley, *op. cit.*, p. 180.

oriental fakir who, before he passes into his hibernat-
ing trance, announces when he shall awake, strongly
impresses upon his mind the day or the hour of
his return to consciousness and fulfils his prediction to the letter, — far more wonderful cases than
those of Ireland, said McCosh, but produced in the
same way by the influence of the imagination upon
the voluntary muscles.   Both self-hypnotization
and the entrancement of subjects in a revival
crowd arise primarily from the same predisposing
circumstances ; namely, the distraction of attention
from the manifold experiences and concerns of life,
and limitation of the field of consciousness to a
single subject or a single object and the prolonged
centralization of the mind thereupon.   Under these
conditions inhibitive control soon vanishes and entrancement in susceptible persons succeeds.

The stages of these psychic processes in religious cases were definitely observed in the revival
of 1859 in Ireland, and are recounted in Gibson's
" Year of Grace."[1]   There was first an awful apprehension of impending evil, a fearful looking
forward to judgment and fiery indignation, accompanied by crushing pressure in the region of
the heart, inducing despairing cries and groans of
agony.   Then followed a period of fierce wrestling,
sometimes real, sometimes imaginary, with the evil
one, whose personality was apprehended with terrible distinctness.   Then there came a transition
out of the deep depression into a calmer state of

[1] p. 72.

feeling, and some object earnestly desired stood
out before the view.   Now appeared the entranc-
ing vision, with mutterings of "O Blessed Jesus,
come, Thou art my hope, my all; wash me in the
precious blood," etc.   In this stage images flitted
before the mind with all the vividness of reality.
There was an evident excitation of the ganglia
connected with sight.   Then there ensued a sense
of relief, a feeling of lightness, the assurance of
forgiveness, prompting to an outburst of praise.
The last stage was one of great languor and exhaustion, showing what a tremendous output of
nervous force, freed under excitement, had been
expended in these strange psychic experiences.
Not only delicate women, but strong men, were un-
fitted for work for days.

The temporary loss of leadership on the part of
the higher brain centres under great excitement in
a revival crowd has manifested itself also in what
is known as "the gift of tongues," or glossolalia.
It was never a "spiritual" phenomenon, but probably always a perfectly natural one, whether it
appeared in the first century or the twentieth.
The day of Pentecost and the years that follow
constitute a period when vast primitive populations
were in the throes of the greatest religious revolution that ever has been known among men.   A
great hope and the prospect of a new life of
achievement and of character were, for the first
time in this world, breathed into the soul of the
common man.   Criticism may well stand with un-

covered head in the presence of the unparalleled
stirring of emotion in that early age of exceedingly
imperfect knowledge of all the psychic processes.
It is one of the many marks of the splendid sanity
of the Apostle Paul that he regarded the gift of
tongues as a low order of spiritual endowment.
He puts the enthusiasts who were thus affected
last of all in the array of orders that God hath
set in His church,[1] and he advises the Corinthian
people to desire most earnestly greater gifts
($\tau\grave{a}$ $\chi a\rho\acute{\iota}\sigma\mu a\tau a$ $\tau\grave{a}$ $\mu\epsilon\acute{\iota}\zeta o\nu a$).   Though they might
speak with the tongues of men and of angels, if
they were without that love which doth not behave
itself unseemly, they were only sounding brass and
a clashing cymbal.   And he declares that though
on occasion he had been caught up into the sev-
enth heaven of the mystical consciousness, and
had himself spoken with tongues, howbeit in the
church he would rather speak five words with
the understanding that he might instruct others
also than ten thousand words in a tongue.   It required an immense amount of practical sense and
intelligent insight in that early time for a man of
the Apostle's mystical temperament to take this
stand.   But he saw the unfruitfulness of this phenomenon and the injury that was being inflicted
through it upon the higher life of the Corinthian
congregation.

   "Spiritual" speaking with tongues has probably
been commonly due to the loss of rational self-con-

[1] Cf. I Cor. xii. 28 f.

trol on the part of primitive, ignorant, highly excited individuals in a crowd which has been stirred
religiously to its depths.   The "gift" was a feature
of the first flush of Mormon fanaticism, where it
was observed and described.[1]   The witness testifies as follows :   " Those who speak in tongues are
generally the most illiterate among the ' saints,'
such as cannot command words as quick as they
would wish, and instead of waiting for a suitable
word to come to their memories they break forth
in the first sound their tongues can articulate,
no matter what it is.   Thus some person in the
meeting has told an interesting story about Zion,
then an excitable brother gets up to bear his ' testimony,' the speed of speech increasing with the
interest of the subject : ' Beloved brethren and
sisters, I rejoice, and my heart is glad to overflow-
ing — I hope to go to Zion, and to see you all
there and to — to — *O, me sontro von te, sontro von
terre, sontro von te.   O me palassate te,*' etc."

This example is open to the charge of being a
more or less conscious imitation of the more
natural and useful New Testament instances of
the day of Pentecost.   But this " gift " has long
been one of the regular accompaniments of demon
possession in the interior of China, where no imitation of New Testament models has been possible.
In primitive China when the supposed " spirit "
enters the subject, " the man's eyes close tightly,

[1] Cf. Hawthornwaite, "Adventures among the Mormons," 1857,
pp. 88–91 ; quoted in Riley, "Founder of Mormonism," p. 270.

his whole body trembles, his hands and feet continually move, his hair loosens from the braid — then he begins to speak, and is able to talk not only in his own dialect, but in others as well." [1]

The explanation appears to be that the subjects are, usually, devout but unlearned and ignorant people who lack power of expression of the emotions which crowd upon them in seasons of great religious excitement.   Under the pressure of overwrought mental condition rational control takes its flight, and the overheated brain breaks forth in articulations more or less unconscious, including odds and ends of languages and dialects with which the mind of the individual has become somewhat familiar.   Thus, among the early Mormons, the "tongues" were identified by the few critical listeners, notably an old trapper, as in some cases snatches of Indian dialects.   In China snatches of mandarin and other dialects were discriminated.

I have illustrated the theory which is here set forth with examples of a non-pathological character.   I am not saying that there may not be pathological elements which would enter into the explanation of particular instances.   There may often be.   The visions of Swedenborg and Mohammed were probably partly due to epileptic physical condition.   I am only saying that essentially we are dealing here with phenomena of normal crowd psychology.   There are instances,

[1] Article, "Demon Possession," *Fukhien Witness*, June, 1904, p. 7.   Published at Anglo-Chinese College, Foochow, China.

like the cases of blindness and dumbness in the Irish revivals, which unquestionably proceed from an organism that has been thoroughly weakened by great and prolonged emotional orgy. These cases never occurred except in persons who had been struck down a number of times by "conviction of sin." In many instances of morbid revival hysteria, too, the chief cause may be actual disease and degeneration of function, so that there may appear under unusual excitement a thoroughly abnormal instability of nerve centres.

The most important purely pathological phenomenon of superemotional revivals is insanity. Of the mental causes of insanity, the largest numbers are usually attributed to grief, terror and religious excitement.[1] The revival is not a form of religious mania, as some alienists have held,[2] but it presents far too many cases for the study of the alienist. I do not know that accurate statistical inquiry has ever been made anywhere into the percentages of religious lunacy which may occur in the various denominations. There is a priori probability, however, that the larger number of cases would fall within those sects which are prone to highly emotional methods. One would not expect to find much religious abnormality of this sort among the Quakers, for example.

Both conversion and religion are in themselves

---

[1] Cf., for example, Mayo-Smith, "Statistics and Sociology," p. 224.

[2] Cf. Boris Sidis, "The Psychology of Suggestion," p. 354, note,

normal and healthful and sane. The percentage of the insane was perhaps never higher in any country than during the days of revolution and popular renunciation of faith at the close of the eighteenth century in France.[1] The comforting and tranquilizing influence of undefiled religion upon society is too evident to require argument or even comment. But religion or religious method worthy of the name will neither weaken the will nor enfeeble the rational powers. And it is at least extremely probable that the highly emotional revival has weakened the sense of responsibility and the efforts at control in many persons of incipient insane impulses. Every unnecessary religious melancholiac or maniac is, so far forth, a lamentable commentary upon defective religious method.

The purely melancholiac cases, some of them reaching into mania, which we have observed under Wesley, Finney, Edwards and others, were in certain instances, it will be remembered, effectually cured by the revivalists themselves. The method followed in each instance was precisely that of the heathen exorcist. The priests of the Nichiren sect among the Japanese Buddhists, who have unusual strength of mind and force of will, are most successful practitioners in the same art of mental suggestion. Their specialty is the expulsion of fox spirits.[2]

[1] Cf. Wigan, "The Duality of Mind," p. 427.
[2] Cf. Nevius, "Demon Possession," p. 202, quoting Dr. Baelz, of the Imperial University of Japan.

Joseph Smith, Jr., was in the habit of treating early Mormon demoniacs in the same manner. A paragraph from his journal reads precisely like those which we have already quoted from Wesley's journal of the Bristol demoniacs. A man named Newell Knight was attacked by the "power of Satan" and was subject to "curious actions while thus afflicted."[1] "I went," says Smith, "and found him suffering very much in his mind, and his body acted upon in a very strange manner, his visage and limbs distorted and twisted in every shape and appearance possible to imagine, and finally he was caught up off the floor of the apartment and tossed about most fearfully. His situation was soon made known to the neighbors and relatives, and in a short time as many as eight or nine grown persons had gotten together to witness the scene. After he had thus suffered for a time, *I succeeded in getting hold of him by the hand*, when almost immediately he spoke to me and with very great earnestness required of me that I should cast the devil out of him, saying that he knew that he was in him and that he also knew I could cast him out. I replied, 'If you know that I can, it shall be done,' and then almost unconsciously he rebuked the devil and commanded him in the name of Jesus Christ to depart from him, when immediately Newell spoke out and said that he saw the devil leave him and vanish from his sight. This was the first

[1] Smith's "Journal," p. 50.

miracle that was done in this church." Wesley
was so cautious and so doubtful of the strange and
obscure effect of his own presence and influence
upon the Bristol sufferers that his account is very
modest and impersonal, although it was obviously
the power of his own personality which wrought
the cure. He even distinctly remarks that he leaves
every one to his own judgment of the matter.
But Smith sets himself up as a miracle worker on
the instant.   It is a simple incident, but it discrimi-
nates accurately the characters of these two widely
disparate religious leaders.

There seems to be a common explanation for
all these cases which display such striking simi-
larity. The incipient melancholia or mania became religious by the process of auto-suggestion.
The weak mind was overmastered under revival
pressure by ideas of grievous sin and apostasy
and of impending wrath and penalty.   And it was
the healing power of strong mental impression
which exorcised the obsessing demon — for the
demon even in China· is only an overmastering
idea — and restored the normal balance.

There is a single phenomenon more which I
wish to bring to the attention of the reader for the
purpose of offering a natural explanation. The
outbreak of impulsive action in revivals, originating almost always among the least self-controlled
of the congregation, may be interpreted in terms
of psychological law.   All revolutionary movements, whether religious, political or industrial, no

matter how carefully and wisely they may have been discussed beforehand by intelligent and well-balanced reformers, are subject to this law. Garrison, George William Curtis and John Brown were all prominent in the initiation of the anti-slavery crusade. The first two were thoughtful, responsible men. John Brown was a man of earnest sincerity, but an impulsive fanatic who did not reckon with the consequences. And he struck the first blow. So the Reign of Terror was inaugurated by the unorganized horde who sacked the gunsmith shops of Paris and then stormed the Bastile.

It is a matter of frequent observation on the part of those who are familiar with revival crowds that, ordinarily, the first to fall under the influence of the speaker and of the environment are the relatively impulsive, less rational, less responsible elements in the audience. It has sometimes been a source of chagrin and mortification to the intelligent, high-minded revivalist that this should occur. But it does usually occur under the free operation of the revival method, and it has often been an obstacle to the spread of pure and undefiled religion among sober and cultivated persons who have witnessed the phenomenon. For example, I have known a very promising religious awakening to be nipped in the bud in a moment by the sudden movement towards the altar of a recently discharged convict in whom the community and the audience had little confidence, and who was evidently temporarily overcome by the magnetism of the preacher. The most impressionable elements in a community come to be very well known and need not be of a criminal or vagabond type at all. They may be only the most nervously unstable and suggestible. When the movement toward religion in a community originates among them, as it commonly does under revival leadership, there is frequently positive injury done to the cause.

And there is only the most rudimentary psychological principle involved in all these cases.

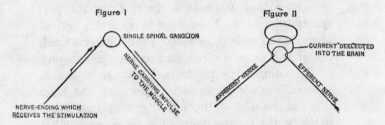

Figure I — SINGLE SPINAL GANGLION — NERVE CARRYING IMPULSE TO THE MUSCLE — NERVE-ENDING WHICH RECEIVES THE STIMULATION

Figure II — CURRENT DEFLECTED INTO THE BRAIN — AFFERENT NERVE — EFFERENT NERVE

Who are they who give way immediately to impulse? They are the relatively untrained elements of society, those whose spinal ganglia and lower brain centres are more highly developed than the higher rational and volitional faculties that have their throne in the gray matter of the cortex. When the sensation passes along the afferent nerve, the impulse to action is at once delivered over the efferent nerve to the muscle. But if the higher centres of inhibition are well developed, and the current of sensation or a part of it is deflected into the brain, the sensation or complex of sensations is detained, so to speak, and the whole cortical apparatus of the cerebrum may be brought to bear upon the matter in the process of reflection. The brain may decide that it is proper for the muscles to act, and in that case will reënforce the impulse. Or it may inhibit the impulse, and the whole life of reflective action is begun. The least self-controlled, with whom impulsive social action commonly originates, are they whose higher faculties of inhibition are not regnant.

Step by step the domain of the mental is being reduced to law and order. In this and the preceding chapter we have seen that certain revival phenomena, widely believed to be supernatural, reveal uniformities which fix them in the category of the natural. So far as their relation to a genuine religious experience is concerned, the most that can be said of them is that they may sometimes be the concomitants of such experience but ought never to be mistaken for it. They and other phenomena like them deserve to be thoroughly sifted by criticism. They ought to be met everywhere as Paul met them in the church at Corinth. He had to face disorders of a similar character and the opposition of those who said that in checking them he was resisting the Holy Ghost. We are all moved by the Spirit of God, said the Corinthians. The spirits of the prophets shall be subject to the critical discrimination of the prophets, said Paul.[1] God is not a God of mental chaos but of rational peace and joy.

[1] I Cor. xiv.

It would be superficial to speak of such an investigation as this as involving the elimination of the supernatural from the process of regeneration. We have only segregated a few phenomena of conversion at white heat and interpreted them in terms of the psychic process. We have discovered that certain alleged phases of religious experience cannot be reckoned as divine except as the whole process of evolution from the animal to the spiritual is itself divine. It is not our task to enter into the deeper question of whether the conversion experience in its entirety is a natural product. Even if it were possible to sound the depths of the human spirit in the hour of religious crisis and reduce the whole realm of the mental to relations of coexistence and sequence, we should not then be free to affirm that we had eliminated the supernatural. It would still be open to the philosophic religionist to declare, — All's law, but all's God.

CHAPTER XII

CONVERSION BY SUGGESTION

It cannot escape the notice of the patient investigator that the literature of revivals abounds with records of the lapsed, the backsliders, those who have fallen from grace. In those churches where the probation system after revival is employed, the shrinkage between the number of registered probationers and the number of registered church members occasions much comment and anxiety. Many thoughtful clergymen in these sects have determined definitely, as a result of their own experience, that accessions are likely to be of more stable and useful quality if quieter and more rational methods are employed in winning men than those which have been traditional in their denominations. It seems to be as true of spiritual fruit as of natural that it maintains a state of excellent preservation longer when it is garnered by hand than when it is swept from the tree by a storm. Here, too, I do not offer it as a complete explanation, — for many professed converts who return to the old paths might perhaps have been advanced in the higher life by a wiser system of probationary nurture, — but I regard it as extremely probable that a great number of the lapsed are such because they were simply victims of the powerful forces of suggestion and imitation which are at work in every typical revival, and were not converts in any high sense whatever.

There is a far greater amount than people generally believe, I think, of conversion by suggestion, which is only that and nothing more. The typical revival lends itself readily to this consummation. There is always the stage of preparation in which the one overshadowing interest is held before the mind of congregations for days or for weeks. The fervor and intensity are greatly heightened by the united prayers and expectations of the church. When the crucial moment arrives and the great assembly has met with common purpose and hope, there are all the conditions present for the easy control of the most suggestible. They are precisely those which the hypnotist seeks after.[1] Every effort is made to secure fixation of attention upon the subject and the speaker. Distraction of mind is guarded against by the revivalist, who seeks to have fresh air let into the room before the sermon, and enjoins perfect quiet even to the cessation of the movement of fans in the hands of the women of the audience. The monotony which results is a prime condition of suggestibility, and the effect of it is seen in that profound silence which passes over a great assembly when the speaker has it under oratorical

[1] Cf. Boris Sidis, "The Psychology of Suggestion," p. 61.

mastery. It is frequently so perfect that you can hear the buzzing of a fly or the slight sputter of an arc light.

The limitation of voluntary movements is of course very complete in such an assembly, and the shrinkage of the field of consciousness to the consideration of the one supreme theme is brought about in exceedingly skilful ways by experienced men. It is well known also that the employment of symbolic images immensely increases the emotion of an audience. The vocabulary of revivals abounds in them — the cross, the crown, the angel band, hell, heaven. Now vivid imagination and strong feeling and belief are states of mind favorable to suggestion as well as to impulsive action. It is also true that the influence of a crowd largely in sympathy with the ideas suggested is thoroughly coercive or intimidative upon the individual sinner. There is considerable professed conversion which results in the beginning from little more than this form of social pressure, and which may never develop beyond it. Finally, the inhibition of all extraneous ideas is encouraged in revival assemblies both by prayer and speech. There is, therefore, extreme sensitiveness to suggestion.

When to these conditions of negative consciousness on the part of an audience there is added a conductor of the meetings who has a high hypnotic potential, such as Wesley or Finney, or who is only a thoroughly persuasive and magnetic personality, such as Whitefield, there may easily be an influence exerted upon certain individuals of a crowd which closely approaches the abnormal or thoroughly hypnotic. When this point is not reached, there is still a great amount of highly acute though normal suggestibility to be reckoned with.

And the methods in detail frequently heighten the effect which is here described. At the close of his sermon, the revivalist usually asks for what he terms immediate surrender, to be announced by uplifting the hand or rising to the feet or signing a card or a movement towards the after-meeting, while the impression is kept up by the very silent departure of the congregation. Sometimes the audience is detained in this tense state of mind, and the process of "influencing the seeker" is carried to a refined extreme.[1] The people are requested to sing a hymn full of pointed suggestion and fervent emotion, while the "seekers" are invited to kneel at the altar. The conductor of the meeting or certain of the workers especially chosen for the purpose kneel also, with the hand on the shoulder or on the head of the person under conviction, and repeat in solemn, measured cadence a few well-tested sentences of revival interrogatory and admonition, such as, "Won't you trust Him?" "Jesus saves you now!" "Trust and obey!" "Only believe!" "Give yourself to God this moment!" Emphasis is always laid upon sur-

[1] Cf. Starbuck, "The Psychology of Religion," for a similar description of a process which I have frequently observed.

render of the will. Of course there are those who, under these exceedingly impressive circumstances, yield with a high motive, reason assenting to the step. There are such men and women, especially of an older generation, in all the churches, who have been drawn by this process of crude suggestion into what has been for many of them a broader and a better life. But the number of them has never been great enough to relieve the method of odium, and there can be no question that there has been much harm done to society by this wholesale hypnotization of weak or recalcitrant wills. The difficulty of training the mass of men to act individually and collectively with deliberation and with a strongly volitional purpose is sufficiently enormous without the undermining of such intelligent effort as there is by a seriously defective religious method.

Particularly is this to be deprecated when we consider that positive, deliberated decisions to rise from a lower plane of life to the practice of the lofty ideals of the Christian religion in the aggregate contribute enormously to the strengthening of both individual and social character. But reliance upon the power of crude, crowd suggestion produces far too many purely negative converts, passive suggestibles all, with whom any implanted idea leads at once to the fulfilment of the same, who " act and reënact the old farce of being converted at every revival" and who fall from grace with facility and despatch when the temporary stimula-

tion of suggestion is removed.   In the method as
it is often baldly employed there is nothing religious
whatever.   It is even practised by some members
of the medical profession who perceive the curative
possibilities of psychic influence in certain cases
with which they have to deal.   But the process of
endorming habitual drunkards and other disso-
lute persons has achieved only moderate success.
Without frequent application of hypnotic suggestion, a relapse is likely to occur.   And even if
permanent reclamation should follow in any particular instance, it would hardly be correct to speak
of the method as religious.

It will not surprise the reader to learn that these
passive revival suggestibles are almost always the
subjects who experience the mental and motor
automatisms.   This is naturally so for two reasons.
These persons are most easily deprived of their
own power of inhibition, and under the stimulation
of fear or great excitement, the primitive reflexes
— the prostration, the trances, the convulsions —
will appear.   Furthermore, if the desirability or
divine worth of these peculiar excitations is made
much of in the meeting, or even indirectly hinted
at, as it frequently is, these persons are they in
whom the suggestion will most quickly bear fruit.

Now the injury of such hypnotic procedure is
not confined to the weak creatures who are most
often affected by it.   There are men and women
of a higher mental and moral grade who are temporarily brought under its sway and under the

thrall of great revival excitement, who feel such
shame and repugnance when the reaction follows
that they are inclined to discard not a faulty and
vicious method, but religion itself. And they
often do. There have been instances of that sort
within my own acquaintance, but I prefer to use a
few of the impersonal illustrations which Starbuck
has gathered.[1] I have no doubt that any reader
will recall more than one instance of his own
knowledge.

One correspondent writes thus of the forces
which led to his conversion at fifteen. " My will
seemed wholly at the mercy of others, particularly
of the revivalist M——. There was absolutely no
intellectual element. It was pure feeling. There
followed a period of ecstasy. I was bent on doing
good and was eloquent in appealing to others.
The state of moral exaltation did not continue.
It was followed by a complete relapse from orthodox religion."

Another observer writes of an exciting revival in
which the meetings were held until the early morning. " Some persons in the midst of the excitement lay prostrate on the floor. One crawled on
hands and knees about the aisles, and some went
into trance. I know that one young man who
was a teacher in our school went to the board soon
after — the writer is a member of the school
board — and told them that he was very sorry for
and ashamed of the part he had taken, that he was

[1] " The Psychology of Religion," p. 165 f.

not fully himself at the time. A seventeen-year-old girl lay in what they called a trance for nineteen hours and has never been able to take more than one study in school since. Three of those who took a very prominent part seem to have grown cold and are seldom at the place of worship."

One young man who had been overwrought under the power of a revivalist called it a "gold-brick" deal and said that he had hardly been in church since.

We have also in this uncanny power of the hypnotic personality a means of explanation of the mysterious influence of men of thoroughly superficial character and ability upon a revival crowd. Professor Coe[1] has written of the evangelist who would cry out at the critical moment to a packed and breathless assembly, " See them coming, see them coming," when as yet no single individual had started for the altar. And the poor sheep heard his voice and followed, but it was not the voice of a shepherd.

And that other religious hypnotist whom we have all seen,— his custom was to walk with measured tread through the aisles of the crowded church, and carefully picking his subjects, touch them on the shoulder or speak a word in the ear, and draw them by purely psychic leadings into a step of whose significance they had no comprehension and the weakness and false pretence of which they later laughed to scorn. . . . Measured by its

[1] "The Spiritual Life," p. 144 f.

effect upon character, the burly fist of Peter Cart-wright — occasionally employed to bring an especially vicious and cantankerous sinner to a realizing sense of his shortcoming — was a far better instrument than the uncanny eye of the modern apostle of religious suggestion.

It has more than once been a source of reproach and scandal to the church that some professional evangelist, who has won large numbers of converts, has been afterwards revealed as having been all the while living a criminal or at least utterly unworthy life. It is easy now to see why such a career is entirely possible. The most remarkable example of a man of this species that has ever been brought to my attention is one La Roy Sunderland, who in the middle of the last century was a prominent clergyman in New England and particularly influential in the antislavery movement.[1] He was an exceedingly able lecturer upon what was then called mesmerism or magnetism. Under the first sermon which he delivered after he entered the ministry, almost the entire audience was struck down entranced upon the floor by "the power of God." It is said that a wide range of reflex phenomena practically always appeared under his preaching. In the later years of his life he was tried for slander and falsehood by four ecclesiastical conferences and several courts. He always

[1] The following facts are contained in two signed editorials by Dr. J. M. Buckley, the *New York Christian Advocate*, May 28 and June 4, 1885.

defended himself and he always won his case.
Judges would warn juries against his malign influence, but it made no difference.   He was
promptly acquitted.   Finally he gave up religion,
on the ground that he had proved its sweet influences to be the product of mesmeric fraud!   In
1836 M. Poyen came to New York from Paris and
aroused great interest by the practice and exposition of the principles of mesmerism.   Sunderland
applied to him for instruction, but soon found that
his own ability was quite equal to the Frenchman's.
Sometime after there visited him at his home two
friends of his earlier days.   One of them was a
young woman who had been influenced in his
meetings.   I now quote his own words of description.   "I recognized her as one of my converts
who had been entranced under a sermon I had
preached in 1824. . . .   When the opportunity
came, I asked her if she had heard M. Poyen. . . .
'Oh, yes,' she said.   'And I have often been entranced in the same way by my husband.' "   Sunderland asked to see her in that condition.
"Whereupon she immediately complied, and lean-
ing back in her chair, closed her eyes. . . .   In a
few moments she appeared to be in a state of
ecstatic joy, when she grasped my hand and said,
'Oh, Brother Sunderland, this is the happiest state
I ever was in.   It is heaven.   And do you remember how I went into this state under that powerful
sermon you preached in our church in Scituate
Harbor years ago?   I was then caught up to

paradise as St. Paul was. . . . Yes, Brother Sunderland, and this is the same heaven, the same as when my soul was converted and filled with the love of God.' "

And I lay particular stress upon this matter here because, while the employment of irrational fear in revivals has largely passed away, the employment of the hypnotic method has not passed away. There has rather been a recrudescence and a conscious strengthening of it because the old prop of terror is gone. And it cannot be too vigorously emphasized that such a form of influence is not a " spiritual " force in any high or clear sense at all, but is rather uncanny and psychic and obscure. And the method itself needs to be greatly refined before it can ever be of any spiritual benefit whatever. It is thoroughly primitive and belongs with the animal and instinctive means of fascination. In this bald, crude form the feline employs it upon the helpless bird and the Indian medicine-man upon the ghost-dance votary. When used, as it has often been, upon little children who are naturally highly suggestible, it has no justification whatever and is mentally and morally injurious in the highest degree. I do not see how violent emotional throes and the use of the art of suggestion in its crude form can be made serviceable even in the case of hardened sinners, and certainly with large classes of the population the employment of this means is nothing but psychological malpractice. We guard with intelligent care against quackery in physiological obstetrics. It would be well if a sterner training and prohibition hedged about the spiritual obstetrician, whose function it is to guide the far more delicate psychological process of the new birth.

It may be important to add a single caution with respect to this much-reviled practice. Suggestibility and the tendency to imitation are by no means altogether evil. They are qualities which are instinctive in the human spirit and will never be banished from their seat. The finest social natures will always possess them, but as the mental evolution of the race goes on, these qualities will come under the perfect dominion of reason and the will. The art of normal suggestion itself will become more and more refined until in therapeutics, in education, even in religion, it will be skilfully employed "to set the conscious will in the right direction."[1] But in each of these fields of cultural activity, how wise and dexterous must the practitioner be!

[1] Moll, "Hypnotism," p. 364.

CHAPTER XIII

THE PASSIONAL AND THE RATIONAL IN RELIGION

WE have long grown accustomed to thinking of the body of man as a product of evolution. The structural resemblance to the lower animals, the various rudimentary survivals in the human frame, point unmistakably to a common physical origin for brute and man. But many well-informed persons have perhaps not entirely habituated themselves to the thought of the development of mind by a gradual process. And yet later researches in the psychology of men and animals, in anthropology, in philology, leave little doubt that the mind of man is an evolution as truly as the body. With the progressive differentiation of the nervous system in the animal world appear progressively higher psychical characteristics. The animal mind culminates in the active development of instinct and emotion, with the faint beginnings of intellectuality.

In the life of the child, sensation, perception, emotion, imagination, rational judgment, manifest themselves gradually and successively. "The stealing in of that inexplicable light — yet not more light than sound and touch — called consciousness, the first flicker of memory, the gradual governance of the will, the silent ascendency of reason, — these are studies in evolution, the oldest, the sweetest and the most full of meaning for mankind." [1]

In the life of the race the instinctive and the emotional and the imaginative function and strengthen long ages before the rational comes to its throne. The primitive man may have had all the mental potentialities of the highly civilized, but his endowments assuredly have manifested themselves gradually, with the broadening of environment and the deepening of experience. There is a vast distance between the primitive and the most highly developed modern type of mind. There is also a marked difference between types of mind in the same modern population at the same moment. By taking account of the indefinite series of gradations from lowest mental faculty to highest, it is possible to discriminate with clearness a number of psychological classes in any population. [2] We are concerned in the study of religious revivals principally with two types, the emotional and the rational. These are popular designations and not precise scientific terms, but they will perhaps suffice if somewhat exactly defined. By the emotional type I mean that part of the population, religious or political, in which instinct, habit,

---

[1] Drummond, "The Ascent of Man," p. 119.
[2] Cf. The *Psychological Review*, 1901, July, "A Provisional Distribution of Population in the United States," or the "Inductive Sociology," p. 86 f., Giddings.

suggestion, feeling, imagination, belief, are dominant in mass and in control. This type frequently
exhibits great power of deductive reasoning, but
its premises are usually beliefs and not propositions inductively established. It is not devoid of
critical intelligence, but is not habitually ruled by
it. At its best, its power and its danger are in
its moral passion and not in its rational judgment.
On the other hand, the critically intelligent type,
if it naturally flowers in a population, without
suffering atrophy of any of its constituent elements, is a higher product of the evolutionary
process than the emotional. Deep feeling, sensitiveness to objective suggestion, a chastened
imagination, are not trodden under foot of the
rational, if the development be true to nature's
plan. These constituent elements are, however,
guided and governed by clear thinking and
vigorous powers of inhibition. It is happily true
that the group of individuals who are habitually
swayed not by sentiment or emotion, but by common sense and reason, who in every emergency and
crisis of experience stop to think, is a steadily
increasing class in the United States and in the
other great modern nations. The emotional type
is on its way to perfection, but is still characterized
by certain prominent mental traits of primitive man.
And these still have power to burst all bonds of
rational control. The type of critical intelligence,
so far as it has become naturally established, has
approached more nearly to the evolutionary climax

of mind. The instinctive, the impulsive, the primitive are not eliminated, they are only subordinated to a higher power. Stimulation is no longer followed immediately by action, but rather by reflection, and later, if need be, by action. Fact and truth and sound judgment act as a check upon too ready belief and overpowering emotion.

And just as mental life in general rises through the instinctive and the emotional to the gradual perfection of reason and will and conscience, so the more ideal spiritual experiences of the race exhibit similar stages of growth and progression. It would be difficult to demonstrate that religion was originally instinctive in the human breast. But there is abundant evidence that the yearning of the human spirit for the help of a higher power, and for communion with a higher power, began very early and was very intense from its beginning. But long before the stage of religious yearning was reached, the human race passed through a terrible and irrational experience of dread relation to spiritual beings with which their primitive minds peopled the world. The origin of religion has often been attributed to the feeling of man that there was something wrong in him. It would be truer to attribute it to the intense feeling of early man that there was something wrong about the unseen and the unknown. The experiences of storm and flood and wild beasts and powerful enemies and disease and hunger and death were ascribed to the supernatural malignity of unseen beings like himself, but vastly more powerful and evil. That primitive religious belief was strongly rooted in fear has long been evident to the student of pagan religions. What hope and trust there might have been were more than half concealed and arose only in the face of some un-looked-for benefit, some unexpected deliverance. The evil spirits were legion, and the good spirits were few. Fear sat on the throne of the human soul and hope as yet scarce lifted up its head. But this is not all of the matter. Back of the emotion of fear was the expectation of evil. But back of hope, when it first began to dawn out of fear, was the expectation of and the desire for life, for self-preservation. And side by side with the strengthening of this instinct for continuing exist-ence, the sad circumstances of the pain economy to which early man was subject developed in him a sense of dependence upon a good power that was other than himself and greater than himself. Religion in any high sense was therefore born of mental need and longing. And this is only another way of saying that they seem to be right who hold that the tap-root of religion is feeling and emotion.

But it would be difficult to prove that reason played no part in laying even the earliest founda-tions of religious faith. It is significant that the brute, which has a wide range of emotion, but only the faint beginnings of reason, has in correlation therewith no religion at all. It is significant that, coincidently with the evolution of higher human intelligence, there should arise the worship of the invisible. At first the inherited capacity in man for taking thought was feeble, while the capacity for feeling and emotion was hereditarily powerful. But it is likely that always, consciously or half unconsciously, feeling posited premises in reason even as it does to-day.[1] From the earliest period of purely animistic interpretation of the unseen and the unknown, to the most modern elucidation of the dogmatic theologies, reason has at least been a servant of religious emotion. And it has been most useful, not in creating systems of religious metaphysics and philosophy, but in keen and patient criticism of the materials which feeling and emotion have often deposited in wild disorder at its feet, and in those careful inductions of fact which have furnished the ground of rational religious progress. Religion has always been something more than emotion, and as the ages have passed and the intelligence of man has grown and strengthened, reason has become more than a servant. Clear thinking and emotion are now true comrades in religion.

In these modern days religion is often defined in terms of love to God and man. A beautiful illustration of the increasingly insinuating influence of intelligence in guiding and controlling emotion is found in the history of the impressive part which reason played in the birth of true love in this world. Love is the outgrowth of parental affec-

[1] Cf. Brinton, "The Religious Sentiment," p. 87 f.

tion, as Henry Drummond and John Fiske have so brilliantly shown, but there was a considerable development of intelligence among early humans before parental affection was born. Mr. Lester F. Ward and Professor Franklin H. Giddings have both called our attention to the possibility of explaining much of mental evolution by the early association of men.[1] It was the social life of the early human which stimulated the higher intellectual activities, the power of sustained attention, of generalization, of judgment. The rapid growth of mental activity in association was paralleled by the rapid increase in the complexity of brain and nervous system. And it was the consequent slower development of this delicate and intricate mental apparatus which made necessary the long period of helplessness of the human as distinguished from the animal offspring. A considerable measure of human intelligence was antecedent to active parental affection.

Now primitive affection did not blossom into love until mere maternity became true motherhood. The human race was long in this world before the tender and unselfish care of children became common. It was not intelligence primarily which suggested motherhood and laid the foundation of love. Natural selection was fundamental in the process. The tribe whose women showed the slightest variation towards the domestic virtues and whose young were consequently more tenderly cared for, would

[1] Cf. the " Principles of Sociology," p. 229, note 2.

increase more rapidly in numbers, and would fare better in the stern struggle for existence. But natural selection only pointed out the way. A relatively strong human intelligence, already developed in association, soon came to be its colaborer. Alexander Bain has said that the earliest and most constant sign of reason is working for a remote object. It must have become increasingly evident to the intelligence of early mothers that the new self-sacrifice for the sake of offspring was *worth while*, not only in the interest of tribal survival, but also because of the intense satisfaction which came with the growth of human love in the soul. Natural selection and reason worked hand in hand in the development of that highest human affection which most closely approaches the divine. There must have been many primitive mothers, whose congenital tendency towards true maternity was not yet strong, who made willing and intelligent choice of the harder path of self-sacrifice and duty for the sake of tribe and child and love.

Professor Borden P. Bowne, in his criticism of purely emotional religion, has said that love itself abides in the will rather than in the feeling, and its distinguishing mark consists in the set purpose to please and to serve.[1] The statement is genetically true. And the corollary thereof is equally true, that love abides in the intellect as really as in the will or the affection. Love first manifested itself in maternal self-sacrifice and was at least partly

[1] "The Christian Life," p. 92.

a product of rational judgment and intelligent purpose. That is, love arose as the individualistic motives began to be socialized and put under the control of the reason. Indeed the whole growth of sympathy and of the higher passional nature in religion is almost directly proportional to the growth of intelligence. And so even if a man declare that religion is love and naught else, it might be readily shown that religious love, too, is a complex passion and arises as certainly out of reason and volition as out of feeling. Reason has always gone hand in hand with emotion in the development of the higher life. If it has not had a controlling influence, it has had a modifying influence. Emotion has on the whole been more powerful because it has had a far longer period of animal and human heredity behind it. Reason has functioned late in animal and human life and has not yet come to its maturity with a great majority of every population, but it has nevertheless steadily strengthened its rule over mankind.

Now there have always been those who have observed that reason is as yet a comparatively feeble instrument and who have therefore ardently discredited its services, particularly to religion. They would trust rather the instinctive and the emotional, which are the older and the tried faculties of the human mind. But if the truth were told, there has been in religious history fully as great cause to distrust emotion. For an unmeasured period of primeval time the mental and spiritual life of man was clouded and distorted by the spectre of fear. This dread emotion is not without purpose in the evolutionary process, as has often been shown. " Fear-thought" was the mother of forethought among animals and men and protected both against enemies and against the scourges of nature. Not even in religion was early fear altogether an evil. One calls to mind the discussions of Walter Bagehot[1] with respect to that primitive time when the human race was soft, incoherent, lawless, unorganized, mentally plastic, and needed the yoke of custom to strengthen its fibre. It was the religion of fear that fixed the yoke with a sanction so awful that none dared disobey. But it was an experience of nightmare and of horror nevertheless, and many peoples never escaped from the yoke into variation and progress and enlightenment. And this is one reason why we have the arrested civilizations of the world. Every one knows, too, that the crude fear element in religion lingered far into modern life, long after its usefulness had entirely disappeared. It was only in the last century that it began to fade out of the religious life of the most highly civilized peoples. We have had abundant evidence in this book of the part it has played in the revivals of the past in " extracting fruits for repentance." The conception of a God who would consign men to an everlasting, torturing perdition has its direct, primitive ancestor in the conception of the Fijian god who habitually devoured the

[1] " Physics and Politics," p. 56 f.

souls of the dead. Hell-fire torment and never ending punishment are no longer preached and no longer believed by faithful and intelligent modern ministers, even by those who do not at all accept in its entirety the philosophy of Universalism. Common sense and reason have revolted against it. It has had its day in the modern world, but it was far too long a day. Crude fear and ignorance are twins of darkness, and when the true light of the knowledge of eternal things at last floods the earth, both flee away. But mankind was in the darkness so long before the dawn, that there is an immense amount of slumbering survival still in every population. In the presence of panic or pestilence or premonition of impending doom, it frequently manifests itself with its old-time energy of fury. Many a revival appeal has been enormously strengthened through the unconscious arousing of these sleeping dogs of human fear. And the effect of this dread emotion in modern life is almost invariably evil. It produces weakening physiological disturbances in assimilation and nutrition. The shock of it causes dissociation of the nervous centres and morbid and irrational forms of involuntary action. It puts an end for the time being to the empire of the will over the muscles, and in many cases permanently lowers physical and mental vitality. Reason is as powerless before it as the self-controlled Darwin was before the puff-adder in the London Zoölogical Gardens. There was a thick glass plate between the scientist and the adder, and he had firmly determined not to allow even a tremor if the snake struck at him, but the moment the adder darted its head, his resolution went for nothing, and he sprang back several feet.[1]

But in the face of the havoc which fear has wrought in the world, there are not wanting even now distinguished apologists for the application of terror preaching and the revival method to at least a certain type of sinner, the utterly wicked, the desperately vile. There are individuals who need it and who are better for it, it is said.[2] Even if this were true, it would not be practicable to segregate these individuals from the mass of their fellows, and administer the emotion and the method solely for their benefit. Certainly for society it would be far better that these be left to the ultra-orthodox pains of everlasting death, or, more reasonably, to the tender mercies of a Heavenly Father, rather than to foster permanently in our modern life such highly dangerous forms of social and religious

[1] "The Expression of the Emotions in Men and Animals," p. 38.

[2] For example, William James, "The Varieties of Religious Experience," p. 162: "But the deliverance must come in as strong a form as the complaint, if it is to take effect ; and that seems a reason why the coarser religions — revivalistic, orgiastic, with blood and miracles and supernatural operations — may possibly never be displaced. Some constitutions need them too much." Also p. 333, op. cit. : "Or are different functions in the organism of humanity allotted to different types of man, so that some may really be the better for a religion of consolation and reassurance, while others are better for one of terror and reproof ?"

procedure. But I am not convinced that this is the more excellent way even with the most hardened and recalcitrant sinner. I think it is the wide experience of Dr. William S. Rainsford with men of this character which has led him to a conclusion with which I heartily concur. " Terror at its worst cannot make men hate sin, though it may now and then frighten a man from sin — a sin that, even as he leaves, he loves. But the knowledge that he is causing pain to some one else can make a man not only hate sin, but finally turn from it forever." [1] For good or ill the thunder and the gloom of Sinai have given place in religion to the sunlight and the beauty of Calvary. And that it is so is no doubt well. It is in line with all mental evolution and social progress. The whip of fear is put aside. It is not for free men, but for cowards and for slaves. And it is more and more coming to be seen that it is the supreme function of religion to develop and strengthen men both brave and free.

Of course my reader understands that it is of crude, irrational fear that I have been speaking. But instinctive emotion is never wholly wrong, is never wholly displaced. It may well be that in this time of revolt and of fierce reaction against a conception of God that erred widely from the truth, the pendulum has swung too far. I think it is so. Side by side with the preaching and the teaching of the love of the Heavenly Father we

[1] In a little book, " Good Friday Meditation."

need a sterner emphasis than of recent times upon the essential justice of the universe and of law and of God — that punishment does not await the verdict of an eternal assize, but that every hour of his life a man is at the judgment seat, and every day he lays up penalty in character.

Not alone fear, but other forms of intense emotion are destructive of the higher life. This is particularly true of the feelings aroused by a highly vivid and unrestrained religious imagination. When reason is not strong enough to subdue the colors, to sift the images, to criticise the visions, doctrine and practice speedily reach a dangerous extreme. Jonathan Edwards, psychologist, was profoundly aware of it, and therefore spoke of the imagination, it will be remembered, as "the devil's lurking place, the very nest of foul and delusive spirits." And the "affection" aroused through the imagination and built upon it instead of upon "spiritual illumination or discovery" he believed to be worthless and vain, however elevated. "Like imperfect sleep," said Saint Teresa, "which instead of giving more strength to the head doth but leave it the more exhausted, the result of mere operations of the imagination is but to weaken the soul." Now the revival of the past is responsible for the purposive cultivation of much of this sort of imagery and consequent violent but irrational emotion. The exaggerated descriptions of hell and heaven, of death-bed scenes and the judgment, have encouraged in multitudes of minds the baneful tendency to exalt the figure above the fact, the picture above the thought. Revival crowds have far too frequently been encouraged to drift in the current of dream and ecstasy upon the rocks of frothy and spurious emotion. Image and vision have been cherished for their own sake and not for any higher purpose, and the immediate and permanent effect has been not only to enfeeble the nervous system, but also the will and the soul. The resulting emotion has been little more than religious intoxication. This is an illegitimate use of the imagination which can be kept within bounds only by the stern criticism and control of the rational judgment.

But neither fear nor these merely sensuous feelings of which I have just spoken are the whole of religious emotion. And there are many who would distrust these baser forms who would still in general have confidence in the passional nature rather than the rational. They would maintain that the propensity to scale the frosty peaks of reason is indicative of a cold, calculating, selfish individuality, that a man is not at his best until he is flooded by high emotion. Warnings against the intellect frequently appear in contemporary ecclesiastical writings, and the more conservative section of the religious press and of the pulpit often represents itself as an enemy to the extended use of reason in the spiritual realm. They agree, as Francis Bacon did, with the heathen in the fable of the golden chain that judgment is not safe in this sacred sphere. They are at one with Dryden in his poem on the religion of a layman: —

> " Dim as the borrowed beams of moon and stars
> To lonely, weary, wandering travellers,
> Is reason to the soul."

The fair mysticism of Clough is their refuge: —

> " Away, haunt thou not me,
> Thou vain philosophy.
> Little hast thou bestead,
> Save to perplex the head,
> And leave the spirit dead.
>
>   *   *   *   *   *
>
> Why labor at the dull mechanic oar,
> When the fresh breeze is blowing,
> And the strong current flowing,
> Right onward to the eternal shore ?"

No matter what exact form this philosophy may take, the underlying theory always is that the passional is the peculiar channel of divine communication. It is a dangerous doctrine. Even the partial acceptance of it drove so skilful a protagonist as Jonathan Edwards into a theological *cul-de-sac* from which he never extricated himself. "Assuming, as he did, that the action of the Spirit in the revival was extraordinary, manifested in bodily effects, and always distinguishable from human activity, he was obliged to admit that the tendency of this divine action was to excite inclinations which if gratified would lead to confusion. Human judgment and discretion must therefore come to the rescue, in order to prevent the unlimited influence of the divine." [1] But Edwards' practical sense served him well, though it played havoc with his theology. Human emotion is deeper and older than human judgment and discretion, but not on that account more divine. Human passion and impulsive action need constant curbing by human forethought and prudence. The safer doctrine is that neither the passional nor the rational is the channel of special supernatural communication, or else that both are, through a real though insensible union of divine influence with the human at the springs of action. It is a shallow religious philosophy that is able to trace the supernatural in the "affections," but cannot trace at least dawning divinity in the developing reason of mankind.

If there is any test of the divine in human life, it is not feeling, it is conduct. This has been repeated often, but there is little present danger of its becoming trite in practice, however it may be in speech. Action that is true and beautiful and good can make impressive its claim to divinity as mere feeling never can. The power to become the sons of God is evidenced not chiefly by emotion, however pure, but by straight thinking and right living.

I have no inclination to overstate the case for the human intellect. The capacity for taking thought and consciously adjusting one's self to facts — which is the essence of reason — unfolds slowly

[1] Allen, " Jonathan Edwards," p. 208.

with the progress of the race in knowledge and experience. Errors of thought are frequently as profound as errors of emotion. The forms of logic are vain things for safety if the premises be untrue. Even in the scientific stage of its development, reason is far from being the perfect tool which it is often represented to be. There is no such thing as absolute accuracy of observation. The statistical average of observations is the nearest we can come to it. Scientific induction begins with a guess and sometimes ends with one. And scientific dogmatism is no better than any other kind. But, nevertheless, as knowledge and experience have grown and reason has become mature, the rational has steadily reached towards the headship in human life. And the evidence of the inner emotional consciousness is the safer when searched through and through by the inner light of reason, and the evidence of both is surer when tested objectively and scientifically by the evidence of external nature.

It becometh not religion to disparage reason. She owes too great a debt to it. Theology is of course only the philosophy of religion, but Christian theology is reasonable. It has no other claim upon the attention of men. Christianity has never been simply emotional fervor, much less mere fanaticism or superstition. From Origen to Harnack it has vindicated its right to exist by triumphant intellectual appeal. And even when men have fought like mental gladiators for conceptions

of God and the universe which were utterly errone-
ous and which have passed away, the tonic effect
of it upon social as well as religious progress has
been immeasurable.   The Calvinistic pulpits of
early New England established not only the Puritan conscience, but the critical Puritan intelligence,
and both have been exceedingly important factors,
and will ever be, in the political and social evolution of America.   The despised husks of theology
have many times proved strongly nutritive for the
mental life of a people, and the mastication thereof
has had momentous reactions upon religion.   Since
the century of the Protestant Reformation, discussions about civil liberty and discussions about religious faith and freedom have gone on together,
and have sounded the death knell of political and
ecclesiastical dogmatism at the same time.   It is
the modern age of rationality which has been the
champion of the individual rights of the human
soul in both these fields of human thinking and
activity.   The polity of discussion, as Bagehot
calls it, is at the root of modern progress.

Within the sphere of creed and doctrine, reason
is the element which has given growth and vitality.
Genetically, belief is a product of emotion, and
many a religious dogma has had little truth or
knowledge at its foundation.   There are beliefs
most dear to us and most necessary to happiness
and sanity in living which reason has never been
able either to demonstrate or to destroy.   But there
have been others which the rational sense of man-

kind has justly criticised into decay, and in many instances scepticism of the nobler sort has sifted and clarified belief and made it a far better instrument of religious propagandism. The church plays no fitting part if she attempts to thwart honest doubt and inquiry and discussion. They are the breath of life to her in the modern world. It will never do for the church to preach psychical degeneration while science is perfecting the reason. A contest of that sort would be very unequal, for science would have the whole course of mental evolution on her side. It will be well for religion if in the future we shall hear less of "barren intellectualism" and more of the spiritual duty of mental growth.

The dominance of the rational will not mean the death of religion, as M. Vacherot and Professor Ribot and other distinguished thinkers would have us believe.[1] Theoretic faith and formalism and spiritual deadness arise through conceit of the understanding and not through a wise and humble

[1] Cf. M. Vacherot, " La Religion," pp. 313, 436, *passim :* "Religion answers to a transient state or condition, not to a permanent determination of human nature, being merely an expression of that stage of the human mind which is dominated by the imagination." Also Ribot, "Psychologie des Sentiments," p. 310: "Of religious sentiment, properly so called, nothing survives at last but a vague respect for the unknowable X which is a last relic of the fear, and a certain attraction towards the ideal which is a relic of the love, that characterized the earlier periods of religious growth. To state this more simply, religion tends to turn into religious philosophy." Both quoted in James, "The Varieties of Religious Experience," p. 502.

use of that important faculty of the soul. Imagination and feeling will never be suppressed in religion any more than in the total mental life. They are both valuable products of the evolutionary process, and it is impossible to conceive an environment, terrestrial or heavenly, in which they would not have utility and to which they would not have adaptation. But they do need to be guided and chastened by the criticisms and inhibitions of higher faculties than themselves.

The passional in religion will never be overthrown. Even the primitive and instinctive emotions themselves do not perish; they are only rationalized and socialized. New and characteristic emotions of the intellectual life appear. In the future, as in the past, we shall be moved to action by aroused feeling. It will be as true as ever in the religious life that men will be stirred again and again to the depths of their souls, and the baser obstructions and impediments to the highest usefulness will frequently be swept away as by a flood. But there is an emotional philosophy which has had its day. This is its poetic embodiment : —

"If his heart at high flood swamp his brain now and then
'Twill be richer for that when the tide ebbs again."

That is true Celtic philosophy, and it has made the original Celtic strain what it is to-day, a beautiful and highly valuable element in the life of another people, but having no practical sense of headship of its own. It is the function of the blood to enrich, but not to swamp, the brain. Emotion may sweep away the baser inhibitions which beset a man, but it should never sweep away that climax product of the mental life, the capacity to reflect between stimulation and action and the power to apply all the knowledge and experience which the individual possesses in that critical period of decision.

It is idle to argue which we could better do without, the passional or the rational in religion. As well dispute the steady and permanent helpfulness of the White Nile, which flows the year round from the chain of Nyanza lakes, because in its season the Blue Nile, swollen and muddy, comes to the rescue freighted with the rich soil of the Abyssinian mountains. The land of Egypt in our day could ill afford the loss of either. As well dispute whether the furnace or the helm is most essential in the ocean steamer. But if it is the question of which shall be trusted as a guide to port, reason ever more tends to become the rudder of human life.

I would take straightforward issue with those who still hold that the subconscious, the imperfectly rational, the mystically emotional, in spite of all its vagaries, is, par excellence, the channel of the inflow of divine life. I realize that I am at this point running counter to the philosophic "perhaps" of that distinguished psychologist, Professor William James, in his splendid inductive study of the varieties of religious experience. As a static investigation of religious types, I know none that is superior. But Professor James' "twice born" people, with their impulses and impressions, their visions, their hallucinations, their divided purposes, their strange subliminal incubations suddenly bursting into consciousness, their sense of impotence in the hour of decision and their tendency to abject self-surrender, are a human type on its way to perfection. A careful dynamic study would find them to be mentally immature, rationally and volitionally imperfect, and I, for one, cannot believe that the feet of the supernatural deliberately choose to tread the slime of the subliminal, the lower mystical marsh lands of the human spirit, while avoiding the sunlit hills of full rational consciousness. It is far easier to believe that the influence of the divine is increasingly evident in the whole process of mental evolution.

Just as the struggle for the life of others comes to control the struggle for life, but so that neither influence is lost to human progress; just as altruism everywhere displaces crude force and yet has its root in the physiological vigor of the early conflict; so the instinctive and emotional in religion give way to the rule of the rational, but never to the destruction of that which is primary and fundamental. For the truly rational life is not only a thoroughly ethical life, which is usually taken for granted, but it is also a profoundly passional life. The deepest emotion is usually under the control of the reason. The juror who holds himself firm against the fervid appeal of the defendant's attorney because of the sense of responsibility he has for the welfare of the community and for the supremacy of law probably has the capacity for far greater sympathy with the prisoner at the bar than the juror who weakly and tearfully yields to the appeal.

In full maturity the rational and the mystical dwell together in the same spirit, but ever so that the latter is undergirded and guided by the former. There is a lofty mysticism, chastened by the critical habit, of which one may speak only with the deepest respect. It was a quality of Beecher, of Brooks, of Martineau, and of those terrible mystics, the Puritans. The practical reason was strong in these men, but nevertheless they refused to shut themselves up to the testimony of the senses. They possessed and they cultivated an inner consciousness of things which eye had not seen nor ear heard. This perfect fusing of the two chief mental traits in the same nature is the real climax of mind. If either be bred out or atrophied, there is something lacking which the course of mental evolution should have made permanent in a man.

CHAPTER XIV

AN APPLICATION TO THE UNITED STATES, AND
OTHER CONCLUSIONS

THE revival method has normally been one in which feeling is dominant in mass and in control. The great religious revivals have been intensely emotional in character. The best of them have been saved in a measure from extreme excesses by the rational guidance of highly gifted and well-balanced men of the type of Wesley and Edwards. In all of them there have been many genuine changes of moral nature. The records abound with examples of persons who were living in open wickedness or in intellectual disbelief or in absolute indifference to higher ethical and religious things, who were suddenly brought, under the influence of the revival wave of emotion and appeal, to the point of mental and moral transformation with respect to the whole subject. And in a multitude of cases the change of attitude was permanent. These facts are of profound importance and no doubt deserve the somewhat exclusive attention which they have received from religious historians. The question of the great value of many revivals to particular individuals is not especially raised in this book.

It has hitherto received its meed of analysis and discussion. But most of the examples, both of temporary and permanent transformation, do afford to the observer of social phenomena substantial evidence of the high development of impulsive personal action in the revival. It is not a movement of deliberation, of criticism, but of feeling and of impulse. And that has always been its weakness and its danger. It has frequently led to holy excesses of excitement, to merely sterile emotion, to the primitive, and often to the pathological. Under its influence men have too often yielded, not to the higher motives, but to the lower. Far too frequently they have been moved, not by intelligent insight into the evil of their ways, not by a sense of unworthiness and sin, not by true volitional action towards a new and higher life, but by fear, by suggestion, by imitation, by social pressure, by a flood of feeling overwhelming the higher cerebral process.

It is a grave error to think that you can touch the sensibilities alone and have any appreciable effect upon the conscience and the character. You must touch the intellect as well, and primarily. There is a necessary crudeness about religious groups that are built up by the emotional revival method unless there follows a most careful and intelligent training in true piety in order to establish what the pure revival movement cannot give, an equilibrium of character. Emotional devoutness leads easily to fanaticism. "Holiness" experts and professors of entire sanctification are notoriously hard to get on with. They are the real spiritual defectives and not their fellow-members of the church at whom they often rail accusingly. We have seen this moral egotism cropping out in our inductive studies more than once. It is always a product of moral passion uncontrolled by common sense and reason. The emotional revival fosters it, sometimes in persons who would not otherwise be subject to it. William Tennent read a paper before the synod of Philadelphia in 1740 to prove that many of his fellow-ministers were "rotten-hearted hypocrites." William Tennent would not have done this except under the pressure of revival passion. It will be remembered that Whitefield in New England became censorious to a degree. But this was not natural to Whitefield. Davenport cultivated this spirit in Connecticut to the point of insanity, but the demon left him to shame and contrition when the gust of overpowering religious excitement had ceased to blow.

The emotional revival has never taken into account the proper function of the will in conversion. Emphasis has been most unfortunately laid upon impulsive and mystical self-surrender. Men and women have been urged to become as "drift logs on the current of divine purpose," as "nothing in the floods and water spouts of God." They must "surrender all," their intellect, their talents, their social pleasures. One evangelist has been in the habit of relating to great audiences of young people the story of a friend of his, "a master and lover of Greek." On his conversion he gave up all, and the last to go was his Greek, but he let that go too ! There has been a great deal of this, and the suggestion of abject surrender has been potent in professed conversions just because it fits so beautifully a type of mind that is very common in every population. There are large numbers of persons whose rational and volitional processes are so imperfectly under control that when they attempt to use them in time of religious storm and stress, or at any other time of great emotional agitation for that matter, they fail utterly. Blackness and darkness and tempest and the sound of a trumpet and the voice of words is the only response. They are plunged more deeply than ever into fear and perplexity and gloom. The lower cerebral processes will not work in harness with the higher. It is only when they cease to think and cease to will and cast themselves unreservedly into the current of the subconscious and mystical in their natures that they find relief. And your professional revivalist, though not a trained psychologist, has had a very practical experience with the mental life of congregations. He knows what his crude methods will accomplish with this type. A suggestion of the impotence of the human will, of the power that comes through complete surrender, an explosion of the ice-jam at the heart through the dynamite of emotion, and you get your result. And sometimes it has been a helpful result religiously to the individual. There are many who have dated their spiritual birthday from such an experience. But there are also many, the record of whom has not been so carefully kept, who have been spiritually injured for time if not for eternity by this process. And there is a grave social danger in such a method of training large elements in a population. The man who yields unquestioningly and uncritically to impassioned appeal in the crisis hour of his religious life will do it in the crisis hour of his political life. And that is the vice of democracy.

The type who yield impulsively in a revival are they in whom the higher cerebral processes are imperfectly organized. They do better when the simpler automatic cerebral centres are allowed to act freely. But it is not a type to be encouraged or strengthened in a population. It is not only better for society, but for men's own souls, that they should employ all their wit and will in the struggle for the higher life. Though they fail, they are in the hands of an all-seeing and merciful God.

Impulsive self-surrender is injurious to a wholesome and normal religious experience. It was not cultivated by the great Head-Master of Christianity. "If any man *will* to do my will," said Christ, "he shall know the doctrine." It was this method which gave spiritual birth and nurture to Abraham Lincoln in the darkest hours of the civil war. And it is the only ideal method. Any other but turns the world of religion and politics alike over to the rule of the subconscious and the passional.

Deliberative self-devotion is quite another matter. Whether it characterize the lover, the patriot or the Christian disciple, it is rational and sound in psychology and in life. It is self surrender, but of the higher kind. The man is conscious that he has his hand on the windlass as he lowers the boat into the sea. The element of value in the baser sort of surrender survives in an attitude of mind. Huxley has likened the sitting down before a fact as a little child, of being prepared to give up every preconceived notion in its presence, to the truth embodied in the Christian conception of surrender to the will of God.[1] And there is worth in the figure and in the comparison. The spirit of simply, humbly following where truth and fact in nature and experience shall lead is the beginning of wisdom in both science and religion. Your proud, self-sufficient intellectualist goes as far astray religiously as his impulsive brother at the opposite mental pole. There are very few well-balanced men who do not at one time or another in their careers come to the point where Toplady's imagery means something to their searching and perplexed spirits : —

> " Rock of Ages, cleft for me,
> Let me hide myself in thee."

It is coming to be clearly seen that the old-time

[1] " Life and Letters," Vol. I, p. 235.

revival method is pedagogically vicious for the religious culture of children. In many respects children are little primitive people brought down to date. It will not do to carry the analogy too far, for the environment of feeling, of intelligence, of conduct, as manifested in the elders of the community, and the environment of nature, too, is very different for the modern child from that in which the primitive races lived. But in important ways the mental life of childhood and youth does reproduce with singular exactness the whole course of mental evolution in the race. The little fellow on the floor with his toys has in him more than we like to admit of the crude selfishness of the savage, and the real social instinct of sympathy and helpfulness and self-sacrifice, which is potentially present in him, develops slowly through thwarted effort and disappointment and the necessity for comfort and guidance and many another experience, sweet and bitter, all the way along. He is peculiarly susceptible to the primitive emotion of fear, and one of the cruelest things in the world is to instil into his plastic mind the image of it. Senseless stories of the hobgoblin, the bogey-man and the witch may remain to torture him for years. The shock of a frightful dream has been known to plunge normal children into epileptic fits, just because the dream is so extremely real to the impressionable little brain.[1] The child has the capacity for far more intensely vivid imagination

[1] Cf. Angelo Mosso, " Fear," p. 226 f.

than the full-grown man or woman just because of his plastic and undeveloped mental and nervous organization. Fact and fancy frequently blend in one for him as they do for primitive man. He is highly imitative and suggestible. In a crowd of other children he will mechanically yield his little will to any trusted leader. A friend of mine once experimented with an infant Sunday-school by requesting all those who were sure that nobody could be saved who did not believe that Isaiah wrote the whole of the book bearing his name, to lift up their hands — and every hand went up. An elderly gentleman whom I once knew said to his little granddaughter, " Would you like to have grandpa take you out into the woods to hear the birds sing ? " And she answered, " Yes." And he said, " Would you like to go out into the woods and see a man cut grandpa's head off ? " And she said, " Yes."

The experience and environment and mental organization of the child are relatively simple, as with the savage. In an assembly of his kind he yields to excitement, to hypnotic personal pressure, to a vivid idea, with the most unconscious readiness. To employ upon these delicate and impressionable little beings any of the crude machinery of a revival is an unseemly perversion of pedagogical principle and a trespass upon the rights of childhood.

It seems to be determined that the high tide of adolescence, immediately following the age of puberty, is exceedingly favorable to revival conversion. It had long been a matter of observation, before any thorough scientific studies were made, that youth is preëminently the time of accessions to the church. All denominations have sought to make adolescence fruitful in additions to membership, and the revival churches in particular have regarded this period as peculiarly auspicious for their labors. Contrary to a somewhat widespread opinion, the employment of the emotional method in conversion even at this advanced stage of early life is fraught with grave danger. The high tide of adolescence is noteworthy in at least three respects—for the extraordinary development of the capacity for sentiment and emotion, for the emergence in strength of the sexual passion and for marked ethical and religious storm and stress. It is a period characterized particularly in females by a tendency to overconscientiousness, apprehension, morbidity and hysteria. It is a time when there is needed the most delicately skilful ethical and spiritual training of which parents and churches are capable. It is true that the mental and moral temper of adolescence lends itself readily to the excitement of revival, but it is also true that such a form of religious persuasion is extra-hazardous at this stage of human life. The sudden increase of emotion needs to be met with the calmness of rational control. It is no time for the shock of fear or the agony of remorse. The only result of such misguided religious zeal is likely to be a strengthening in many cases of those tendencies, especially in females, towards morbidity and hysteria, towards darkness and doubt.

So far as the budding of the sexual instinct at this period of life is concerned, there is something also to be said. The psychological investigations conducted at Clark University have made it clear that at the age of puberty there is an organic process at work which pushes forth into activity at nearly the same time the sexual and the spiritual. There is no proof, however, of the causation of the latter by the former. But it does appear to be true that the two are so closely associated at the point in the physical process where they branch in different directions, that at that critical period any radical excitation of the one has its influence upon the other. The writers of religious hymns have sometimes unconsciously taken advantage of this fact of physical development to arouse the human love passion beside the spiritual. A few years ago at the greatest camp-meeting gathering of young people in America, where thousands between fourteen and twenty-five come together for social intercourse and inspiration, by all odds the most popular hymn, sung all along the sea-shore and about the grounds, was the following :—

" Blessed lily of the valley — oh, how fair is He !
    He is mine, I am His.
Sweeter than the angels' music is His voice to me,
    He is mine, I am His.
Where the lilies fair are blooming by the waters calm,
There He leads me and upholds me by His strong right arm.
All the air is love around me — I can feel no harm —
    He is mine, I am His."

Now I submit that with our present knowledge of the delicate interrelation of the sexual and spiritual in adolescence, such hymnology does not indicate the wisest nurture of the human soul.

We have had our attention called to the sensuality which broke out in the midst of the great religious excitements in Kentucky. There are many other facts of observation indicating that the over-stimulation of religious sentiment among the young frequently arouses the human love passion much more fiercely than the divine. It is natural that it should be so from what we know of adolescent psychology and from what we know of the inhibitive effect of religious excitement upon the higher centres of control. Frederick W. Robertson, in one of his essays, refers to this singular alliance of the animal and the spiritual, which conducts the "unconscious victim of feelings that appear divine into a state of life at which the world stands aghast." It is responsible for the vicious heresies of free-love and "spiritual" wifery and Mormonism. Only the ignorant would hold these phenomena to be to the discredit of religion. But they do teach us to be on our guard in religious method, that we may not adopt that form of effort which unconsciously drags men down to the level of the phallic worshippers of the ethnic faiths.

The steadily increasing predominance of women in modern churches is coming to be viewed with anxiety, if not with alarm. There are aspects of the matter which are in no wise discreditable to

the sex. I launch no shaft of unworthy criticism
at religious womankind. The most influential
makers of moral authority in any state are
mothers. And many women have shown themselves capable of the highest things in reason and
in self-control. But if one may speak of types of
mind and not of individuals, it is within the truth
to say that woman is a creature of intuition, of
mystical emotion, rather than of intellect and
rational inhibition. Perhaps sex enters into the
mental constitution as well as the physical, and
this seeming differentiation is permanent. But I
do not lean entirely to that interpretation. For
ages woman was the slave of man. She had no
will of her own, no environment and no experience that would develop in her those later mental
products of the evolutionary process which grew
to strength in her lord and master. But she is
gaining rapidly in the modern age what is important to perfect her characteristic endowments.
She will never be man. Woman she will always
be, and love will be her sceptre and home will be her
throne. But the time will come when she will be
less impulsively emotional, less highly suggestible
than she is now. And this leads me to add a
word with respect to the relation of the revival
method to the predominance of women in the
churches. It has been an important factor in the
result. Woman is easily swayed by emotion. Her
mental constitution is fertile soil for external suggestion by a speaker or by the example of a

friend. And it is not at all wonderful that the drawing of the gospel net should reveal so frequently an excess of the feminine among the multitude of fishes. I think that this matter has not received the attention which it deserves on the part of those who are interested in the increase of manhood membership in the churches.

The conclusion seems to be that the revival has established its own peculiar type of religious experience and not that which is truly normal and universal. It has not created this type out of nothing, for the material is at hand from which to build it. In every population there are relatively large numbers of the "twice born," persons subject to especially violent pulses of growth, in the midst of the shock of which unutterable things are heard, indescribable visions of glory are seen, and sometimes strange motor phenomena are experienced. This condition is not an ever present one with this class of persons, but there is in them an existing mental tendency towards the emotional life and its primitive manifestations. In time of revival excitement, of course, this is the element which is most characteristic, which comes at once to the fore, and which is established by tradition as the only perfect and sufficient type. Its weakness and its limitations are clear. It is a mental segment of humanity. Its experiences are simply impossible to thousands of genuinely religious persons. And it is no cause for lament that this is so. It is well for the world.

The dramatic and instantaneous and convulsive personal experience of conversion is a single kind. Its philosophic basis is the inner experience of emotion as something incontestably divine. And it has all the defects of its philosophy. Conversion in the New Testament is a phenomenon in which thought and will and conduct play the chief part. The essential meaning of μετάνοια is a change of mind on reflection. The word which essentially signifies to *feel* repentance is μεταμέλομαι, and was used of Judas when he impulsively cast the thirty pieces of blood money on the floor of the temple. Conversion itself is a volitional word.

The sudden and convulsive type of religious conversion has never been universal. Certainly the founder of Christianity did not foster it. His method with the disciples and the people was education and discussion, the reported incident of the stampeding of the demon-spirits and the swine of Gadara to the contrary notwithstanding. It has not especially characterized the Catholic and Episcopalian and Lutheran denominations of Christians, nor the Puritan churches either, save as there has been leakage into these sects of alien principle and practice. These churches have employed more or less effective, though sometimes dangerously formal and lifeless, methods of religious education to the exclusion of the revival, taking advantage through confirmation and other means of the spiritual phenomena of adolescence.

And there has always been still another class of

persons who have never known religious struggle and who have never needed special catechetical instruction or confirmation of purpose at a certain stage of career, but have blossomed into maturity spiritual as naturally as into maturity mental or physical. This group comes from stock which is mentally well balanced in heredity, and, more important still, which has maintained in the household a simple and rational family religion. This was the sort of home that produced Edward Everett Hale and made it possible for him to pronounce the ideal Christian testimony: "I always knew God loved me, and I was always grateful to him for the world He placed me in. I was always glad to tell Him so and was always glad to receive His suggestions to me. . . . I had no idea whatever what 'the problem of life' was. To live with all my might seemed to me easy; to learn where there was so much to learn seemed pleasant and almost of course; to lend a hand, if one had a chance, natural; and if one did this, why, he enjoyed life because he could not help it, and without proving to himself that he ought to enjoy it." [1]

Candid investigation will compel a true bill against the revival of the past on the evidence of its having violated the fundamental principles of education. Its normal tendency is not to strengthen the intellect and the will, but rather to submerge

[1] Quoted in Starbuck, "The Psychology of Religion," pp. 305, 306.

both under billows of suggestion and emotion. It is a thing of impulse rather than of reason. When allowed full sway in a population, its manifestations become primitive and ultimately so grewsome and grotesque that they can no longer be associated in the thought of earnest men with soundness of method or of mind. Whenever in the past, as has sometimes happened, genuine good has been done in society through the revival, it has been directly in proportion to the control which the reflective processes of individual leaders have exercised over what is essentially impulsive social action. When, as in recent times, certain of the forms of revivalism are maintained under the name of "missions" or "retreats" or even greatly modified "evangelistic services," while reason remains dominant in mass and in control, the essential nature of the movement is so changed that the terms of description applicable to the great religious awakenings of the past no longer suffice.

We must not be blind to the utility of impulsive or sympathetic action in primitive times. This was the method that established civilization in every part of the world. In those early days it was responsible for great harm, but for greater good. Let us hope that men are rapidly outgrowing it now, that it will soon pass entirely away and that we shall not see its recrudescence save in the most dire emergency of national life. Rational like-mindedness, the polity of discussion and intelligent public judgment, is at the root of social progress.

So must the order be with the revival churches which have wrought well for humanity through the use of a primitive method among primitive populations, which otherwise might long have waited for the touch of the higher life. They must go on from the emotional to the rational. "Churches that fail to maintain their hold on the highest regions of human thought are inevitably destined to wither and die. No degree of evangelistic zeal can compensate for the loss of intelligent and rational faith." [1] A religious method more or less suited to early conditions, when sympathetic like-mindedness was, so to speak, in a virgin state in great populations, might easily become a menace to a modern nation in the modern age.

Early in this study I have alluded to the decline of revival over large areas of the United States, particularly in the centres of population where social organization is highly perfected, where the environment is complex, the interests many, communication easy and education within the reach of all the people. The accession of knowledge, the sense of security, the measure of well being — which have come with a more highly specialized and effective social organization in these modern industrial communities — have on the whole transformed beneficently the primitive emotional nature of man.[2] In individual cases the reaction is too violent, and prosperity and enlightenment beget the

[1] Hugh Price Hughes.
[2] Cf. Giddings, "Inductive Sociology," p. 244 f.

lust of the flesh and the pride of life. But in the main it is not so. For the mass of the people the new life social is begetting a new life mental and, eventually, let us hope, will beget a new life ethical and spiritual. But in nothing does the change more quickly appear than in the growth of calm and disciplined habits in religion. Any attempt to maintain the extravagantly emotional methods of other days breaks down utterly and inevitably in the midst of city life.

But it would be much too wide a generalization to maintain that this condition is true of the entire nation. It is not. There are many lines of evidence which converge in proof that we are still an emotional people. We are an empire, with varying measures of economic and social development in the different parts. We are civilized and barbarous at the same time. We have millions of primitive black men and more millions of primitive white men, both native and foreign born. We have Kentucky and Kansas and Colorado, and then we have Massachusetts. But not to speak of the contradictions of localities, there are not wanting indications that the mental mode of our entire population is still emotional. The churches in which feeling, belief and authority are dominant have by far the largest membership. The "solid South" as well as certain "solid" portions of the North bear eloquent testimony to the reign of prejudice instead of independent thought in politics. The feuds in the Southern mountains, the

lynchings of black men and white on both sides of
Mason and Dixon's line, the mob spirit in industry,
attest the rule of impulsive social action over great
numbers of men.

In what civilized country do evidences of religious fanaticism more abound? Modern spiritualism had its rise here, and nowhere has it spread
with so consuming a flame. The minds of unnumbered thousands were overwhelmed by the fantastic
arguments and vain imaginings of the Vermont
farmer, William Miller. And in our time the tide
is still rising. The Mormons have fastened themselves upon great stretches of our western country
and upon great numbers of simple, primitive people with the grip of "revelation" and authority.
The commercial and the hypnotic have swallowed
up the rational with the multitude of followers of
the "prophet" Dowie. And I have by no means
exhausted the record of monomania and credulity.
It is partly due, I know, to the extraordinary freedom to think and freedom to print and freedom to
act in America upon the most false and chimerical
hypotheses if they are only advanced in the name
of religion. And for this there is no remedy in so
out-and-out a democracy. The excess of liberty
has its advantages in the end. But such evidence
would not abound if there did not exist in our
population a great volume of unrestrained imagination and emotion which are always the predisposing causes of fanaticism.[1]

[1] For an informing discussion of this subject, cf. *Century Magazine*, December, 1903, " Fanaticism in the United States," Buckley.

And what of the political errors of our democracy? They are not so many or so vital as Lecky thought. But there are enough of them to give us pause and impel us to a study of the cause. The craze for cheap money and for wild-cat banking, the struggle of frenzied feeling between debtor and creditor which lies at the base of our rather humiliating financial history, the antislavery movement in its leading phase, and that sad burst of sentimentality which clothed the recently emancipated freedman with the political powers of a developed Anglo-Saxon freeman, are all instances of the acceptance of the leadership of emotion on the part of a nation. Though God maketh the wrath of man to praise Him, though there was disclosed on both sides in the Civil War a wealth of spiritual sacrifice and of mental and material resource which have demonstrated for all time that we are one people and a great people, nevertheless these are no justification for bloodshed and passion and sectional strife. The path of reason, too, leadeth onward and upward, but never through such wilderness of woe.

And the bearing of this upon religious method? Take Kentucky for an illustration. No state of the Union is more notoriously subject to waves of impulsive action in politics and also in the administration of justice and the practice of religion. Extravagant and exciting revivals have vied with neighborhood feuds and community lynchings to satisfy a primitive lust for emotion. And there is some reason to believe that it would not be difficult to establish a correlation between the religious fury of this population and its judicial and political fury. I offer the following only as a bit of evidence to light the way of future research in this field. The attention of the reader is called to the accompanying map of the state of Kentucky by counties. The dots represent the number of lynchings in each county from 1882 to 1903, a period of twenty-two years.

The bunching of instances in the counties of Logan, Simpson and Todd will not escape the eye. The detailed figures are as follows : [1]—

1882–1903

Total number of black men lynched in the state
of Kentucky 95
Total number of white men lynched in the state .
of Kentucky 61
In all 156
In the county of Logan, 10 blacks and 4 whites, . 14 in all.
In the county of Simpson, 3 blacks and 3 whites, 6 in all.
In the county of Todd, 3 blacks and 3 whites, . 6 in all.
Total 26

The population of Kentucky by the census of 1900 was upwards of two millions. The population of the three contiguous counties — Logan, Simpson and Todd — was upwards of fifty thousand. That is, in a region containing only one-fortieth of the population of the state and not

[1] These are taken from an exhaustive study of lynchings made by Dr. J. Elbert Cutler of Yale University.

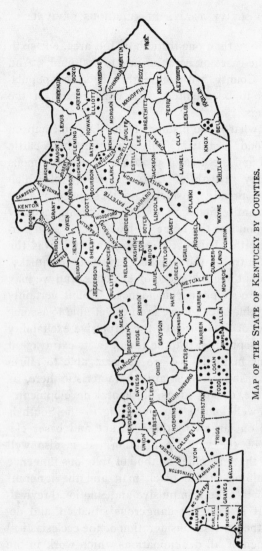

MAP OF THE STATE OF KENTUCKY BY COUNTIES.

The dots indicate number of lynchings in each county, 1882-1903.

much more than one-fortieth of the area, one-sixth of all the cases of lynching are to be found. And Logan County, with one-eightieth of the population, is to be credited with one-eleventh of the lynchings.

And what is the history of this Logan, Simpson and Todd locality? This was the chief battle ground and the area of propagation of the famous Kentucky revivals of 1800, the record of which we have already considered in these pages. During the entire first half of the nineteenth century this region was the home of bloody feuds, and during the latter half of the same century it was the great centre of the lynching spirit in Kentucky. This is but a single piece of evidence, and we may have here simply a coincidence. But it certainly is a striking one. If we are not yet able to assume that one of the causes of the impulsive excitability of this population is to be found in its extravagant religious methods, we are at least able to affirm that exciting revivals are characteristic here, as elsewhere, of low areas of mental development.

It is well known that lynching in the South is carried on largely by the ignorant and baser elements of the white population. It is also well known that the chief method of religious influence and training of the black man and the ignorant white man alike is impulsive and emotional revivalism. It is a highly dangerous situation, and deserves the earnest consideration of the ecclesiastical statesmen of all denominations which work in the

South. It will be impossible to protect that part of the nation or any other from the epidemic madness of the lynching mob, if the seeds of it are sown in the sacred soil of religion. The last thing that the superstitious and impulsive negro race needs is a stirring of the emotions. That is easy and meaningless. What they need is a strict religious discipline that will keep their passions in check and build them up in chastity, industry and integrity. The whites in the feud belt are not suffering from an absence of religion, but from the wrong kind. Their preachers are great " soul savers," but they lack the practical sense to build up their emotionalized converts into anything that approaches a higher life.

There is no problem which confronts the people of the United States into the solution of which a right religious education does not enter as an important factor. The great mass of wage-earners in this country need a form of spiritual training which shall help to develop in them a better poise of mind than they now possess. The cause of labor is invariably set back when its programme is carried out by hasty and impulsive action. Now and then a strategic strike is a powerful influence in the direction of better wages, a better organization and remedial legislation. But its success invariably follows upon rational methods, upon passion kept in control. The economic as well as the moral and religious future of the wage-earning classes depends upon their capacity for deliberation. For ill-advised and emotional action they have capacity in plenty.

The field of religious evangelism is suddenly widening among the primitive populations of our dependencies. The Cubans are still the quasi-wards of the nation, and the Philippinos are bound to us by stronger ties. The missionary to these people will be sure to find that proneness to excitability, to hasty and ill-considered action, is one of their most characteristic traits. And he will do well to modify any traditional religious method with this fact in mind. It should not weigh too heavily upon his spirit, however, if tremendous outbursts of emotion do now and then follow upon his careful preaching of the word of life among the child races of the earth. When they first break away from that comparatively low stage of mental and moral evolution at which their progress has so long been arrested, it would be a marvel of method as well as of grace if they could at once master the deepest instincts and habits of their primitive natures.

The vice of religious, political and industrial democracy is emotionalism in the wide sense of that term. I do not mean that we can have too much of the right kind of emotion. Sentiment which is deep and true and held in leash of the reason is as valuable an asset for a nation as for an individual. But there is no virtue which a free people needs so much as rational self-restraint. The sheet anchor of permanent liberty in a democracy is moderation of mind. It is in this mental atmosphere that the Christian spirit of brotherhood will best flourish. And the church most powerfully contributes to the realization of the ideal of its Master, which strives to be a real centre of social control. In the main it has been that in the past, and well deserves the gratitude of every lover of his country. But the work of restraint in the nation is by no means accomplished. The subliminal consciousness of primitive man still slumbers in our population.

> "The jungle is wide and the cub he is small,
> Let him *think* and be still."

CHAPTER XV

THE NEW EVANGELISM

THE Germans have a maxim which recites the impropriety of emptying the child out with the bath. Is conversion out of date as well as the old-time revival? In this critical study of a religious method I have taken the reality of the conversion experience for granted. Investigations in religious psychology, so far as they have gone, have established it as firmly as have the observations and deductions of theology. I suppose that no scientific man now doubts that conversion is a normal human experience with at least very large numbers of persons in every population.

There is reason to believe that the religious impulse unfolds as naturally in the life of the child as the social impulse, and that careful nurture will usually show fruitage in spiritual decision and church membership at an early stage of adolescence. Although there may be pulses of growth even in the young, on the whole this form of conversion is a gradual process which manifests itself, not in crises, but in the normal evolution of character. When the hidden element of faith in a Heavenly Father and devotion to righteousness in personal and social relation rises to sovereignty, we call it conversion. It is the budding of the higher life of the human soul.

There is no longer scepticism on this point. But sudden, dramatic, climacteric, convulsive changes of character in later life under the influence of religion still occasion some controversy. There is as little cause for it here. Every human being, young or old, is an exceedingly composite product. There are multitudes of human minds which never pass through normal growth, religious or other. They issue into physical maturity only half trained, mentally or spiritually. They are a bundle of unified and conflicting tendencies still, some good and some evil. Instinct and impulse at one end of the scale and aspiration and ideal at the other, or the power of forming such ideal or aspiration, have long lain dormant in their spirits. And there is not the slightest reason to doubt that it often happens in the lifetime of such men that some new influence brings sudden glad release to these suppressed elements of character, and arouses them into such activity that the individual's whole conduct from that time on is transformed.

This is the type of religious experience which appears so frequently in revivals. There has been in the past a tendency to think of it as involving more of the supernatural than is contained in the gradual process of divine unfolding through religious education. It is a theological question, and I will not raise it further than to suggest that Jerry

McCauley once made a profound remark to a friend of mine when he said, " Far be it from me to limit the grace of God, but I never yet knew a man to be permanently reclaimed who did not have a good mother." This unique evangelist, who ran to such good purpose the " spiritual rough-house " for lost men, had exceptional opportunities for the study of human nature, and he has left a valuable bit of testimony. The power to become the sons of God has indeed been implanted in men by other than human hands. To one man, the immediately miraculous only is supernatural. To another, the divine immanence is natural or supernatural according as you view it. And if He be immanent in heredity, which is the essence of Jerry McCauley's philosophy, why not a silent partner in that whole complex influence which awakened the man in the critical hour? And as to the relative supernaturalness of sudden and gradual conversion, if God be in the thunder, why not equally in the still small voice ?

The only question with respect to remarkable conversions of the revival type is as to the number of them that naturally occur in a population. Inductions of this variety of religious experience have not yet covered a sufficiently wide range. The statistics are either selective or only indicative. Students and soldiers and saints have furnished much of the material, and we have not yet established a true average experience. And so perhaps one man's guess is as good as another's. And it is

THE NEW EVANGELISM 311

mine that the number of cases of sudden and startling conversion which would normally occur in a
population is greatly exaggerated.

I do not deny that there are many instances in
which the volcanic burst through the crust of habit
and of the old, imperfect life, is the only way out
into newness of character. I do not deny that
humble conviction of a lost and helpless state must
precede a spiritual resurrection with some persons.
I do not deny that there is a great volume of imperfectly suppressed imagination and emotion in every
population which easily finds vent in unusual sensory and motor phenomena *under certain circumstances*, though normally there is inhibition enough
to control them. But the circumstance which has
enormously added to the number of cases which
would naturally appear is the revival method. It
is very easy to "experience a doctrine," and there
has been much of that, as Professor Coe has explained, in the matter of awful conviction of sin.
But it is easier still to experience an experience.
For many people it is only a step in a crowd from
control of emotion to loss of inhibition and to imitation half-unconscious. And anything which is
traditionally held to be unusually mysterious or
divine is copied with alacrity in a revival assembly.
That exquisite spiritual analyst, Jonathan Edwards,
long ago called our attention to this in the
"Treatise concerning the Religious Affections."
"A rule received and established by common con-
sent has a very great, though to many persons an

insensible, influence in forming their notions of the process of their own experience. I know very well how they proceed as to this matter, for I have had frequent opportunities of observing their conduct. Very often their experience at first appears like a confused chaos, but then those parts are selected *which bear the nearest resemblance to such particular steps as are insisted on* [the italics are not Edwards']; and these are dwelt upon in their thoughts, and spoken of from time to time until they grow more and more conspicuous in their view, and other parts which are neglected grow more and more obscure. Thus what they have experienced is insensibly strained, so as to bring it to an exact conformity to the scheme already established in their minds. *And it becomes natural also for ministers*, who have to deal with those who insist upon distinctness and clearness of method, *to do so, too*." [1]

It is no more difficult to establish a religious type by selection than any other kind. And that this has actually occurred in the multitude of commonplace cases which make up the vast majority, I have no manner of doubt. And we may look, I think, for a great decrease of these special and startling experiences with the more careful training of children in religion, with the slowly strengthening mental quality of the average man, and with the progressive decline in the old-time revival. The

[1] Cf. also William James, "Varieties of Religious Experience," p. 200.

new evangelism will not concern itself with the reproduction of by-going, if not by-gone, types in method and experience. It will be thoroughly interested in the relatively small number of genuinely sudden and startling metamorphoses of character which are not artificially induced by the revival. But it will not model itself completely in accordance with them.

The great crises of awakening in America in the eighteenth and nineteenth centuries have lent aid and comfort to a human proneness towards intermittency of spiritual interest. They have accentuated the seemingly rhythmical transition of populations from the tropical to the glacial in the religious life. The tendency of the method has been to suppress the rational and the self-controlled in men. And there is a consequent reshaping of evangelistic ideals.

The days of the emotional stampeding of a town are passing away in religion just as they are in politics. As the voting population grows more rational, the campaign attitude and manner of appeal of the political parties is undergoing a change. Torchlight processions and the oratory of the "spellbinder" are giving way to a sober consideration of candidates and principles through the medium of newspaper discussion and clever and illuminating advertisement in unusual forms. There is also an immense amount of careful personal work done with new voters, man to man, face to face, eye to eye. Great audiences can still be brought together to listen to exceptional men whose reputation for knowledge and clear thinking is well known, but "spread-eagle" emotional appeal is rapidly losing its power over men in the more intelligent sections of America. Outward political enthusiasm is not so great, but actual political thinking and public judgment were never so strong.

Even in politics great meetings will still have a value in a refined and rationalized form. And I am not therefore deaf to the logic of this book when I express the belief that in religion likewise men will never in this world forsake the assembling of themselves together. Even in heaven, where there is no temple, we read that they still unite in choral song to Moses and the Lamb. As long as the social instinct lasts, so long will men seek one another's company in public gathering for the mere joy of it, not to speak of the utility of it. The crowd is natively a primitive thing. But there is no reason why it may not be moulded into a more rational instrument of helpfulness and inspiration. And in this form it will still serve religion. The emotion of the crowd will give the grip of reality to spiritual teaching. It will arouse them that are at ease in Zion. It will melt the ice of indifference and leaven the soul life of multitudes yet unborn. But the crowd will no longer be employed to lay bare the primitive in man. There will be, I believe, far less use of the revival meeting as a crass, coercive instrument for overriding the

will and overwhelming the reason of the individual
man. The influence of public religious gatherings
will be more indirect, more unobtrusive. It will be
recognized that hypnotization and forced choices
weaken the soul, and there will be no attempt to
press to decision in so great a matter under the
spell of excitement and contagion and suggestion.

It will become increasingly clear that crude, crowd
coercion is a cowardly as well as a destructive
agency for pressing men into the kingdom. The
way of courage and of helpfulness is the way of
tactful personal approach of man to man. Noble
individual character will become more and more
the supreme power of suggestion and of attraction
in religion. The revival is founded upon the educational fallacy that there is one right method for
the mental and spiritual development of all men,
whereas every pupil in church or common school
is a new problem in salvation. No two lives need
the same touch or the same moulding. One by
one, each must be led out into his own life spiritual.
We are beginning to appreciate how great is the
practical skill and wisdom in suggestion required
of him whom we sometimes erroneously call the
secular teacher. We must set our standards as
high for the leaders and workers in religion.

The new evangelism places the emphasis upon
the native religious impulse of children and youth.
Its guiding light is the psychological insight of
Jesus, "Suffer the little children to come unto
me and forbid them not, for of such is the kingdom

of heaven." Jonathan Edwards said that if children are not born again, they are no better than young vipers.

> "Conceived in sin, O wretched state,
> Before we draw our breath,
> The first young pulse begins to beat
> Iniquity and death."

The Christian Nurture of Horace Bushnell harked back to Christ with its proposition "that the child is to grow up a Christian and never know himself as being otherwise." He is born from above when he is first born into the world if we have eyes to see it and skill to lead the way in the divine unfolding. He is a tangle of the animal and the spiritual, and the struggle for possession begins no man knows how early.

The most important phase of mental development in a child is the growth of the sense of personal fellowship with a world of beings other than himself and outside of himself. The progressive accommodation of his own little spirit to other spirits like himself is the essence of character building. The motive that impels him to the development of the social impulse which leads to the growth of character is the need of sympathy and help for the better ordering of his life. Now the religious impulse is only a differentiation of the social impulse, and the religious motive is a differentiation of the social motive. Conversion is the climax of the "unselfing" process. The time comes when it is seen that visible help must sooner or later fail, and human sympathy will not suffice. The need of a divine power is felt in the soul, and lo, the God-consciousness is awake. This development cannot be, should not be, hastened unduly, but no man may say how early it will appear under the simple, rational nurture of an intelligent Christian home. A sound family religion furnishes the only sufficient basis for healthy evangelism. And next after this we shall strive to bring the content of religious instruction in church and Bible school up to the psychological and pedagogical ideas of our time. We shall gather the children between the ages of ten and fourteen into classes, under the most perfect leadership that the churches can command — wise and noble men and women who are able to teach boys and girls that they are born for the higher life of religion and the church just as they are born for the higher life of politics and the state; that enrolment for citizenship in the spiritual kingdom of the invisible Father is as natural and sensible as enrolment in the voting population of the nation.

Such a training as this, which follows nature's time and plan, will probably require no cataclysm, no upheaval, no crisis, no mechanical revival emphasis, no yearning after experiences that are normal enough to a few people of mature life but not to the vast majority, either adults or children. There will be no fixed "age of discretion," though we shall, no doubt, make special endeavor to establish right choices through church membership at

that period of rather swift maturing of social sympathy which occurs with boys and girls in early
adolescence.[1] This is exceedingly important in
order to give the plastic mind of youth a "set"
towards lifetime habits of religion. And it will be
well if this can be accomplished before the emotional tide of adolescence swells to its flood. The
best sort of a Christian life is the product of the
gradual dawning of a sweet and trustful God-consciousness upon the maturing mind and heart of
a human being. "The child who is early taught
that he is God's child, that he may live and move
and have his being in God, and that he has, therefore, infinite strength at hand for the conquering
of any difficulty, will take life more easily, and
probably will make more of it, than one who is
told that he is born the child of wrath and wholly
incapable of good."[2] From the conception of a
kingdom of heaven which suffereth violence while
the violent take it by force, we are passing on to the
formula of evolution physical, mental, spiritual, —
first the blade, then the ear, then the full corn in
the ear.

The ideal way is the path of Christian nurture and
not of revival rupture. But we must not gaze so de-
votedly at the perfectly ideal as to miss the plainly

[1] Cf. Coe, "Education in Religion and Morals," a book of unusual
practical helpfulness on this whole subject of the ethical and spiritual
training of childhood and youth.

[2] Edward Everett Hale, a part of quotation cited in previous
chapter.

practical. There is no good reason why an assembly of young people, who are no longer children, may not be so reasonably and judiciously directed and controlled upon the day which the church may set apart for the public sealing of self-consciousness in religion, that the mere inspiration of numbers added to the earnest and rational advice of a godly pastor may not furnish the last touch of emotion which shall determine conduct and character.

And what of that great multitude, who for generations to come, because of unwise parenthood or imperfect methods or sheer wilfulness or some other cause, will continue to pass out of the home and out of the church of childhood and youth into adult maturity without God and without hope and perhaps without love to man? Are the days of "crowd" evangelism altogether done? I do not so believe. But the emphasis of preaching and the manner of winning men to a more normal and rational life will undergo modification. The new evangelism will speak less of the soul's depravity and more of its infinite worth. There are a few instinctive criminals in society whose heredity and environment have left them very little of the image of God. But we shall not allow their existence to determine the content of religious doctrine. Preaching will declare a sincere respect for human personality, not as something dead in trespasses and sins, but as "a distinct expression of the thought of God." The new evangelism will therefore honor the moral initiative of men, not seeking to entrap it or override it or coerce it or engulf it. This profound esteem for the volition of another has frequently been wanting in the revivals of the past. " A man may be ever so gross and vulgar, but when you come to deal with the deepest that is in him he becomes sensitive and feminine. Brusqueness and an implied familiarity may do very well when dealing with his brains, but without tenderness and courtesy you can only approach his heart to shock it. . . . To know and remember the surpassing dignity of the human soul — for its own sake, for its God-like elements, for its immortality, above all for His sake who made it and gave Himself for it — this is the first axiom to be remembered." [1]

A supreme effort will be exerted to make men in this age *think* rather than feel, to think of the utter abnormality and folly as well as the wickedness of violating the divine order through sinning. Thus the source from which flows the emotional impulse towards newness of life will be deepened and widened. Salvation will no longer seem to be a means of escape from the sharks of perdition, but rather will appear to be the natural fulfilment of a worthy life.

The new evangelism will proclaim the modern and not the mediæval view of the character of the Heavenly Father. It will interpret Him to men not as a God who was alienated from a guilty race

[1] Drummond, "The New Evangelism," pp. 280, 281.

until the blood of the cross disposed him once again to favor, but as a God who was verily in Christ, reconciling the world unto Himself, revealing thereby a Father's mighty, suffering love that will not by any means let the sinner go until at last it draw him upward and homeward. Thus shall we have restored to us a strong sense of the reality of a personal God in the world, for the practical loss of which in a multitude of minds a false theology and an imperfect science of impersonal force and impersonal law have been co-responsible.

The earnest preaching of great truths in their modern light, a straightforward appeal to the intellect and conscience of men, liberalism attuned to faith and spiritual service, a passionate devotion to the highest ethical ideals, a social rather than an individualistic church that shall truly set men on work for the kingdom of heaven — this is the programme of the new evangelism. The converts may be few. They may be many. They will be measured, not by the capacity of the preacher for administrative hypnotism, but rather by the capacity for unselfish friendship of every Christian man and woman. For the influence upon the world of growing men in our time is to be more and more the indefinable and the unobtrusive influence of personal character. Here lies the crux of the question for modern evangelism.

There is need in the American population for such a message and for such spiritual endeavor.

For though there be no radical national decline in morals or religion, yet there is a considerable measure of popular indifference to the church and an unwholesome lack among multitudes of men of a genuinely living faith in the Invisible and Eternal. And righteousness is by no means firmly set upon the throne of our industrial splendor. Surely there is nothing which will sooner put to shame the sordid materialism of an intensely active and commercialistic nation than the fearless and intelligent proclamation and practice of the principles which controlled the human life of Christ. It is inconceivable that the righteousness and love of God, revealed in the character and activities of Jesus of Nazareth, have lost their power of individual and social regeneration.

There are not lacking signs in England and America, as well as in other countries of the world, that the so-called age of scepticism is warming towards an age of faith. The gentle heat has touched already some mature men of science and many young men in the colleges and universities. The transformation is at once intellectual and spiritual. There are those also who interpret certain contemporary sounds of a going in the tops of the mulberry trees as presaging the return of great numbers to faith. Whether they be true prophets or no, certainly they have a vision of the goal of an aggressive and rational evangelism — the spiritual vivification of the multitude.

But of this I think we may be confident. The days of religious effervescence and passional unrestraint are dying. The days of intelligent, undemonstrative and self-sacrificing piety are dawning. To do justly, to love mercy, to walk humbly with God, — these remain the cardinal tests of the divine life in man.

> "And every virtue we possess and every kindness shown,
> And every thought of holiness is His alone."

Religious experience is an evolution. We go on from the rudimentary and the primitive to the rational and the spiritual. And, believe Paul, the mature fruit of the Spirit is not the subliminal uprush, the ecstatic inflow of emotion, the rhapsody, the lapse of inhibition, but rational love, joy, peace, long-suffering, kindness, goodness, faithfulness, meekness — *self-control*.[1]

[1] ἐγκράτεια, strength within, self-mastery.

THE END